PROFESSIONAL CARS

Ambulances, Hearses and Flower Cars

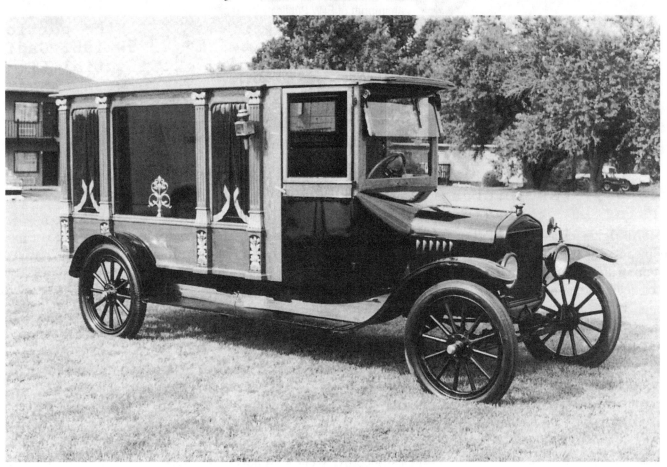

Gregg D. Merksamer

Published by

700 East State Street • Iola, WI 54990-0001
715-445-2214 • 888-457-2873
www.krause.com

Our toll-free number to place an order or obtain
a free catalog is (800) 258-0929.

Library of Congress Catalog Number: 2004100740

ISBN: 0-87349-642-6

Designed by: Wendy Wendt
Edited by: Brian Earnest

Printed in United States

Dedication

For their encouragement of my endeavors, this book is dedicated to my parents Norman J. and Geraldine F. Merksamer, my late sister, Gail Linda Merksamer, and my loving wife, Lisa Lachover-Merksamer, who was an especially steadfast source of optimism through the most exhausting and demanding phases of this project. As this book goes on sale we are celebrating our 10th wedding anniversary and every day I hope it is just the beginning of a long life together.

In Special Remembrance:

JOHN RYAN KEEL
October 5, 1984 - December 25, 2002

Here was a true procar prodigy, who had grown up across the street from the LaPorte Cemetery in Freeland, Michigan, become captivated by the cars going in and out of the gates and could identify the coachbuilders that built them by the time that he was 3 years old.

Impressing all who met him as an exceptionally polite and incredibly detail-oriented young man with a greater mastery of the subject than enthusiasts two or three times his age, he made an indelible mark as a videographer and meet judge at Professional Car Society events and a contributor to PCS publications. He left us much too early and he is sorely missed by the many friends he made in our circle.

Don Keel photo, courtesy Tim A. Fantin

John R. Keel with his 1973 Superior Cadillac Crown Sovereign combination coach "Ravenna," which was one of four professional cars owned by this 18-year-old enthusiast. This image was taken just a couple of weeks before his tragically premature death on Christmas Day, 2002.

Acknowledgments

A work of this depth and scope would simply not have been possible without the enthusiastic assistance of a great many people in the Professional Car Society, the Society of Automotive Historians, and the funeral coach, ambulance, and limousine industries. The following firms and individuals were unfailingly generous in providing extremely rare imagery, invaluable leads, and interesting personal reminisces regarding their own professional vehicles or the vehicles that served in their communities, and I am profoundly in their debt.

Accubuilt Inc., Lima, Ohio—Don D. Cuzzocrea, President and CEO

Michael Bedard, Limousine & Livery Manager, Lincoln Professional Vehicles

W. Rance Bennett, W.R. Bennett Funeral Coach, Lowell, Michigan

Nick Bliss, Editor, *The Minute Man Monitor*, Indiana Chapter Professional Car Society

Stuart R. Blond, The Packard Club, Fords, New Jersey

Thomas J. Brown Jr., PCS, Schertz, Texas

Joe Bunn, Sales Administration Manager, Accubuilt Inc.

Cadillac Professional Vehicles—Mike McKiernan

Tom Caserta, Meteor Motor Car Company, Piqua, Ohio

Timothy J. Cenowa, PCS, Shelby Township, Michigan

Paul Cichon, 1990-92 President, PCS, Hampton, Connecticut

Richard J. Conjalka, PCS, Merrillville, Indiana

Crestline Coach, Saskatoon, Saskatchewan

Dave Csimbok, PCS, Carteret, New Jersey

Rick & Maggie Davis, PCS, Winona, Ontario

Edward J. Defort, Editor, *American Funeral Director*, Lakewood, New Jersey

Ralph H. Dunwoodie, SAH, 1924-2003

Eagle Coach Company, Amelia, OH - Michael R. Kellerman, President

Ken Earnest, Marketing & Advertising Manager, Accubuilt Inc.

John Ehmer, President, Professional Car Society, Pittsburgh, Pennsylvania

Tim A. Fantin, PCS, Merrillville, Indiana

Federal Coach, Ft. Smith Arkansas—Tania Kordis

Christopher G. "Kit" Foster, Treasurer, Society of Automotive Historians

Larry Gustin, Assistant Director, Communications, Buick Motor Division of General Motors

George Hamlin, Co-founder and Chief Judge emeritus, PCS, Clarksville, Maryland

Dwight Heinmuller, Co-founder, Professional Car Society

Image Coaches, Warsaw, Indiana—David & Heather Marshall

Indianapolis Motor Speedway Hall of Fame Museum

Howard Johnson, Johnson Memorial Funeral Directors, Bessemer, Alabama

Fred Kanter, Founder & President, Packard Industries, Boonton, New Jersey

Jerry W. Kayser, Kayser's Chapel of Memories, Moses Lake, Washington

John R. Keel, PCS, 1984-2002

Mike Krehel, Spitler Incorporated, Montoursville, Pennsylvania

Tony Karsnia, Archivist, Professional Car Society, St. Paul, Minnesota

Krystal Enterprises, Brea, California—Edward Grech, President, CEO and founder

Terry Lange, PCS, Santa Ana, California

Jeremy D. Ledford, President, PCS Volunteer Chapter, Lebanon, Tennessee

Graeme Lemin, PCS, Oak Park, Victoria, Australia

Steve & Gene Lichtman, PCS Mid-Atlantic Chapter, Mt. Airy, Maryland

Mary Little, Ingersoll, Ontario

Rich Litton, PCS, Moorestown, New Jersey

Steve Loftin, PCS, Clinton, Oklahoma

Robert Logan, National Sales Manager, LCW Automotive, San Antonio, Texas

C. Marshall Long, PCS, Reynoldsburg, Ohio

Don Lunn, Lunn Funeral Home, Olney, Texas

Fred Mackerodt Public Relations, Montvale, New Jersey—Marie Hayden

Keith Marvin, SAH, Worcester, Massachusetts

Walter M.P. McCall, Editor, *The Professional Car*, Windsor, Ontario

Joseph P. McDonald, PCS, Rock Falls, Illinois

Thomas A. McPherson, founder, Specialty Vehicle Press

Jason Meyers, Curator, Museum of Funeral Customs, Springfield, Illinois

Moby's Eureka Autos, Gallipolis, Ohio

Jose Molina, President, Royal Coachworks, St. Louis, Missouri

Gerald T. Nesvold, PCS, Pitman, Pennsylvania

Old Cars Weekly, Iola, Wisconsin—Ron Kowalke, Keith C. Mathiowetz, Angelo Van Bogart

Mark Patrick, Curator, National Automotive History Collection, Detroit Public Library

John R. Perkins, PCS, Rochester, Minnesota

John Rabold, Former President, Indiana Chapter PCS, Indianapolis, Indiana

Lloyd & Karen Ray, PCS, Council Bluffs, Iowa

Road Rescue Ambulances, St. Paul, Minnesota

Daniel P. Reynolds, PCS, Barton, Vermont

Dr. David Richards, PCS, Bloomfield Hills, Michigan

The James L. Schwartz Home for Funerals, Mifflinburg, Pennsylvania

Richard Shelly, Imperial Coach, Pittsburgh, Pennsylvania

Standley Sipko, PCS, Dupont, Pennsylvania.

Specialty Hearse & Limousine Sales Corp., Plainview, New York—Terry, Scott & Jim O'Neill

Lyle Steadman, PCS, Brigden, Ontario

Craig Stewart, PCS, Wood Ridge, New Jersey

Alvaro Casal Tatlock, SAH, Montevideo, Uruguay

Noel Thompson Library, CCCA Museum, Hickory Corners, Michigan

Dale K. Wells, 2001-3 President, Society of Automotive Historians, Kalamazoo, Michigan

Bernie Weis, Editor, *The Arrow*, Pierce-Arrow Society, Rochester, New York

Roger D. White MD, PCS, Rochester, Minnesota

A.L. Whinery, PCS, Sayre, Oklahoma

Bob Winegardner, Engineering Records, Accubuilt Inc.

Peter Winnewisser, SAH, Cazenovia, New York

Jan Witte, Chster, New York

David E. Wolfe, Kalkaska, Michigan

Fred Wolfinger, vice president for sales, Eagle Coach Company

Donald F. Wood, 1935-2003

Craig Zweibel, Accubuilt Inc.

I am especially grateful to Edward J. Defort, Walter M.P. McCall, and Thomas A. McPherson for respectively granting permission to reproduce images from the *American Funeral Director* magazine, the official Professional Car Society publication *The Professional Car*, and the Eureka, Flxible, and Superior books published by Specialty Vehicle Press. I also want to express my appreciation for the consistently excellent photo processing service provided by Donna & Jim Hobson of Church Street Photo in Vernon, New Jersey.

Though their images are not credited in factory-issued prints, the outstanding skill of the photographers affiliated with funeral coach and ambulance builders should be acknowledged here. The ones whose names are known to us include:
Bob Bowsher, chief photographer, Superior Coach Corporation, Lima, Ohio, 1969-1980
Lyle Eshleman, Eshleman Studios, Sterling, Illinois, (The Eureka Company, Rock Falls, Illinois)
James Kloss, official photographer, The Flxible Company, Loudonville, Ohio

Contents

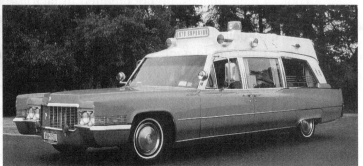

Introduction

Perhaps it is the air of mystery that has surrounded the afterlife since the dawn of abstract thought. Or the adrenaline that is sent pumping when an ambulance dashes down a busy street with lights and sirens blazing. Or the gasoline that courses through the veins of every car enthusiast, compelling us to learn more about the vehicles we know the least about. Or an impish, Tom Sawyer-like reverie where we speculate how many friends, reflected in the number of limousines taking part in the procession to the cemetery, will show up for our funeral. Whatever the reason, it is plainly evident that "professional cars"—a relatively-recent term encompassing hearses, ambulances, flower cars, service or "first call" cars, invalid coaches, six-door limousines, "combinations" that can be converted from funeral coaches to part-time ambulances, and any other type of vehicle involved in mortuary, emergency or livery service— are enjoying more attention from the old car hobby than they ever have before. An Indiana art teacher named Terry Sheedy, whom I met at the Professional Car Society's 1996 International Meet in St. Paul, Minnesota, may have said it best when he asserted that his three-owner, 33,000-mile 1976 Miller-Meteor Cadillac landau hearse was "great for meeting people. Kids come up and have a friendly idea about it because it's a different-looking car; nice and shiny with a vinyl top and big hubcaps. It's Mom and Dad who go and hint that it's the kind of car Grandma went out in. But at a car show, people are curious and they want to come up and look inside."

There was, of course, a time not very long ago when the only people attracted to a retired funeral coach or ambulance were rock bands, painters, plumbers, and surfers seeking a cheap carryall showing fewer miles than most other cars of the same vintage. On those rare occasions that a hearse appeared at an old car meet, its ghoulish aspects inevitably got more interest than history or artistry. As a result, the Antique Automobile Club of America barred them from taking part in its painstakingly judged events for nearly 20 years. The idea that these vehicles deserved more serious treatment did not reach critical mass until 1973, when Canadian journalist Thomas A. McPherson gathered 2,000 catalog images, factory photos, and advertisements together (he had gotten hooked on the subject as a 10-year-old, after receiving a stack of mortuary magazines from a funeral home that was cleaning house) and authored *American Funeral Cars and Ambulances Since 1900* for Crestline Publishing. Though the subject matter's "acquired taste" character made this 352-page tome an initially slow seller and it went out of print fairly quickly, it found a fervent following among funeral directors, emergency medical technicians. and other procar cognoscenti who affectionately nicknamed it "The Black Book" and "The Bible." The book is still held in such high esteem after 30 years that a secondhand copy in good condition can command hundreds of dollars in an online auction. Given this reality, it is certainly good news that several other worthy books on the topic written by McPherson, Walter M.P. McCall, and Richard J. Conjalka have also been

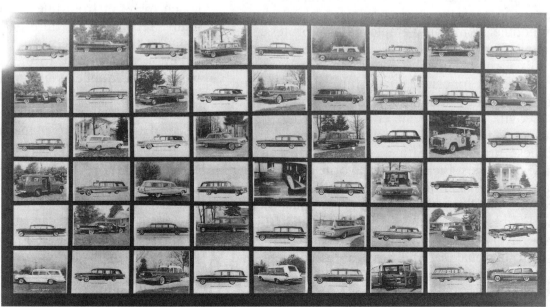

One of the most endearing aspects of ambulances and funeral cars is that they were usually built to individual order on any make of chassis that the purchaser desired. The incredible variety of unique vehicles that have been created as a result of this custom is epitomized by this intriguing mosaic of Cadillac, Chrysler, Chevrolet, Oldsmobile, Buick, Pontiac, Mercury, Lincoln and International Travelall professional cars offered by National Coaches of Knightstown, Indiana in 1960.

Richard J. Conjalka collection

published in the last decade, and I encourage readers who enjoy this book to examine my bibliography and seek these titles out as well.

Another important step towards a wider acceptance of hearses and ambulances in old car hobby circles took place in 1976, when a pair of Packard enthusiasts from Maryland, Dwight Heinmuller and George Hamlin, founded the Professional Car Society to champion authentic preservations and restorations, establish formal judging criteria and re-direct the public's attention to the craftsmanship and aesthetics of vintage ambulances and funeral vehicles. This feat was primarily accomplished by prohibiting the display of caskets, skulls, and other macabre miscellany at club activities. Having served as PCS publicity chair since 1993, it is a great source of pride to me that the Society's membership rolls have nearly doubled over the last decade to more than 1,100 people in 15 countries, and that our eagerly anticipated international meets can attract up to 100 vehicles from all over the United States and Canada each summer. While the rare, magnificent cars you'll see are incentive enough to attend a PCS national or regional chapter-sponsored event, it should also be noted that the people you'll encounter at these gatherings are among the most generous and friendly you are likely to meet, reflecting the fact that so many of them hail from the funeral directing and paramedic professions where the number one priority is assisting those in need.

If this book is serving as your basic introduction to professional cars, it may come as a surprise to learn that mainstream auto manufacturers like Cadillac, Lincoln, Buick, and Oldsmobile have never built their own hearses and ambulances. Though the following chapters are organized around chassis make in deference to novice enthusiasts who will likely approach the subject as a fan of one brand orn another commonly employed as a professional car platform, it is hoped that the accessibility of this format will give you an awareness of and appreciation for such great funeral coach and ambulance body builders as Henney, Eureka, Sayers & Scovill, Superior, Silver-Knightstown, Miller-Meteor, and Flxible—especially since so many of these firms elected to focus their skills on one make of chassis. Picking your favorite coachbuilder may well come down to how Cotner-Bevington became an Oldsmobile specialist, or that Siebert and Flxible were renowned for Fords and Buicks, respectively, or how Henney and Packard constituted the professional car industry's most-admired and exhalted partnership from the mid-1930s through the early 1950s.

As an artistically inclined "algebra notebook" auto designer who reached driving age during the era of diminished expectations in the late 1970s, I was always fascinated that coachbuilders constructing procars were completely dedicated to satisfying individual customer tastes and requirements regardless of cost, time, or difficulty. These builders maintained carriage trade traditions of craftsmanship that most enthusiasts assumed were lost forever when the "Golden Era" of custom-bodied passenger cars from firms like Willoughby, Judkins, Murphy, Brunn, and LeBaron came to an end in the 1930s. Having also spent a decade as the official compiler of the Professional Vehicle Preview issue put out by *American Funeral Director* magazine each November, I remain convinced that there are few sights in the modern automotive world more awe-inspiring than watching a brand-new Cadillac DeVille or Lincoln Town Car "coachbuilder sedan" arrive at a firm like Accubuilt, Eagle, or Federal, get stripped down to its most-essential sheetmetal, then get locked into a giant framing jig where it is cut, stretched, raised, and otherwise transformed into a funeral coach.

The body structure of a top-of-the-line "commercial-glass" hearse may incorporate as many as 400 specially fabricated components, ranging from an oversized windshield to extra-tall side windows and reduced angle pillars. And after the car has been welded together, the builder will be happy to finish the exterior in any color the customer desires. I can still recall a 1994 visit to the S&S/Superior plant in Lima, Ohio, where a brand-new six-door limousine was being repainted in a 1959 Cadillac color, because that was how the funeral home had set its cars apart for more than three decades. Because it is not unusual for a funeral coach to be in front-line service for 15 years, the many second- and third-generation craftspeople found at these builders are especially proud of the attention they devote to the rear door dominating what is often dubbed the "ceremonial" or "working" end of the hearse. John Phillips, testing a Superior Cadillac Sovereign funeral coach for the July, 1994 issue of *Car and Driver* magazine, remarked with well-justified admiration that its rear door "slams shut, appropriately, with the vault-like finality of a Mosler safe. It may be death's door, but it's beautifully assembled."

Given that funeral cars and ambulances are built in small volumes to individual customer order and you will probably never see two identical coaches unless they were part of a fleet, another theme I wanted to emphasize in these pages is that every professional car has its own unique and interesting story to tell. These vehicles are profoundly personal manifestations of a funeral firm's self-image or a community's pride in providing its denizens with up-to-date ambulance service, so I felt it was important that my photo captions pass on any information I managed to obtain about an individual car's original owner, service history, post-retirement adventures, and restoration. Whatever issues we might have with the Internet, it has proved its worth as a research tool by allowing me to take an old photo of an ambulance or funeral coach, type a window nameplate number into a search engine, and quickly obtain a lead on where the car had seen service.

As far as the future is concerned, it has sometimes been asserted that the best days of the professional car industry are behind us. While it is true that the typical ambulance is now a utilitarian breadbox on a truck chassis, many funeral homes are now controlled by cost-focused chains and the increasing popularity of cremation and ceremony-free "direct disposals" will have some effect on the demand for new funeral vehicles, it is also obvious that presentation will continue to remain a top priority in a profession where identity-diluting changes will never be accepted without protest. An interesting object lesson in this idiom can be found in the recent experiences of Daniel M. Isard, whose business appraisal firm The Foresight Companies analyzed how much money funeral firms in a 23-home market might save by leasing their vehicles from a jointly-owned cooperative. Though his study concluded that such a pooling of resources would allow the mortuaries in the sample to reduce the number of hearses they needed from 28 to 14, the

number of limousines from 25 to 10 and the number of lead cars from 25 to 16, allowing each participant to put $40,000 in the bank and save an average of $28,000 per 100 casketed calls, Isard also recalled in the November, 2002 issue of *American Funeral Director* that "one man in the back of the room raised his hand (and) asked 'how many of the autos are going to be Robin's Egg Blue?' I said, 'None. They would be black or silver or white, but a uniform fleet so they could be interchangeable.' He got up and left the room. Another hand went up, 'Cadillacs or Lincolns?' I said I didn't care as long as the fleet was interchangeable, (and) more people got up and left." Despite the logic of his case, the incident convinced Isard that "funeral directors think of their cars as an extension of their real estate, regardless of the cost," and it also confirmed how little things had changed since *American Funeral Director* asserted in a March, 1935 professional car industry overview that a funeral director's rolling stock should be compared "to a storekeeper's window. In his window the tradesman puts his finest wares and displays the best selling arguments for his merchandise. Similarly, the funeral director must consider his automobiles as a constantly-viewed advertisement. Thousands of people see the hearse and funeral cars daily, more than will ever visit the funeral home or have actual experience with a director's services. People consider these automobiles as examples of the funeral director's business habits. If kept in immaculate condition, the natural conclusion is that the director maintains the same high standards in other things."

— Gregg D. Merksamer, May, 2004

Funeral coach and ambulance collecting got a big boost in the old car hobby when the Professional Car Society was founded in 1976. The organization's annual International Meets, like this 1999 event that attracted a record 104 vehicles to Lancaster, Pennsylvania, traditionally end with a sky-piercing "sound and light" show.

Gregg D. Merksamer photo

9

Chapter 1

A Look Back at History

Centuries before the motor vehicle was even conceived, caring for the sick and arranging respectful farewells for the dead ranked among the highest priorities of civilized peoples. Though professional medics and morticians play a far bigger role in handling these duties than family and friends do today, humanity has spent most of its history on more intimate terms with death and illness and our funerary traditions reflect this to a great extent. Using the color black to signify mourning, for example, is thought to have originated among ancient Europeans who believed that painting their skin black would disguise them from recently expired spirits that might try to take control of their bodies. Conversely, there is evidence that early Africans coated their bodies with chalk for the same reason.

The close relationship that the living once had with the dead is further symbolized by how the word that we

Offering quiet running and simple operation, battery-powered ambulances were serving in several American cities by the beginning of the 20th century. This Riker Electric made headlines when it transported President William McKinley to the hospital after he was shot in Buffalo, New York, on September 6, 1901, though it did not prevent his death eight days later. The foot-operated gong beneath the driver's seat afforded warning of the vehicle's approach in the days before Klaxons and sirens.

NAHC, Detroit Public Library

apply to a funeral vehicle—*hearse*—traces its roots to a rake, or *hirpex*, used by Roman farmers every day. Also called a "harrow" in Saxon England, or a "herse" after the Norman invasion of 1066, this tool was made of wood or iron with triangular bracing for the row of teeth it used to break up ground. Since it looked like the candelabras used in Norman funeral services when it was inverted and held aloft above the bearer's head, the same word was eventually applied to both. Placed on the coffin lid during the funeral procession, it grew gradually in size through the Middle Ages to accommodate more candles honoring new saints and new holidays, and evolved into a wheeled vehicle, spelled "hearse" in Middle English, by the 16th Century. Obviously, the slow pace equated with respect at modern funerals was an act of simple practicality when the proceedings included an easily extinguished candelabra was part of the cortege.

In the same way that "funeral" is descended from the Latin *funeralis* or "torchlight procession," the word "ambulance" is descended from the Latin *ambulare*, meaning to walk or move from one place to another. The first use of a vehicle to transport an injured person is difficult to pinpoint, but it is known that the Anglo-Saxons put a hammock-style litter on the back of a horse-drawn cart around 900 A.D, with two attendants sitting on each side of the patient to apply braking chains to the rear wheels on precarious downhill grades. As the lurching and swinging must have been unsettling to a sick passenger, 11th century Normans came up with the idea of suspending a stretcher on poles between two horses moving single-file.

The large volume of casualties produced in wars has always given strong incentive for improving transportation of the injured. King Charles V of Spain equipped his armies with "Ambulancias" during the Siege of Metz in 1553 (the term had actually been coined earlier, to describe the field hospital tents introduced when his grandparents, King Ferdinand and Queen Isabella, fought the Moors in 1487), but these big, heavy vehicles were stationed to the rear of armies and used for transporting surgeons and their equipment, and were typically not sent into the field until the battle had ended. It was not until Napoleon's 1797 campaign in Italy nearly 250 years later that a talented military physician named Dominique-Jean Larrey devised a lightweight, relatively smooth-riding, two-wheeled ambulance equipped with air ventilation, windows, a mattress, and a pillow that could retrieve wounded soldiers while the shooting was still going on. These vehicles became known as *ambulances volantes* or "flying ambulances," because they were teamed with fast-moving "flying" artillery

units and, in the eyes of some troops, seemed to fly through the air as they swept into action. For an encore, Larrey also came up with a camel litter ambulance for Napoleon's 1798 campaign in Egypt.

Across the Atlantic in the newly independent United States, important cultural changes were taking place that would have a fundamental effect on funeral practices and the sort of vehicles used to carry the deceased to their final resting places. When America was a mostly rural, Puritan society centered in New England, burials were handled directly by family and friends, who dressed the corpse, placed it in a coffin built by a local craftsman and carried it to the graveyard themselves. These were typically crowded, nasty places carved out of a neglected corner of the village square or churchyard, where stark slate slabs carved with skulls and other fearsome symbols warned the wicked that fire-and-brimstone awaited them at the Last Judgement.

As the country transformed into a more secular, multi-ethnic, industrialized society spread across a continent during the late 18th and early 19th centuries, Americans began to think of death as an elevated form of afterlife, Our Father's reward for good deeds performed on behalf of one's family, community, and country. These emerging ideals were materially manifested in the creation of beautifully landscaped new cemeteries run in a more business-like fashion, with the costs of land acquisition, landscaping and maintenance financed through the sale of burial plots.

As the burial ground moved from the local churchyard to larger cemeteries on the city's periphery, the undertaker became more than a carpenter or furniture maker who built coffins as a sideline: he became a livery man who hired vehicles.

From the very beginning, funeral professionals equated conservatism with sensitivity, so their horse-drawn hearses went through major visual changes fairly infrequently. The last big transition prior to the automobile's appearance took place during the 1870s and 1880s, when the light, narrow-bodied, oval glass-sided hearses that had dominated the previous half century were succeeded by more massive looking and elaborately carved eight-column "funeral cars." In either case, "Belgian Black" horses were favored for pulling these vehicles due to their calm demeanor and gentle disposition, and they were always a most imposing sight with their plumed headdresses and black velvet robes. The number of horses pulling the hearse proved an easy way to ascertain the status of the deceased, with four or more horses signifying a wealthy person while a person of modest means would warrant one horse and a pauper would be wheeled to potter's field in a hand cart. The properly equipped funeral establishment would also have a plain or sunburst-paneled service wagon for "first calls," a fleet of passenger carriages for mourners, and a small, white hearse for handling the all-too-frequent funerals of children.

Starting with President Abraham Lincoln's June, 1861 founding of a United States Sanitary Commission to select military surgeons and develop field hospitals for the Union forces, the Civil War years witnessed many advances in ambulance development. The two-wheeled "Finley" ambulances initially used, which proved so fragile and rough riding under battlefield conditions that they were soon dubbed "avalanches," were replaced within a year by sturdier, four-wheeled "Rucker" ambulances that could carry four recumbent or 10 seated patients. Dr. Jonathan Letterman, serving as the first Medical Director for the Army of the Potomac, formulated the first truly official ambulance design and construction standards in history for "An Act to Establish Uniform System of Ambulances in the Armies of the United States" passed by Congress in 1864. That same year, the first Geneva Convention developed a standard symbol for signaling the neutrality of battlefield ambulances, which were given safe conduct by displaying a red cross on a white background.

While it remained more common in America's rural areas for the doctor to make a house call to a sick or injured patient than it was for the patient to be taken to the doctor (in such cases, family or friends usually loaded the sick or injured person into a farm wagon using his or her own mattress, which could be burned afterward to ward off contagion), the lessons learned on Civil War battlefields proved invaluable for urban emergency care. The Commercial Hospital in Cincinnati, Ohio, now known as Cincinnati General, is credited with establishing America's first hospital-based ambulance service by 1866, and former U.S. Army surgeon Dr. Edward B. Dalton founded New York City's first ambulance service at Bellevue Hospital in 1869.

The operation was organized along military lines for maximum effectiveness, with each ambulance assigned to a warden to ensure that they were always ready for action. A good "snap" harness could get a horse ready to run within 30 seconds and the ambulances themselves, manufactured by the Abbott-Downing Company of Concord, New Hampshire, were relatively maneuverable and lightweight at 600 to 800 lbs. apiece. Manned by two surgeons and a staff of drivers who were paid $500 a year plus room and board, the ambulances were usually called to action by a telegraph from a police station and

equipped for any conceivable contingency with a pull-out floor to receive the patient, two tourniquets, six bandages, six small sponges, blankets, splints, a quart of brandy, a pair of handcuffs, and a straitjacket. Though these rigs were making good time if they covered a mile of crowded city street in 5 minutes, and stopping was always challenging, the Bellevue service proved a great success.

Self-propelled emergency vehicles were already in service by 1900. On February 24, 1899, the *New York Herald* reported that "five prominent businessmen" had donated a battery-powered ambulance with a 1,600-lb. curb weight and 16-mph top speed to the Michael Reese Hospital in Chicago, and within the year St. Vincent's Hospital had taken delivery of New York City's first electric ambulance from Frederick R. Wood and Son of 219 West 19th Street. In addition to 44 battery cells delivering a 20-30 mile range and a top speed of six, nine, 13 or 16 mph depending on the chosen gear, this 4,000-lb. conveyance had a pair of 2-horsepower motors suspended on the rear axle, slide-out litters, 10-candlepower electric interior lighting, and a speaking tube between the surgeon and the driver.

Fitting a convenient curbside loading stretcher, the Lying-In Hospital of New York placed another Wood Electric into service on March 1, 1900, and when William McKinley was shot in the Temple of Music at the Pan-American Exposition in Buffalo, New York, on September 6, 1901, the newspapers devoted lots of ink to the Riker Electric ambulance that transported him to the hospital. Though it did not prevent his death eight days later, it was thought to be the first time that a U.S. president had ridden in an automobile.

Given that ambulance operators embraced the automobile fairly early on, it is ironic that the closely allied funeral business was probably the last American profession to employ horse-drawn vehicles in significant numbers. While the August 8, 1900, issue of *The Horseless Age* carried word that Philadelphia undertaker Oliver H. Blair had placed an electric funeral wagon built by Fulton & Walker into "successful use" and intended "to add five more," electric cars simply didn't have the range to reach a cemetery on a city's outskirts, and concerns about noise, soot, and smell compelled many cemeteries to ban gasoline-powered vehicles—even if they hadn't, why would any family in mourning want to rush a loved one to their final resting place at 15 or even 20 mph? In spite of the naysayers, there were still a few forward-thinking funeral directors, usually in cities where poor roads were less of a factor, who transferred their old horse-drawn hearse bodies to passenger car or light truck chassis with the help of a local blacksmith or mechanic. Until the Association of American Cemetery Superintendents lifted its ban on automobiles at its annual convention in October, 1909, most of these early one-offs proved their worth in "first call" or service roles, such as retrieving the deceased from the place of death or taking delivery of a coffin at the railway station. A typical pioneer in this respect was Stephens & Bean of Fresno, California, which ran a 1905 Rambler Type 1 Surrey locally fitted with a boxy casket receptacle on the left side of the body and a pair of right-side bucket seats for the driver and funeral director. The July 4th, 1906, issue of *The Horseless Age* reported that this car had accomplished one 100-mile journey in 5 1/2 hours, while a 50-mile trip "on which a corpse was conveyed" was completed in just 3 hours.

It is generally believed that the first entirely horseless funeral in America occurred in Chicago on January 15th, 1909, when a leading undertaker named H. D. Ludlow organized an all-car procession honoring the last wishes of Wilfred A. Pruyn, a longtime taxi man with lots of friends in the Automobile Livery Chauffeurs' Union. As Ludlow had not previously worked with motor vehicles, he turned to livery service owner Charles A. Coey (who also operated one of America's first driving schools and the Chicago Thomas Flyer distributorship), who improvised an appropriate conveyance by mounting a four-column Cunningham horse-drawn hearse body onto a 12-passenger Thomas opera bus chassis. It proved so successful that Ludlow used it for another 13 funerals over the next nine weeks, after which Coey replaced it with an even larger, more splendid motor hearse wearing a brand new Cunningham body on March 22, 1909.

Since the funeral directing community was so closely-knit by its own schools, periodicals and annual conventions, long-established builders of horse-drawn hearses could not help but notice and respond to the trade's increasing interest in motor vehicles. Crane and Breed of Cincinnati, a leader in the funeral supply field since the time it manufactured America's first metallic burial cases in 1853, was the first American firm to market a commercially built, gasoline-powered motor hearse on June 15, 1909. "The demand for it has arrived. WE cannot avoid it. YOU cannot. Nobody can," the company proclaimed upon the cover of *The Sunnyside*, stating that "those people who continually ride in automobiles object to the long and (to them) uncomfortably close and slow carriage journey. They want speed—the smooth glide to the cemetery, same as downtown or anywhere else—and especially in larger cities … The demand is perfectly natural, and if you cater to that class of trade you are bound to supply it." The vehicle's mechanical specification included a water-cooled, 30-horsepower, four-cylinder engine with triple-magneto ignition and a 30-mph top speed that was "faster by fifteen miles than any hearse should go," a three-speed transmission with a "fool-proof" multiple disc clutch running in oil, heavy-duty "noiseless" chain drive ("we shall take no chance on a shaft-driven machine," Crane & Breed proclaimed, "which is very well for pleasure, but not so good for business"), 36-inch wheels with the customer's choice of pneumatic or solid tires, and a 130-inch wheelbase channel steel frame whose running boards could be fitted with removable wire flower baskets.

Though the front seat had no roof or doors and the casket compartment was plainly carved with a column at each corner and crossed Cycus leaves on the side panels, the concept's basic novelty was emphasized with an odd-looking, mound-like rooftop sculpture inspired by the tomb of the Roman general Scipio. More conventional flat-top models, including a triple-duty Combination Hearse, Ambulance and Casket Delivery Wagon making maximum use of the costly motorized chassis, were on sale by September. By the end of 1911 Crane & Breed had elected to focus on body building, adopting Winton mechanicals fitted to a special 152-inch wheelbase increased-strength chassis built for it by the famous Cleveland firm. This would mark the first of many formal and informal alliances between a professional vehicle builder and a mainstream carmaker, though the majority of early firms preferred to assemble their own chassis using mechanical components sourced from suppliers to the auto industry at large.

James Cunningham, Son & Company of Rochester, New York, already one of America's longest-established and best-regarded builders of horse-drawn carriages and funeral coaches with origins dating back to 1838, emerged as another early leader in the movement towards gasoline-powered professional cars. Respectively offering easier operation and greater range than the steam and electric emergency vehicles that had come earlier, its Model 774 became America's first commercially built gasoline Auto Ambulance when it was announced in funeral trade journals on April 15th, 1909. Resting on a 126-inch wheelbase chassis, the coachwork touted a stained mahogany interior with electric dome lights, two attendant seats and a linoleum-surfaced floor, as well as a roofed-in driver's seat with a windshield, roll-down side curtains and foot-operated warning gong. Power initially came from a four-cylinder Continental motor making 32 horsepower, though a 40-horsepower overhead-valve unit built by Cunningham took its place within a year. A semi-closed Auto Hearse based on Cunningham's Style 793 Mosque deck body also debuted in August,

Concerns about noise and smell initially barred gasoline automobiles from most American cemeteries, so the first home-built cars in funeral service proved their worth in workhorse roles such as retrieving the deceased from the place of death or taking delivery of coffins at the railway station. Stephens & Bean of Fresno, California, ran this 1905 Rambler Type 1 Surrey fitted with a boxy casket receptacle on the left side of the body and a pair of right-side bucket seats for the driver and undertaker. If desired, the original touring body could be re-installed in about 30 minutes so the vehicle could be used for pleasure as well as business.

Thomas A. McPherson collection

In order to avoid spark plug problems and the often-dangerous prospect of hand-cranking a gasoline engine, the Kings County Hospital in Brooklyn, New York, opted for a White steamer chassis when it placed Ambulance No. 7 in service around 1908-09. The body could accommodate up to four patients on two levels, but it must have been frighteningly coffin-like to ride to the hospital in the lightless lower compartment!

Nathan Lazernick photos, NAHC, Detroit Public Library

Having built carriages since 1838 and horse-drawn funeral coaches since the Civil War, James Cunningham, Son & Company of Rochester, New York, was another early motor hearse builder that felt that the transition from the feed loft to the gasoline pump should not compromise traditional standards of construction or aesthetics. This stately Model 807 casket wagon, attractively finished in light gray with gold trim and sunburst-pattern side panels, was completed in 1910.

Bernie Weis collection

1909, with a White steam car chassis initially employed to insure appropriately quiet and smooth operation at procession speeds as low as 2 mph.

In spite of the progress made, horse-drawn hearses continued to outsell motor-driven types 8 to 1 as late as 1915, and the leading makers hedged their bets by building horse-drawn and horseless funeral vehicles side-by-side. While the mortuary trade's basic conservatism had a lot to with it, an equally important factor was that only large urban firms could afford to spend between $4,000 and $6,000 for the first auto hearses being sold at a time when a quality horse-drawn version could be bought for around $1,500. In spite of its greater cost, a motor hearse could also be expected to last only a few years before it needed to be replaced, and other major impediments included the cost of employing experienced chauffeurs and the fact that an auto hearse could go no faster than any horse-drawn carriage taking part in the cortege. Firms that managed the initial outlay, however, soon discovered that a car-based hearse was much easier to maneuver and stop in city traffic than a horse-drawn coach, and it could pay for itself by handling more funerals in a given time period.

While there were many firms throughout North America that crafted funeral cars for largely-local clientele, an exceptionally large share of the 160 firms engaged in this work were located in Ohio and Illinois, not only to take advantage of the many auto makers and component suppliers in Michigan and Indiana, but also the extremely skilled hardwood carvers of Scandinavian ancestry found in the region's carriage and furniture industries.

Even though fully enclosed driver's compartments had became common by the time the gasoline pump displaced the feed loft in mid-teens, the conservative nature of these builders and their customers saw to it that most early motor hearses maintained a strong visual resemblance to their horse-drawn predecessors. Their elaborate, Victorian-style bodies were truly awe-inspiring demonstrations of traditional hand craftsmanship with their intricately carved columns and drapery panels, which were inevitably complimented with leaded or beveled glass windows and an ornate pair of brass or silver-plated coach lamps that could be 4 feet tall on the fanciest coaches. Henney, to cite just one example of the standards in place, would lavish three weeks on the paintwork alone, applying 21 coats of primer, color, and varnish to a durable, hardwood-framed body covered in hand-hammered metal panels.

While the professional car industry might expect to serve only a few thousand customers each year and most of them would want a vehicle built to special order, there

were still efforts to realize economies of scale through technological and marketing advances that could, in the spirit of Henry Ford's Model T, bring purchase costs down and expand the size of the overall market. It is significant that the first big builder of budget-priced professional cars, Maurice Wolfe of the Meteor Motor Car Company in Piqua, Ohio, had more experience in the auto business than the carriage trade where earlier players had gotten started. Wolfe acquired the Clark Motor Car Company of Shelbyville, Indiana, in 1912, renamed it Meteor and moved its manufacturing operations to Piqua. After debuting "assembled" touring cars and roadsters with six-cylinder Continental or Model engines priced from $1,050 to $1,375 in the summer of 1914, Wolfe made an even bigger splash by introducing the industry's first reasonably priced funeral coach/ambulance combination in 1915, billing it as a "$2,800 car for $1,750" with its 45-horsepower Continental six, Stromberg carburetor, Delco self-starter, removable flower rack, and two sets of rear compartment drapes, with one set being gathered silk for funerals while the other was plainly finished for ambulance service.

As Meteor lead the charge toward more affordable funeral cars at home, World War I dramatically boosted the demand for American-built motor ambulances overseas. An initial fleet of 10 Model T Ford ambulances, likely Manchester, England-assembled touring cars retrofitted with crude plank bodies made of packing crates, was serving in France as early as August or September, 1914, and the numbers soon increased when it was seen how a prompt evacuation of the wounded boosted morale in the trenches. By 1917, the American Field Service had 1,100 mostly Ford-built vehicles tending to the wounded on the Western Front.

Though the Ford ambulances used in France looked somewhat comical with their short wheelbases and extremely long rear overhangs, the combination delivered superb maneuverability in tight quarters and a surprisingly comfortable ride for the patients. The canvas-topped wooden bodies were officially rated for three stretchers, but up to 10 casualties could be carried out of a particularly savage battle by using the fenders and running boards. Operators also appreciated how the Model T could keep moving on flat tires if some shrapnel was encountered on the battlefield.

The General Motors Truck Company was another firm besides Ford that offered the advantage of scale, delivering 8,512 vehicles to the U.S. Army through 1919. About 5,000 units of this total comprised the Model 15 ambulance that had already proved its worth in the British army and "Black Jack" Pershing's Mexican campaign against Pancho Villa, and an improved Model

16 launched in 1918.

Back in the States, a dependable mode of transportation between the patient's residence and the nearest medical facility was urgently needed, and local funeral directors soon emerged as the most logical providers of such services as they were used to handling crisis situations, had a telephone that was answered on a 24-hour, 365-day basis, and were typically the only other people in town besides the doctor with advanced training in natural sciences like anatomy, chemistry and pathology. Furthermore, the funeral director was inevitably the only person with equipment and vehicles that could move immobile patients and transport them to a hospital in a reclined position, which was especially important in isolated locales where the trip might take several hours.

Expanding their staffs with Red Cross-trained personnel or World War I veterans who had served as medics, more than 90 percent of the funeral homes in the United States offered some sort of ambulance service by 1930 and it was frequently free-of-charge as a benefit to the community. Many directors operated "combination" coaches that could be quickly converted from hearses into ambulances by removing the flower rack and replacing it with a stretcher and a pair of attendants' seats (during the 1950s and 60s, this basic concept would be fully developed with bolt-on roof beacons, reversible casket rollers, flush-folding attendants seats, and removable landau panels covering the ambulance signage on the quarter windows). Many directors also outfitted their lead or personal cars as sedan ambulances where the right side door post and right front passenger seat could be removed to make space for a wheeled cot that was secured into place by depressions or post cups in the floor. A number of funeral firms also rented convalescent equipment as a sideline or donated their services to the Purple Cross Emergency Relief Corps founded in the 1920s, which would send large numbers of ambulances to major disaster scenes like mine cave-ins, floods, tornados, and train wrecks, prior to its dissolution in the late 1940s.

The automobile had became a fully accepted element in the funeral procession by the early 1920s and metal was well on its way to replacing wood as the most popular body building material. As a result of this progress and the rising popularity of combination cars that could be used as part-time ambulances, morticians and their customers began to gravitate towards funeral vehicles that resembled other automobiles of the day and the so-called "limousine-style" hearse became the dominant type.

Compared to the old, carved-column hearses that were visually descended from horse-drawn vehicles, the limousine-style coach offered a long, low, and completely modern silhouette that complimented other cars in the funeral procession with its plain steel body panels and full length windows, which were usually fitted with half- or full-length flower trays at beltline level. For added flair, the purchaser could always opt for a contrasting color roof and fender finish, disc wheels, a nickel-plated radiator shell flanked by drum-shaped headlights, leaded or beveled glass quarter windows, and a "landau back" roof with leather-covered D-pillars trimmed with ornamental S-shaped irons. While the underlying structure was still fashioned from finely seasoned and kiln-dried hardwoods, the departure from past aesthetics was further emphasized by the radiused body corners and tucked-under rear ends that became common by mid-decade. These surface transitions, initially wrapped or hammered over the framework, became considerably easier to fashion after the Packards and Nashes built in Bellefontaine, Ohio, by A.J. Miller took advantage of converted tire presses to introduce the professional car industry to hydraulically-formed steel body panels in 1927. Eureka of Rock Falls, Illionois, meanwhile, stressed in its advertising that its limousine-style bodies could be custom-built on "any new or used chassis."

That limousine hearses were less expensive and easier to build than their carved panel predecessors obviously appealed to relatively large and efficient new players like the Superior Body Company of Lima, Ohio, which had been originally established in May 1923 to construct aluminum-paneled bus bodies for locally built Garford Motor Truck chassis. The firm entered the big time after the attractive, well-built ambulance and funeral coach bodies it debuted on Cadillac V-8 and Studebaker Big Six chassis in early 1925 attracted the attention of Studebaker President Albert R. Erskine. Erskine struck a deal where Superior would construct standardized bodies to Studebaker's specifications, mount them on a specially engineered long-wheelbase chassis powered by a 75-horsepower Big Six L-head engine and sell them directly to Studebaker, which would market and distribute them with its 3,000-strong nationwide dealer network. Helped by keen pricing (just $3,550 complete for both ambulance and hearse models) and an extensive installment financing program specially targeted at funeral directors, more the 1,200 Superior-Studebakers were sold during the first year of the alliance and the company was well on its way to becoming the world's largest-volume coachbuilder.

"Getting the casket to and from the coach is considered by many funeral directors the 'zero hour' of the whole service," the Indiana-based Knightstown Body Company asserted in a 1928 trade journal advertisement, and these procedures were sometimes fraught with family-distressing challenges. Though metal or rubber rollers had been built into the casket floor and rear door threshold since the days of horse-drawn coaches to facilitate loading and unloading, pallbearers strained to lift the deceased into the first motor hearses with their high-riding frames and narrow double rear doors. More often than not, the street they had to stand in while performing their solemn task was unpaved and muddy; parking the coach at right angles to the curb could solve both problems, to be sure, but traffic issues usually ruled this option out at urban funerals. Fortunately, the new limousine-style hearses had a second set of doors behind the driver's seat, which inspired the Eureka Company of Rock Falls, Illinois, to introduce the industry's first "Side-Way Burial Coach" in the autumn of 1926. This innovation, developed after hours in the home basement workshop of a five-year Eureka employee named Wilbur S. Myers (who would become the company's president in 1945), featured a swing-out casket table that glided on ball bearings along a Y-shaped track to emerge from either side of the vehicle. In addition to reducing loading height from street level to curb level, side servicing also allowed more uniform spacing between the hearse and other cars parked outside the church or funeral home and reduced the need to maneuver the casket between rows of gravestones once it arrived at the cemetery.

Within a short time, exclusively side-servicing hearses (with the spare tire mounted underneath the rear window like a regular passenger car's) were superseded by more versatile "three-way" vehicles whose casket tables could also slide out the rear door. This basic three-way concept (aside from small refinements like lighter-weight Formica construction and flat-faced rectangular pads for the adjustable bier pins that anchored the casket to the table) would remain unchanged until Superior sold the last series-built examples in 1984. To allow unrestricted table movement, three-way coaches were typically fitted with sliding or tilting front seats, a catch that locked the table at either extreme of travel, and double-width side door openings eliminating the center pillar and partition.

Though Eureka had been the first firm to put a side-loading funeral coach on the market, stressing in its initial promotions that it "strikes a hopeful note and casts none of the gloom inevitably created by rear-loading hearses," the Henney Motor Company of Freeport, Illinois, claimed to be the first builder with a patent on the principle and this difference of opinion spurred some rather spirited battles in the legal and advertising arenas.

The advent of side-servicing funeral cars was just one of several significant developments witnessed in the professional vehicle industry during the 1920s and 1930s. Trade-ins and servicing were addressed more effectively as specialized hearse and ambulance dealers, divided into geographic territories and often drawn from the ranks of successful funeral directors and livery services, began to take the place of telegraph or mail-based sales arrangements that concluded with the purchaser taking delivery at the factory. Firms like Cunningham, Henney, and Meteor that had previously built their own chassis from the ground up began switching to factory-built long wheelbase "commercial" chassis sourced from mainstream carmakers like Cadillac and Buick, though the transition was often de-emphasized by using the body builder's badges on hubcaps and bumpers.

Sayers & Scovill developed an air-conditioned ambulance of sorts in 1935, fitting the partition with a cork-insulated stainless-steel tank that was filled with cracked ice and water that was pumped through a pair of heater cores and 6-volt blower motors using a coolant pump from a machine tool grinder; the tank required refilling after 90 minutes use at 90 degrees, but it proved adequate for a typically short hospital trip until Henney delivered the first mechanically air-conditioned ambulance to the Kreidler Funeral Home of McAllen, Texas, in 1938. Superior welcomed the 1936 model year with a line of Pontiac professional cars that proved so successful they replaced the company's Studebakers after 1937, while the Flxible Company of Loudonville, Ohio, (paralleling Superior in the way that it had branched into funeral cars and ambulances from the bus industry in 1925) began to distinguish its mostly Buick-based offerings with raised hoods, cowls, and headlight stanchions designed to compliment their tall coach bodies.

Henney, having emerged as the biggest purchaser of the moderately priced Packard 120 Series 158-inch wheelbase commercial chassis introduced in 1935, earned the grudging admiration of its rivals by securing an agreement giving it exclusive use of Packard's commercial chassis starting with the 1937 model year. While the coup initially won Henney a commanding one-third share of the total hearse and ambulance market, it also put the company at a fatal disadvantage during the postwar years, when it had to compete against five firms building Cadillac coaches.

While the limousine-style funeral coach had proved itself ideally suited to combination ambulance service and evolving construction methods, there was a measure of nostalgia for the stage presence and painstaking craftsmanship of the old carved-panel hearses. The ultra-prestigious and conservative Cunningham company

The first commercially manufactured motor hearses were extremely expensive, so many rural undertakers built their own by mounting older coachwork on touring car or roadster chassis. The bowed roofline and rounded rear doors on this service wagon, created from a 1912-13 Reo by Kalkaska, Michigan, mortician Lowell M. Clapp, were typical of horse-drawn hearse bodies prior to the 1880s.

David E. Wolfe collection

Maurice Wolfe, founder of the Meteor Motor Car Company of Piqua, Ohio, took advantage of direct mail sales and an "assembled" chassis employing a six-cylinder, 45-horsepower Continental engine and Delco self-starting when he debuted the industry's first reasonably priced funeral coach/ambulance combination in 1915. It was billed as a "$2,800 car for $1,750." A Meteor "Twin Six" offering a 72-horsepower Weidley V-12 for $2,150 went on sale in 1916.

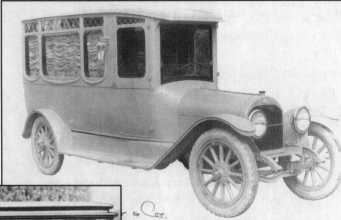

Museum of Funeral Customs

While most motor hearses had fully enclosed driver's compartments by the mid-teens, the conservative nature of the funeral market dictated that a strong visual resemblance to earlier horse-drawn equipment be maintained. With its intricately carved columns and drapery panels, this 1918 Sayers & Scovill Style 195 demonstrated the skilled craftsmanship that had made this Cincinnati firm a leader in the field since 1876.

Moby's Eureka Autos

For the first two decades after commercially built auto hearses and ambulances became available, bodies were typically mounted on a purpose-designed, long-wheelbase chassis of the coachmaker's own manufacture with components from the rest of the automotive industry. The 1923 Meteor 70-horsepower chassis epitomized this construction method with its Continental "Red Seal" six-cylinder engine, Warner transmission, Fedders radiator, Delco ignition system, and Timken axles.

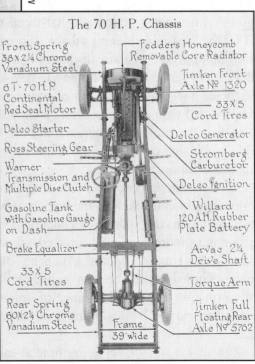

The 70 H. P. Chassis

Front Spring 38 x 2¼ Chrome Vanadium Steel
Fedders Honeycomb Removable Core Radiator
Timken Front Axle No. 1320
6T-70 H.P. Continental Red Seal Motor
33 x 5 Cord Tires
Delco Starter
Delco Generator
Ross Steering Gear
Stromberg Carburetor
Warner Transmission and Multiple Disc Clutch
Delco Ignition
Willard 120 A.H. Rubber Plate Battery
Gasoline Tank with Gasoline Gauge on Dash
Brake Equalizer
Arvac 2¼ Drive Shaft
33 x 5 Cord Tires
Torque Arm
Rear Spring 60 x 2¼ Chrome Vanadium Steel
Frame 39 wide
Timken Full Floating Rear Axle No. 5762

Moby's Eureka Autos

kept building them without interruption all the way up through the time it left the field in 1936. Sayers & Scovill forged an exciting new aesthetic direction for the genre with its 1929 debut of a "Signed Sculpture" town car hearse whose quarter panels featured massive cast-bronze reliefs of an autographed "Angel of Memory" bearing a wreath and Cycas leaf that was created by the eminent sculptor Clement Barnhorn. It was an extremely expensive and exclusive model, with an $8,500 F.O.B. Cincinnati factory price and a one-purchaser-per-territory sales policy, but it inspired an entire decade's worth of imitators embracing Art Deco aesthetics like arch-shaped decorative panels, pontoon fenders, and "beavertail" rear ends. Though the panels on these new-generation carved coaches were more often made of stamped steel or cast aluminum to simplify construction and save weight, most casual observers were convinced that these elements were still fashioned from hardwood thanks to carefully detailed tassels, curtain folds, and tie backs for the "draperies" between the pillars, which were often matte finished as well.

Notable variations on the theme included: the "Art Carved" hearses launched by A.J. Miller as 1934 models, where three beveled French glass windows were situated above plain-surfaced panels on each side of the body and surrounded by an elaborately carved and pinstriped arch with two dividing pillars; Flxible's 1938-41 "Classic A" and "AA" models, featuring two semi-circular arches with filigreed borders and carved drape or beveled glass inserts; the Gothic panel Cadillacs and LaSalles, complete with blue stained-glass windows and Old English rift-sawn oak interiors, introduced by Meteor at the NFDA's October, 1938 Convention in New York City; and the "4-Purpose" combination coach with removable cast aluminum drapery panels that Superior debuted as a $250 option on its limousine style Studebakers and Pontiacs in 1936. Henney was the only major builder that did not catalog a carved panel hearse during this period, but its Packards could be finished as a so-called "Formal Limousine" with vertically ribbed aluminum plaques bearing the owner's name on the side and rear doors and a matching Art Deco motif for the interior woodwork.

Another interesting new body style that appeared in quantity by 1940 was the purpose-built flower car, developed by coachbuilders to counter the disappearance of the open touring cars and phaetons that had previously ferried florals in the funeral procession. As early as the late 1920s, Cunningham had constructed casket wagons that combined pickup-style driver's cabs with low-profile rear decks that were capable of carrying flowers within their perimeter railings. The 1937 model year witnessed Eureka's launch of a full-fledged La Salle flower car featuring a linoleum-lined open well with a protective cover and a trap door for cleaning purposes, a collapsible driver's compartment top made of tan Burbank material, and a matching rear boot behind the flower well that was shaped to simulate a folded convertible top. These open trough models soon became known as "Western" or "Chicago"-style flower cars because Chicago livery services were the first to use them—a big gangster funeral might see a dozen of these vehicles accompanying the hearse.

The "Eastern" flower car debuted by Henney as a 1938 model set a new standard for versatility with a cross-railed, corrosion-resistant stainless-steel deck that could be hydraulically inclined to accommodate different-sized baskets or placed in a horizontal position so a casket could be loaded into the compartment underneath through a drop down tailgate (later versions had a side-swinging, hearse-style rear door). This body style also had a simulated convertible top and a second pair of side doors that allowed a church truck or chairs for the funeral service to be easily loaded. Coupe-style flower cars with painted metal roofs and four-window cabs were added to the S&S, Meteor, and A.J. Miller LaSalle lineups for the 1939 model year, while Flxible had Buick and Cadillac flower cars with single window cabs on sale by 1940. The 1942 Flxible Innovation was a novel synthesis of flower car and carved panel funeral coach styling elements with its coupe-style cab and natural finish walnut side panels, even though its smooth rear deck wasn't capable of carrying flowers and the suspension in civilian car production following America's entry into World War II prevented it from spawning imitators.

The landau look still most commonly associated with American funeral coaches, where a heavily-padded leather, vinyl, or fabric roof with opaque quarter panels is ornamented with S-shaped bows recalling the center-hinged carriage irons used to lower the tops on horse-drawn Victorias in the 19th century, also traces its origins to the 1930s. The Eureka Company of Rock Falls, Illinois, was evidently the first firm to offer the style in 1931. The look did not really catch on as trend, however, until S&S of Cincinnati unveiled a LaSalle-chassied Victoria as a 1938 model, but other firms latched onto it quickly as an inexpensive but effective way to dress up an otherwise simple-looking limousine body. By 1940, visually similar cars with straight funeral coach and combination ambulance interiors were available from Meteor, A.J. Miller, and Henney. Flxible Buicks and Superior Pontiacs, along with the Cadillacs catalogued by both firms and the humble Fords created by The Shop of Siebert in Toledo, could also be fitted with landau bars by 1941, while A.J. Miller added them to its Cadillac flower car when that style switched to a three-window cab for 1942.

In common with the automakers that supplied them with long-wheelbase chassis in peacetime, American funeral coach and ambulance builders made considerable contributions to the country's war effort even though the rapid, costly changeover to military wares left many firms with red ink on their balance sheets in 1942. Flxible's Loudonville, Ohio, factory, in addition to manufacturing gear guards for Liberty ship steam winches, radiator support brackets for M-4 tanks, Goodyear airship control cars and fins, and windshield frame assemblies for Corsair fighter planes, cranked up the production of busses to the point that they were being finished off in the street, with electric cords running out to them from the plant. In Rock Falls, Illinois, Eureka constructed field ambulances and woody wagon-bodied Navy staff cars on the 1.5-ton Chevrolet truck chassis, utilitarian ambulance conversions of the International step van, 15-passenger war workers' busses on Chevrolet passenger car and Ford truck chassis and, most memorably, 50 gigantic 100-passenger articulated busses that were built for the Army Ordinance Department's Chicago branch from auto transport trailers. Superior, turning its Lima, Ohio, facilities over to the manufacture of military busses, box-bodied field ambulances, signal corps and ordinance maintenance vans, rocket launchers, radio installations and ammunition boxes, became the first auto equipment manufacturer in its classification to earn the Army-Navy "E" pennant for Excellence in war production. Presaging the truck-based modular ambulances used by rescue squads today, Henney built almost 3,500 Packard passenger car ambulances with box-like bodies that saw distinguished service in England's bomb-ravaged cities and Civil Defense agencies on the home front. Sayers & Scovill of Cincinnati, known as Hess & Eisenhardt after it was sold to one-time company office boys Emil Hess and Charles A. Eisenhardt, Sr. in 1942, constructed trailers, cargo bodies and standard army truck componentry.

With the return of peace, however, all of these builders were plagued by widespread shortages of raw materials and commercial chassis, dictating that their immediate postwar lineups be severely truncated. The most significant casualties of post-World War II austerity were the Cathedral and carved drape style funeral coaches with their decorative stamped or cast-metal panels, which would not have worked aesthetically with the full-fendered bodies Detroit was rolling out in any event. Landau hearses were far better suited to the new look, since most of their styling differentiation versus regular passenger cars took place above belt line level, and the position they assumed as the industry's dominant body design in this period has never really been relinquished.

The war years had also witnessed considerable price inflation with the cheapest Eureka Cadillac Chieftain end-loading limousine style hearse, to cite just one of many possible examples, increasing from $3,195 in 1942 to $4,953 four years later. There was still no shortage of eager buyers after a 3 1/2-year drought when no civilian cars were built at all, and this created an opportunity for new coachbuilding ventures that focused on cutting, splicing, and otherwise converting sedan deliveries and the new steel-bodied station wagons into inexpensive hearses, ambulances, service cars, and combinations.

In the late 1940s and early 1950s, Memphis, Tennessee, and its environs, a relatively low-wage area in a union-averse "right to work" state (which would also attract the Saturn and Nissan plants to Tennessee during the 1980s) became home to more than half a dozen of these firms, including: Guy Barnette & Company; the Economy Coach Company, whose professional cars were dubbed the "Memphian" line after a name change to Memphis Coach in 1955; Weller Brothers, famous for the "Four-Purpose" ambulance/closed flower car/child's hearse/utility vehicle it began building from the standard-wheelbase Chevrolet sedan delivery in 1948; the Comet Coach Company, which eventually sold its name to Ford for its 1960 Mercury compact and relocated to Blytheville, Arkansas, where it manufactured Cotner-Bevington Oldsmobile professional cars named for company co-founders Waldo Cotner and Bob Bevington; and former Comet Coach partner Jack Pinner's Pinner Coach, which situated its first plant about ten miles southeast of Memphis in Olive Branch, Mississippi. Budget-conscious funeral directors and fire department rescue squads could also take their business to the National Body Manufacturing Company of Knightstown, Indiana, which Vernon Z. Perry founded in 1945 by combining the remnants of the prewar "Silver" Knightstown and Knightstown Funeral Car companies, and the Acme Motor Company of Sterling, Illinois, established across the river from Eureka's Rock Falls factory by F. J. "Fran" Cullins and Don Schultz in 1950. Acme's "Sterling Line" of landau and limousine style hearses, ambulances, combination coaches, and service cars were created by extending the wheelbase of a straight-eight Pontiac sedan delivery 36.5 inches. While Acme left the business less than two years after the sedan delivery was dropped from Pontiac's U.S. lineup in 1953, National built a mind-boggling variety of professional vehicles from Chevrolet, Pontiac, Oldsmobile, Buick, Chrysler, Plymouth, Mercury, Ford and even International Travelall chassis over a 25-year period.

Older builders in Illinois and Ohio that had previously concentrated their skill on the Cadillac Commercial Chassis countered the new competition from down South by proliferating their own inexpensive offerings. Eureka sold small numbers of extended-wheelbase Chevrolets and Pontiacs for a couple of seasons starting in 1949. Meteor followed suit for 1950 with a lineup that included a particularly novel Pontiac flower car with hardtop styling (in December, 1953, the company announced that it was delegating construction of its Pontiacs to Economy Coach of Memphis). In 1952, the Henney Motor Company's long-wheelbase Packard professional cars were joined on sale by a standard wheelbase Clipper "Junior" initially priced at $3,333. Superior had the most successful run in the low-cost field by producing its entry-level coaches in a low-wage venue just like the Memphians, turning to its "Southern Division" school bus plant in Kosciusko, Mississippi, to produce the professional Pontiacs it reintroduced to its lineup in 1953. Production of these cars increased substantially from 34 units in 1953 to 195 the following year and 273 for the completely redesigned V-8 models debuted in 1955. That same year, with competition from Henney-built Packards no longer a factor, Superior's freshly expanded operations in Lima, Ohio, consumed nearly 40 percent of the 1,975 Commercial Chassis produced by Cadillac—an impressive four-fold increase from 1938.

While the customers of an upscale, conservative builder like Eureka were willing to absorb the price differential of an old-fashioned, wood-framed body until the 1957 model year, a new miracle material called fiberglass was rapidly making its mark on the industry. Durable, relatively light in weight, easily fashioned and impervious to corrosion, this reinforced composite allowed even budget market professional car producers to offer a wide variety of body styles without resorting to the expense of steel tooling and surface finishing. It played an important role in the early 1950s appearance of high-headroom ambulances that could transport up to four patients at once without being top-heavy. It also encouraged prevailing trends toward more elaborate exterior styling as the Eisenhower decade progressed, with many coachbuilders following the lead of Detroit's automakers in their adoption of thinner window frames, wrap-around windshields and rear windows, and two- or even three-tone paint jobs—a trend taken to its illogical limits when Miller-Meteor's 1956-58 lineup offered a Crestwood funeral coach whose lower flanks were adorned with a simulated "Mahogatrim" or "Walnutrim" finish. So-called "commercial" glass, with more height

and less tumblehome (the angle at which it rakes towards the top of the roof) than OEM windows, also began to appear as a proportion-enhancer in this era, and Flxible took a big step towards making combination cars look more like straight hearses by becoming the first coachbuilder to fit removable landau panels, easily secured with thumb screws, to the rear quarter windows of its dramatically finned 1959 Buicks. Superior epitomized the era's exuberance to an even greater extent by offering a pillarless hardtop funeral coach called the Beau Monde that could be ordered as a fully enclosed flower car touting a completely unobstructed view of the tributes inside.

Embracing a "bigger is better" business mentality that also spurred Nash and Hudson's formation of American Motors and Studebaker's ill-fated union with Packard, a number of coachbuilders merged with each other or became parts of conglomerates during the 1950s and '60s in order to increase their working capital and lower their component costs. Wayne Works, a Richmond, Indiana, bus manufacturer that was also known for building Divco milk trucks, initiated the trend in January, 1954, when it paid $230,000 to purchase the Meteor Motor Car Company of Piqua, Ohio. After announcing its acquisition of the A. J. Miller Co. of Bellefontaine, Ohio, on March 19, 1956, Wayne Works merged the operations of both firms at Meteor's Piqua plant in time to roll out the first "Miller-Meteor" professional cars as 1957 models. Wayne Works' product portfolio was further broadened with Oldsmobiles when it purchased Cotner-Bevington and its Blytheville, Arkansas, factory at the beginning of the 1964 model year. Flxible (which had already suspended funeral coach and ambulance production once, from 1953 to 1958) permanently staked its future in the bus business by selling its Buick professional car tooling to Vernon Perry's National Coaches in January of 1965. This move came several months after Eureka president Wilbur Myers, in failing health, chose retirement over a costly redesign for Cadillac's 1965 models (featuring such major changes as curved side glass and an all-new perimeter frame), selling his parts stock and three-way casket table patents to Superior for a reported $100,000. This was a remarkable amount, considering that S&S had offered only $10,000 for these assets, but it would pale in comparison to the $13,261,520 spent by Sheller-Globe Corporation, a Toledo-based auto parts conglomerate, in 1968 for a 36-percent stake in Superior Coach, with the remaining balance acquired in a stock swap in 1969.

The June 6, 1964, shuttering of Eureka's Rock Falls, Illinois, operation after 93 years in business left just three significant players producing long-wheelbase Cadillac professional cars within a 130-mile radius of

Compared to the old, carved-column hearses that were visually descended from horse-drawn vehicles, the steel-paneled limousine-style funeral coaches that became popular during the 1920s offered a completely modern silhouette. A three-tone paint finish was used to accentuate the horizontal lines of this 1926 Henney "landau-back" built in Freeport, Illinois.

American Funeral Director

Employing a swing-out casket table that glided along a Y-shaped track to emerge from either side of the body, the Eureka Company of Rock Falls, Illinois, debuted the industry's first "Side-Way Burial Coach," shown here on a Reo Flying Cloud chassis, in the autumn of 1926. Three-way hearses with casket tables that could also extend out the back door were available soon afterwards. In addition to reducing loading height to curb level, side servicing allowed more uniform spacing between the hearse and other vehicles parked outside the church or funeral home and reduced the likelihood that the pallbearers would have to step into a muddy street while performing their duties. A pivoting clamp and adjustable bier pins securely locked the casket into place atop the carrier, which also incorporated polished aluminum wheel wells to accommodate a Bomgardner cot for "first calls."

American Funeral Director

After a decade dominated by simply adorned limousine-style hearses, Sayers & Scovill sparked a carved coach revival with its 1929 debut of the "Signed Sculpture" town car funeral coach. The quarter panels of this extremely expensive and exclusive model, priced at $8,500 with sales limited to one customer per territory, featured autographed, cast-bronze reliefs of an "Angel of Memory," created by the eminent sculptor Clement Barnhorn.

Accubuilt

By the mid-1930s, most coachbuilders had abandoned the practice of assembling their own chassis in favor of long-wheelbase "commercial" chassis built by Buick, Cadillac, LaSalle, or Packard. These photos of Buick's 158-inch-wheelbase Series 60 professional car chassis, taken at the Loudonville, Ohio, factory of the Flxible Company (note the Chevrolet Clipper bus being constructed in the background), highlight the 141-horsepower "Dynaflash" straight-eight engine and coil spring rear suspension added to 1938 models.

NAHC, Detroit Public Library

each other in western Ohio: Superior Coach in Lima, the almost equivalently-sized Miller-Meteor concern in Piqua, and the smaller, more exclusive S&S division of Hess & Eisenhardt situated outside of Cincinnati in Rossmoyne. On average they consumed about 2,500 Cadillac Commercial Chassis a year between them during the 1960s. Flxible Buicks, Kosciusko-built Superior-Pontiacs, and Cotner-Bevington Oldsmobiles accounted for another 1,500-2,000 units per annum with the help of the high-top, standard-wheelbase Flxible Buick Flxettes, Superior Pontiac Consorts, and C/B Oldsmobile Sevilles respectively, debuted during the 1960, 1961, and 1963 model years and a number of one-off creations from smaller builders like National-Knightstown, Pinner, and the Duncanville, Texas-based Trinity Coach Company that was best remembered for its 1966-68 Buicks. The bottommost budget segment of the market, meanwhile, included firms like the Automotive Conversion Corporation of Troy and Birmingham, Michigan, Adam & Hense of St. Paul, Minnesota, the Universal Coach Corporation of Detroit, and W.S. Ballantyne of Windsor, Ontario.

While some 12,000 American morticians were still providing ambulance service in the 1960s, it became painfully apparent in this period that too many lives were being lost to inadequate training and outmoded equipment. With only six states offering standard courses for rescuers and less than half of the country's 200,000 ambulance personnel trained to the level of Red Cross advanced first aid, it was not uncommon even in big cities for the patient to ride all alone in the back behind a driver who might be little more than a funeral home chauffeur. The part-time "combination" coaches most often used as ambulances in small communities had no room to stand up and work on a patient and just a few small cabinets in the partition or wheelhouses for carrying medical supplies. While fire departments in some large cities had operated rescue trucks equipped with rudimentary resuscitation devices since the 1930s, these were usually used to revive firefighters overcome by smoke inhalation and had no patient transport capability. Until AT&T, acting on a recommendation from the President's Commission on Law Enforcement and Administration of Justice, reserved the digits 911 for nationwide emergency use in November, 1967, there was no standard telephone number for dialing assistance in an emergency either and, even then, only 17 percent of the U.S. population had 911 service by 1976.

Releasing its landmark three year study, "Accidental Death and Disability: The Neglected Disease of Modern Society," in September, 1966, the National Research Council of the National Academy of Sciences declared that "expert consultants returning from both Korea and Vietnam have publicly asserted that, if seriously wounded, their chances for survival would be better in the zone of combat than on the average city street." Nearly half of the 700,000 Americans who died from coronaries every year were doing so before they even reached a hospital. With another 115,000 lives claimed annually by auto accidents, falls, drownings, seizures, gunshots, electric shocks and on-the-job mishaps, trauma was now the leading cause of death between the ages of 1 and 37, and it was estimated that 90,000 lives could be saved each year by beginning care more promptly and improving communication between doctors at the hospital and caregivers at the accident scene.

American initiatives to bring emergency care to the patient instead of the other way around were greatly influenced by the experiences of Dr. J. Frank Pantridge, who headed the cardiology department at the Royal Victoria hospital in Belfast, Northern Ireland. After concluding in 1963 that 90 percent of his fatal heart attack cases would survive if they received an electric shock before they reached the hospital, he converted a Daimler ambulance into a mobile coronary care unit staffed with a doctor and equipped with a "portable" defibrillator that weighed more than 100 lbs. While reponse times in the city's narrow streets ran as much as 20 minutes, Pantridge's trial chalked up 10 successful pre-hospital resucitations in its first 15 months and the results received worldwide attention.

That same year, Dr. Eugene Nagel of Miami, once he decided a disease-specific ambulance might not be the best way to deal with pre-hospital cardiac arrest, began training six Miami firefighters to become America's first paramedics. He instructed them in defibrillation, "closed chest cardiac Massage" laer known as cardio pulonary resuscitation, or CPR), intubation (the opening of an airway with a laryngoscope) and the administration of intravenous fluids. To make sure his trainees could communicate with the hospital, Nagel worked with cardiologist Jim Hirschman (who had, in 1965, helped make Miami the first U.S. city with a radio link between its hospitals and firefighters) and a radio expert named Ben Denby, to develop a telemetry packaged called a "biocom" that turned the heart's electrical impulses into an audio tone that could be transmitted to the hospital and converted into an EKG readout.

With its 28-lb. Motorola Business Dispatcher radio unit, 11-lb. nickel cadmium battery, and shock-absorbing, waterproof aluminum case, the first design put into service in March 1967 weighed a whopping 54 lbs., but confirmed the idea had promise. Skeptical city officials, meanwhile, were treated to a memorable demonstration where Nagel laid himself down on the commissioner's conference table and said "let's imagine that I've collapsed in your chamber" and brought in a paramedic unit to monitor his EKG and start an IV drip.

Miami was by no means the only U.S. municipality performing pre-hospital care as the 1960s drew to a close. After St. Vincent's Hospital turned a spacious Chevrolet step van into a New York City's first Mobile Coronary Care Unit in 1968, program coordinator Dr. William J. Grace calculated that the heart attack victims attended to by the vehicle (which initiall carried at least one resident physician) within an hour of the onset of acute symptoms had an 8 percent mortality rate, compared to 21 percent for those whose treatment was delayed by more than an hour.

Dr. Richard Crampton eventually trained the nation's first volunteer (as opposed to fire department) paramedics for the Charlottesville-Albemarle Rescue Squad in Charlottesville, Virginia, in 1970.

Following its formation in 1969, the Robert Wood Johnson Foundation would issue 44 grants to communities throughout the U.S. for the development of EMS systems, helping to significantly increase the roll of rescue personnel in its grant regions. Though the Digest of Surveys calculated that 44 percent of all U.S. ambulance services were still being operated by funeral homes as late as 1978, this was only half as many as had been the case four decades earlier and it was plainly obvious that ambulance work, aided by an influx of skilled medics from the war in Vietnam, was becoming a full-time profession.

With 81 municipalities spread across more than 100 square miles, California's widely-dispersed Los Angeles County would prove itself the ideal venue for realizing the potential of paramedic rescue squads after two separate programs set up shop in August, 1969. The first venture, founded by Dr. Walter F. Graf of the Daniel Freeman Hospital in Inglewood, with the backing of the L.A. County Heart Association, dispatched a step van type coronary ambulance that would travel to the nearest of three project hospitals serving more than 700,000 people within a 10-mile diameter service area, pick up a CCU nurse and travel to the scene of a heart attack (it was not until the third year of the pilot project that paramedics were used exclusively). The second, more famous program, developed by Drs. J. Michael Criley and A. James Lewis at the County-operated Harbor General Hospital in Torrance, was established in cooperation with Battalion Chief James O. Page of the L.A. County Fire Department, which had been responding to medical emergencies since 1928 and had equipped more than 300 vehicles in its fleet with resuscitator/inhalator units in 1960.

It would, however, be the TV series *Emergency!*, produced by Robert A. Cinader for Jack Webb's Mark VII Productions and Universal Studios, that would make L.A. County's paramedics the model for the nation. To ensure authentic story lines as John Gage (Randolph Mantooth) and Roy DeSoto (Kevin Tighe) of L.A. County's fictitious Rescue 51 responded to distress calls in a utility-bodied 1972 Dodge D-300 rescue truck, the paramedics hired to assist the series as technical advisors hosted the show's writers during their duty shifts, with Cinader himself witnessing nearly 1,000 rescue calls. When the first of 129 one-hour episodes aired on NBC in January, 1972, there were only 12 paramedic units in the entire country; by the time the show ended its run five years later (seven two-hour movies of the week were also filmed through 1979), at least 50 percent of the U.S. population was within 10 minutes' reach of a paramedic unit and thousands of EMTs, nurses, doctors and firefighters would credit the series with inspiring their career choice.

In the long run, the paramedic movement's demands for more patient and equipment space would play a crucial role in the disappearance of passenger car-based ambulances by the end of the 1970s. The transition to truck-derived emergency units had actually started fairly quietly almost 30 years before, with basic interior conversions of the Ford F-Series panel, the Chevrolet/GMC Suburban, and the International Metro walk-in van that were sold to various industrial plants, military bases, municipal rescue squads, and other buyers who placed a higher priority on interior space, durability, and a low purchase price than they did on riding quality, styling, or prestige. High-headroom ambulance conversions with raised roof caps made of fiberglass were commonly available by the mid-1960s. High-headroom ambulance conversions of these vehicles, with raised roof caps made of fiberglass, were available from several firms by the mid-1960s, while the Automotive Conversion Corp. of Birmingham, Michigan, charged just $1,095.28 to turn a rear-engined 1961 Chevrolet Corvair Greenbriar into a maneuverable "Amblewagon."

In the spring of 1968, about the same time that America's first paramedic squads and mobile coronary care units were entering service, the Ford Motor Company turned the truck-based ambulance revolution up to full volume by unveiling all-new, second-generation Econolines and Club Wagons whose engines (including optional V-8s) had been moved forward in the chassis to enhance driver comfort and expand the cargo floor by 23 percent. Established builders like Superior, and a legion of new players like Horton Emergency Vehicles of Grove City, Ohio, took to them almost immediately, while the Wayne Medicruiser and Knightstown-built National Pacemaster exploited the versatility of the similarly improved Chevrolet and Dodge vans introduced in 1971. Figuring there was no such thing as too much space when it came to the patient's comfort and the paramedic's convenience, Superior even launched a "61" Series in late 1972 where the body of a Chevrolet G-30 or extended-tail Dodge Tradesman van was sliced down the center from end-to-end and widened 14 inches, yielding a 68.4-inch-wide back door, 84 inches of interior width at beltline level, and a 25-inch aisle between the primary patient and the squad bench.

As was the case with the rest of the auto industry, the U.S. government was also assuming a significantly larger role in ambulance design during this era. This was certainly not surprising given that a lot of federal grant money was available to fire departments, rescue squads, and ambulance services in the 1975-83 time frame for the purpose of purchasing new equipment, so most ambulances were manufactured to the government's specifications even though the rigs bought with grants were actually the only ones required to comply.

The first standards, formulated by the Department of Transportation in 1973 and slated to take effect in the 1974 model year, were dubbed KKK-A-1822. They were heavily influenced by a 1970 report from the National Academy of Sciences' Ambulance Design Criteria Committee that incorporated myriad recommendations from coachbuilders, ambulance operators, medical authorities, and individual states. In addition to stipulating minimum interior dimensions and equipment levels that could realistically only be met by truck and van-based vehicles, the criteria also addressed compliance with Federal Motor Vehicle Safety Standards and ambulance-specific identification issues like colors, lettering, and signage. Backwards "AMBULANCE" lettering across the hood of the vehicle, which looked normal in the rear view mirrors of preceding cars, became a standard item, while a blue six-pointed "Star of Life" was devised to serve as an easily recognized symbol that could be affixed to all ambulances instead of those affiliated with the American Red Cross. The white paintwork used for ambulance exteriors was now accented with a high visibility traffic safety color called Omaha Orange, which was a darker, more distinctive shade than the National School Bus Yellow originally slated to be used. KKK-A-1822 also divided truck-based ambulances into three basic design classes that are still in use today: a box-bodied "modular" ambulance mounted on a light- or medium-duty truck chassis with its own separate cab became known as a Type I; a raised-roof van was classified as a Type II; and a Type III designation was assigned to cutaway van chassis carrying an extra-wide rear body with an aisle between the driver and patient compartments. In stark contrast to the Cadillacs and other passenger car-based ambulances that had come before, all three configurations offered plenty of space for emergency medical technicians to stand up, move around, and otherwise work on their patients more effectively.

The challenges involved in mounting an aluminum box behind a pickup cab or adding a raised roof and extra impact bracing to an Econoline van were comparatively modest ones, and more than 80 U.S. and Canadian firms were building truck-type ambulances by the end of the 1970s. Already wincing under the thumb of bean-counting conglomerates that were intent on trimming staffs and model lines, it was certainly bad luck for Ohio's old-line coachbuilders that the emergency profession's call for more patient and equipment space in ambulances coincided with the first gasoline crisis of 1973, prompting the Federal government to pass a Corporate Average Fuel Economy (CAFE) law and General Motors to start paring excess size and weight from its passenger cars beginning with the 1977 model year. The Cadillac Commercial Chassis, whose model year production totals had already fallen from 2,265 units in 1974 to 1,509 units in 1976 as Federal KKK specifications steered more ambulance buyers into trucks and vans, would certainly not be exempt, and an unusually large number of the last big cars were stockpiled by ambulance and livery fleets that kept them in storage until an older unit was retired. Given that funeral coach and ambulance owners equated size and weight with prestige and capability, it was especially off-putting that the Commercial Chassis underwent the greatest wheelbase reduction of any 1977 Cadillac, shrinking from 157.5 to 144.3 inches.

After the disappearance of car-based ambulances and combinations reduced the demand for Cadillac Commercial Chassis from 2,506 units in 1970 to 864 units in 1979, only the widely recognized nameplates of the great Ohio coachbuilders survived into the 1980s as the conglomerates controlling their fates decided that the returns involved in serving the limited funeral market no longer justified production. Miller-Meteor was the first domino to fall, with the Wayne Corporation announcing on September 10, 1979, that it was shuttering the Clark Avenue plant, unceremoniously dismissing 252 employees and 34 North American distributor franchises. Tom Caserta, who had joined Miller-Meteor in 1962 and worked his way up from prepping cars for

Coachbuilders constructed the first purpose-designed flower cars in the late 1930s to replace the open touring cars and phaetons that had previously ferried floral tributes in the funeral procession. Open-well models were dubbed "Western" or "Chicago" style flower cars because livery services in the Windy City were among the first to use them, while "Eastern" style flower cars had hydraulically inclined stainless-steel decks and opening rear doors or tailgates that could admit a casket when the compartment roof was in the horizontal position. The flower cars built by S&S (top), Miller (bottom) and Meteor on the 1939 LaSalle Commercial Chassis used coupe-style driver's cabs, while the 1939 Eureka Cadillac touted a collapsible convertible top.

Donald F. Wood

Coachbuilders constructed the first purpose-designed flower cars in the late-1930s to replace the open touring cars and phaetons that had been used previously. Open-well models were dubbed "Western" or "Chicago" style, while "Eastern" style cars like this 1940 Meteor LaSalle had hydraulically inclined stainless-steel decks and opening rear doors or tailgates that could admit a casket when the compartment roof was in the horizontal position.

The Landau look most commonly associated with today's funeral coaches, offered by Eureka as early as 1931 and popularized by the S&S Victoria launched in 1938, became the industry's dominant style after World War II. It was easier to build than a carved panel hearse and visually better suited to the full-fendered bodies that began appearing in 1948-49. This Flxible-bodied Buick from the war-truncated 1942 model year also featured "airfoil" front fenders flowing into the doors and a hood/cowl assembly raised 5 5/8 inches to compliment the tall coach body.

Moby's Eureka Autos

Being a low-wage town in a "right to work" state where union membership wasn't mandatory, Memphis, Tennessee, became home to several coachbuilders after World War II that concentrated on inexpensive conversions of Pontiac and Chevrolet sedan deliveries. Guy Barnette & Company offered this extended-wheelbase Chevrolet hearse/ambulance combination in 1948.

delivery to serving as the company's national sales and service manager by 1974, recalled many years later that, following Wayne's final disposition of machines and inventory, "I was the fifth to last person to leave when the doors closed on May 16, 1980, and I was in tears. While a guy from the bus plant named Tom Kessler saved many factory photos, most of the company archives were thrown in a dumpster with cans of paint poured over them. I climbed in and tried to save some of the things they had pitched but it had rained already."

The similarly unappreciated Superior Division of the Sheller-Globe Corporation, which had delivered America's very last car-based ambulance (built from a 1979 Cadillac) to Mayo Clinic anesthesiologist and lifelong passenger car ambulance enthusiast Dr. Roger D. White on February 18, 1980, saw its 55-year-old plant at 1200 East Kibby Street in Lima, Ohio, shut down as well shortly after its 1981 coaches were unveiled at the NFDA convention in New Orleans the following autumn. Fortunately, the firm got a new lease on life fairly quickly after Armbruster/Stageway President Thomas P. Earnhart (whose Fort Smith, Arkansas, plant, in addition to building six-door limousines for the funeral trade, had been manufacturing Buick hearses for Superior since 1975), purchased Superior's name, inventory, and tooling in 1981 and moved production to a new, smaller plant 2 miles away from the old at 600 East Wayne Street. By year's end, S&S funeral coaches previously built in Cincinnati by Hess & Eisenhardt were also being manufactured in Earnhart's Lima facility as well.

While economic turmoil and record-high interest rates made the early 1980s an incredibly tough time to initiate an auto-related enterprise, a number of entrepreneurs saw the funeral business as being relatively recession-resistant and, in several cases, they reduced their risk by reviving some of the grand old names from years past. With the Canadian dollar already putting them at a production cost advantage versus U.S. builders, Toronto area author Thomas A. McPherson and Vancouver, B.C., coach dealer Howard Carter purchased the professional car division of AHA (which had been producing traditionally sized Lincoln Continental hearses in Mississauga and later Downsview, Ontario, since 1978) in the fall of 1980 and, recalling the great Rock Falls, Illinois, builder that had shut its doors in 1964, renamed their venture the Eureka Coach Company Ltd. Building hearses with a limousine-style cut-and-stretch method as opposed to a long-wheelbase commercial chassis used by other firms, Eureka really hit its stride after launching the first commercial glass Buick coaches seen since the 1960s and a Cadillac Concours series in the spring of 1981, ultimately crowning its incredibly diverse portfolio

(including Oldsmobile, Pontiac, and Chevrolet funeral coaches with matching four- and six-door limousines) with a Cadillac town car hearse, touting real wire wheels and a removable driver's compartment roof, that debuted at the October, 1984 NFDA convention in Dallas.

The Miller-Meteor name did not stay on the shelf for long, either, being purchased by Jack Hardesty of the Barron Corporation in Lima, Ohio, for use on a cathedral-style, front-wheel-drive Cadillac Eldorado two-door hearse he was prototyping in 1983. After two of these extremely novel cars were built, a Hutchinson, Kansas-based, builder of van and modular ambulances named Ron Collins took control of the Miller-Meteor brand for use on his company's Cadillac and Buick hearses beginning in the 1986 model year. Back in Hess & Eisenhardt's hometown of Cincinnati, the skilled employees left behind when S&S funeral car production moved upstate to the Superior plant in Lima founded Eagle Coach in the fall of 1981. Starting out rather modestly with Buick station wagons fitted with quarter panel extensions to increase casket floor length and wider-opening rear door hinges that kept the pallbearers from crowding each other, the company gradually advanced to raised-roof, extended wheelbase Cadillacs, Buicks, Mercurys, and Lincolns by the time Michael R. Kellerman purchased the concern in 1989 and increased production into the 200-unit-a-year range.

With the launch of a "New Generation" front-wheel-drive DeVille signaling the demise of both the rear-drive Cadillac Commercial Chassis and the factory-built Fleetwood limousine (succeeded by a front-drive formal built by Hess & Eisenhardt) that shared its 144-inch wheelbase at the end of the 1984 model year, General Motors' second wave of downsizing proved another source of consternation to North American coachbuilders. S&S/Superior, given exclusive use of a new 6CZ90 Commercial Body Package that was basically a stripped-down, standard-wheelbase Coupe DeVille fitting heavy-duty suspension and electrical system components, was the first firm to debut funeral coaches on the new platform in 1984. While these new hearses touted all-independent suspension, rack-and-pinion steering and the world's first transverse-mounted V-8 engine, their stubby hoods, lower roofs, and disproportionately long 146.25-inch wheelbases (shortened to 139 inches in production models while maintaining the display cars' 230.39-inch overall lengths) only reminded conservative funeral directors how much smaller they were than the old rear-drive Cadillacs. The people who liked their looks the least quickly dubbed them "Dachshunds."

While longer overhangs, taller rooflines, and a 1989 engine displacement increase from 4.1 to 4.5 liters would allow much better-looking and performing front-drive Cadillac hearses by the time coachbuilders sold their last "New Generation" platform cars in 1992, the initially poor reception they received encouraged the appearance of larger, less expensive, or more versatile alternatives. As the price of new Cadillac coaches climbed from the $30,000-$35,000 range in 1980 to $50,000-$55,000 by decade's end, a new spate of budget market builders carved a substantial niche converting Ford Crown Victoria, Mercury Grand Marquis, Pontiac Grand Safari, Oldsmobile Custom Cruiser, and Buick Estate wagons into service cars and raised roof mini-hearses. With restrictions on the number of floral tributes that could be left on graves being enforced at more cemeteries, the full-sized casket-carrying flower cars sold in small numbers by Superior, Eureka, and Eagle (currently the only major coachbuilder offering the body style today) were similarly-supplemented by the Chevrolet El Camino "pickup car" and standard-wheelbase Cadillac and Lincoln sedans whose rear roof sections and trunk lids were replaced with stainless steel beds.

Lincoln, parlaying a traditionally sturdy rear-wheel-drive Town Car platform into a commanding share of the booming stretch limousine market, established a foothold in the hearse trade (steadily incresed to nearly 25 percent of total sales by 2003) where it had been essentially absent since the mid-1930s. The first examples offered by S&S/Superior, Eagle, Miller-Meteor, and Allen Coachworks of Laredo, Texas, among other firms, proved especially popular in the South and West where the front-drive Cadillac's claims of superior traction and handling had less resonance. Suburban sport-utilities from the Chevrolet and GMC divisions of General Motors, in addition to being spacious enough to carry the largest caskets and airline shipping cases without costly body modifications, offered true truck durability and the option of four-wheel drive to the rural funeral director.

The Braun Corporation of Winamac, IN, already known for its para-transit conversions, even turned the front-drive minivans launched by Chrysler Corporation as 1984 models into casket-capable funeral vehicles by extending the quarter panels and installing a padded vinyl roof with landau bars. The market for these versatile vehicles really took off after longer-length, V-6-powered Dodge Grand Caravans and Plymouth Grand Voyagers that were big enough to carry caskets without panel quarter stretches went on sale in mid-1987. The extra-plush Chrysler Town & Country launched in 1990 even saw front-line service as a more affordable and less intimidating alternative to the traditional hearse or six-door limousine. The list of companies adding easily

removed casket roller racks and fiberglass flower trays to these vehicles expanded to include Richard Shelly's Pittsburgh-based Imperial Coach (whose lineup also featured an interesting Ford Explorer L-Mini hearse with a quarter panel stretch), David Marshall's Image Coaches of Warsaw, Indiana (now known best for its six-seat hatchback Lincoln "family" hearses), and Joe Molina's Royal Coachworks in St. Louis. "Most of the time, if someone passes away at a retirement village or at a family member's home, you don't want to announce it to the neighborhood," Image's Sales Manager Heather Marshall asserted to *American Funeral Director* shortly after Chrysler debuted an even better, second-generation minivan with roll-out seats and a second, driver's side sliding door as a 1996 model. "Our minivans allow you to make a discreet first call by pivoting the rear quarter windows open and sliding the landau panels off the glass."

In the same spirit Royal Coachworks President Joe Molina said in 1996 that "the idea is to keep these multi-purpose coaches as standard as possible so that they can eventually be sold to a larger segment of buyers versus the more limited funeral coach market. All you have to do is remove the landau panels, pull out the casket floor and re-insert the rear bench seats, and you're ready to go fishing or take the little league team to its afternoon game."

With the van- and box-bodied modular formula compelling no significant visual changes in ambulance design between the mid-1970s and the present day, most of the refinements that took place were related to power trains, vehicle platform choices, and emergency procedures or providers. After the 1973 passage of the Emergency Medical Services Systems Act, enthusiastically championed by Michigan congressman and future President Gerald Ford, provided $185 million over a three-year period to develop emergency medical services in the United States (another $269 million was authorized in 1976), the country was divided into 303 contiguous EMS regions with no geographic gaps, where the selection of facilities that could best function as trauma centers was determined strictly by patient flow patterns versus political boundaries (Dr. David Boyd, who served from 1974 to 1983 as the first director of the Division of EMS at the Department of Health, Education and Welfare, would recall that "we used the same market areas that Levi's and Sears & Roebuck used"). Ambulance services operated by funeral homes and other private concerns, faced with increasingly complex federal and state-level qualification requirements and more-expensive vehicles, were almost entirely replaced by municipal or county-run fire and rescue squads and corporate consolidators. Cool-running, turbo-diesel engines, delivering plenty of low-end torque and capable of serving as an auxiliary power plant at an accident scene, became the power train of choice after a rash of gasoline V-8-powered Ford ambulance fires took place in 1989. At about the same time, many fire departments determined that the transmissions, engines, and suspensions of their cutaway van and pickup-based ambulances were being overburdened with heavy new equipment, like the Hurst "Jaws of Life." Consequently, they began moving up to combination ambulance/rescue trucks whose patient compartment modules were mounted on medium-duty truck platforms like the Freightliner FL60, Navistar 4700LP and GMC Topkick. Some of the biggest units on the market were equipped with four-door cabs and compressed-foam dispensing systems for extinguishing car and dumpster fires, earning them the "rumper" nickname for combining the capabilities of rescue trucks and pumpers.

The downsizing of factory-produced Cadillac limousines, as well as their final replacement by a Hess & Eisenhardt-built front-driver following the 1984 model year, created a big demand for aftermarket stretch limousines that dozens of firms sought to satisfy in an increasingly prosperous economic climate. In the wake of new Federal Trade Commission rules that mandated fully itemized funeral service bills, however, many families that had previously gotten six-door limousines as part of an all-inclusive package were choosing to delete them, so more cars were being fitted-out as "24-hour" vehicles that could also handle business, weddings, and recreational clientele with their reversible center seats, solenoid-released center doors, and hideaway TV and beverage consoles covered with roll-top tambour doors.

Some of the companies stretching Cadillacs and Lincolns, naturally, had more capital and engineering capability than others, and in 1989 a rash of widely reported fatal accidents involving stretch limousines prompted the National Highway Traffic Safety Administration (NHTSA) to commence investigating whether coachbuilders were complying with Federal Motor Vehicle Safety Standards for occupant protection and fuel system integrity. A number of firms, already struggling after the Wall Street crash of 1987, chose to close their doors instead of demonstrating compliance.

The companies left in business by 1990 also saw Canada, without advance notice, close its borders to U.S. coachbuilders until they proved their products met provisions of the Canadian Motor Vehicle Safety Act. In response, S&S/Superior, offering to share the resulting engineering data with competitors who helped defray the expense, became the first firm to crash test a funeral

coach, subjecting one of its commercial glass Sovereigns (because it represented the most radical departure from the rear-drive Cadillac base vehicle) to a 30.5-mph fixed barrier frontal impact at the Transportation Research Center in East Liberty, Ohio, on April 24, 1991. The fitment of a double-width front bier pin, with two parallel rows of mounting pin plates employing hexagonal holes to further reduce the chance of casket movement in an accident, was one of many improvements made to U.S. funeral cars as a result of this and subsequent crash tests, which became a standard part of the coachbuilders' product development process.

In 1989, Lincoln established a Qualified Vehicle Modifier (QMV) program to ensure that Town Car-based limousines and funeral coaches maintained factory-level quality and safety standards after modifications. The conceptually similar Cadillad Master Coachbuilder (CMC) program was in place by the time an aerodynamic new rear-drive Fleetwood went on sale as a 1993 model.

The final decade of the 20th century also witnessed its fair share of interesting developments in the funeral coach and limousine industry with regards to the consolidation of existing builders and the emergence of new ones. Two companies that were better known for building V.I.P. stretch limousines and hotel shuttles in large quantities, Federal Coach of Fort Smith, Arkansas (which inherited many of its employee-craftsmen from Armbruster/Stageway), and Krystal Enterprises of Anaheim, California, entered the funeral coach market in 1989 and 1994, respectively. The former eventually become the leading producer of Lincoln Town Car hearses, while the latter won a following with West Coast and Pacific Rim customers who might save $1,400 in shipping charges compared to a coach built in Ohio.

The Eureka Coach Company Ltd., following a few good years in the mid-1980s as the largest North American coachbuilder, had to close its plant in Concord, Ontario, after company backer Howard Carter died in July, 1988, and the strengthening Canadian dollar decimated exports to the U.S. that had accounted for nearly 80 percent of sales. After the company's Pennsylvania dealer Heritage Coach acquired control in 1989, Eureka production moved to a new facility in Norwalk, Ohio, where, united with Ron Collins under the CCE corporate umbrella, the manufacture of Miller-Meteor professional cars also moved from Hutchinson, Kansas, in the fall of 1992. Both brands would move a second time to Lima, Ohio, after S&S/Superior acquired them in July, 1999, changed its corporate name to Accubuilt, and consolidated the production of all four makes at its massive new Central Point Parkway Manufacturing Facility.

General Motors decided to drop its rear-wheel-drive

Pontiacs got their "postwar" look for 1949, with the flush front fenders, 15-inch wheels and "Wide Horizon" curved glass windshields. The Style 2571 Streamline Sedan was the division's first truck in 20 years, and its blind rear quarters, one-piece left-hinged swinging door, and $1,749 starting price (substituting a straight eight for the standard six-cylinder engine cost just $68 more) made it an ideal platform for this Barnette-bodied funeral coach/ambulance combination.

NAHC, Detroit Public Library

Spitler, Inc.

With their flamboyant tailfins soaring 42.4 inches from the pavement, 1959 Cadillacs are especially coveted in professional car collector circles. The most memorable out of many head-turning creations built from this platform was this likely one-off S&S Park Place flower car, teamed with a matching S&S Cadillac Victoria funeral coach. Both cars were constructed for the Spitler Funeral Home of Montoursville, Pennsylvania. Hess & Eisenhardt, the owner of S&S, debuted this body style in 1957 and built just a few examples through 1961, fitting the first cars with a manually folding soft top based on the design it developed for the U.S. Secret Service's 1956 Cadillac parade vehicles.

Cadillac's switch to a smaller, shorter commercial chassis shared with its factory-built limousines spelled the end of car-based ambulances, especially since it coincided with government standards calling for more equipment and patient space. The significant size difference between these 1976 and 1977 Miller-Meteor Cadillac high-tops makes it clear why ambulance production at the company's Piqua, Ohio, plant fell from 100 units to a dozen in a single year.

Cadillac Fleetwood (as well as the Buick Roadmaster and Chevrolet Caprice used to build "first call" cars and entry-level funeral coaches like the Eagle Alternative and Superior Chancellor) at the end of the 1996 model year to expand pickup truck and SUV production at its Arlington plant. Well aware from 1985's experiences that Lincoln stood ready to steal away its most conservative customers if the 1997 front-drive DeVille did not look as imposing and perform as well as its rear-drive predecessors, Cadillac's Specialty Vehicle Team put unprecedented effort into making sure that the platform's conversion into a funeral coach or limousine was both easy and worthwhile. Its 1994 vintage styling was extensively revised to suggest size and maintain a "family" resemblance to the 1993-96 Fleetwoods that it would be serving within funeral and livery fleets, while the basic stamina of Cadillac's front-drive power train and 32-valve Northstar V-8 engine were demonstrated by dispatching eight 1996 Sedan DeVilles to livery operators in four different U.S. cities for a two-year "real world" durability test placing 200,000 miles on each car. The all-new V4U limousine and B9Q hearse conversion vehicles supplied to Cadillac's Master Coachbuilders, who were also furnished with a 3-inch-thick manual of technical guidelines, featured more than 200 heavy-duty components, a 7,000-lb. gross vehicle weight rating that was only 200 lbs. less than the old Fleetwood's, and an extra-long wiring harness that didn't need cutting or splicing after the wheelbase was extended.

What the 21st century might have in store for the American professional car is open to debate, given that prevailing demographics and cultural trends could steer the fortunes of the funeral, livery, and coachbuilding industries in any number of directions. Thanks to computer-designed internal structures, corrosion-resistant composite exterior panels, and fade-resistant clearcoat paints, as well as the demise of the once-annual styling change, the latest funeral coaches can be used in front-line service for a longer period of time than has ever been possible before, after which a smaller funeral home or an overseas customer (the Caribbean, the Philippines, South Africa, and Poland are among the biggest export markets for secondhand U.S. hearses) might get another decade's worth of work out of the vehicle.

Significant growth in the percentage of U.S. deaths resulting in a cremation, from 5 percent in 1975 to 25.48 percent in 2000, has also spurred a perceptible decline in the demand for new funeral coaches, with the trend especially evident in the Pacific Coast states. A similarly steady erosion in the profit margin realized from the average adult funeral, calculated at 7.63 percent by the Federated Funeral Directors of America in 2002 versus 8.69 percent in 1990, 13.73 percent in 1980 and 13.19 percent in 1970, has also compelled many of the "pop and sons" funeral homes that took the most pride in owning their own hearses to sell out to regional or national conglomerates like Service Corporation International or The Loewen Group, which place a higher priority on sharing expensive vehicles and drivers with as many outlets as possible.

On the other hand, the decline in funeral vehicle sales imposed by the growth of cremation and the rise of funeral service chains might be offset to some extent by an increase in the number of deaths. By the year 2030 there will be 65 million Americans over the age 65 compared to 30 million in 1995, and there is also some evidence that the consumers who embrace cremations and other non-traditional funerals are looking for a more personal service as opposed to a less expensive one. In this vein it is interesting to note that 41 percent of the Baby Boomers surveyed by the Batesville Casket Company (the first of which will turn 65 just eight years off in 2012) wanted their family and friends to "throw a huge party" rather than establish a gravesite in their memory. W. Rance Bennett, a vintage funeral coach dealer and restorer from Lowell, Michigan, also told *The New York Times* in 1996 that "there's a growing trend toward using older hearses. Funeral directors have an interest in antique hearses in the same way we are interested in '50s convertibles," and such vehicles have proven especially popular for the funerals of vintage car enthusiasts and auto dealers. Horse-drawn hearses are even making a comeback as a way to express concern for the environment or a yearning for simpler, less-stressful days gone by.

Another trend that may take hold one day, even though most U.S. funeral coachbuilders are headquartered in places like Ohio and Arkansas where the sentiment to buy American remains strong, is that a generation weaned on the taut handling and rational ergonomics of imported luxury cars might want to take their last ride in a Volvo or Mercedes-Benz. The latest company to explore this possibility is the North Palm Beach, Florida-based subsidiary of the Italian coachbuilder Pilato, which recently commenced U.S. sales of a European-style, glass-sided funeral coach constructed on a Mercedes E-Class platform. "Even before we decided to open an office in the United States a couple of years ago," the company's U.S. President Lorenzo Rusin recalled in September, 2003, "American funeral directors who had traveled to Europe to learn about the industry over there came to know about us. We were getting three or four requests a week from American funeral homes asking how they could purchase one of our cars."

PROFESSIONAL CAR TIMELINE

1900: Philadelphia undertaker Oliver H. Blair puts an electric funeral wagon built by Fulton & Walker into service.

1901: President William McKinley is taken to the hospital in a Riker electric ambulance after being shot in Buffalo, New York.

1909: The first all-car funeral processions take place in Chicago. James Cunningham, Son & Co. of Rochester, New York, offers the first factory-built gasoline ambulance. Crane & Breed of Cincinnati markets the first commercially produced motor hearse.

1913: Sayers & Scovill of Cincinnati, founded in 1876, enters the motor hearse market. A Great Eagle funeral coach built by the U.S. Carriage Company of Columbus, Ohio, is driven from San Francisco to New York City.

1914-18: Thousands of American motor ambulances, mostly Ford Model T's and GMCs, deliver meritorious service in World War I.

1915: Meteor launches an inexpensive funeral coach/ambulance combination billed as a "$2,800 car for $1,750."

1916: The John W. Henney Company of Freeport, Illinois, in business since 1868, builds its first motor hearses.

1920s: Steel-paneled, limousine-style funeral coaches start to dominate the market.

1925: Studebaker begins distributing Superior funeral cars and ambulances built in Lima, Ohio, through its nationwide dealer network. Flxible builds its first Buick professional cars in Loudonville, Ohio.

1926: The Eureka Company of Rock Falls, Illinois, debuts a side-loading funeral coach.

1927: Henney markets its first Nu-3-Way loading funeral coach. A.J. Miller's Bellefontaine, Ohio, plant employs converted tire presses to form exterior body panels.

1928: Kissel partners with the National Casket Company of Boston to market Eureka-bodied professional cars through the traveling salesmen National has calling on funeral homes.

1929: The Sayers & Scovill "Signed Sculpture" sparks a carved funeral coach revival.

1931: Dispute between Henney and Eureka over side service casket table patents settled in Eureka's favor. With Kissel out of business, National Casket teams with Henney to produce attractively streamlined funeral cars on the Reo Royale chassis styled by Count Alexis de Sakhnoffsky.

1933: The Shop of Siebert in Toledo, Ohio, builds its first Ford V-8 professional cars. Meteor switches from a Continental-powered chassis built in-house to a Buick straight-eight chassis, downplaying the transition with its own grille design.

1934: Henney offers "Elecdraulic" three-way casket table operation, replaces its own chassis with a "Progress" line based on the straight-eight Oldsmobile. A.J. Miller launches "Art Carved" funeral coaches.

1935: Cadillac and Packard offer coachbuilders factory-built, long-wheelbase, commercial chassis.

1936: 98-year-old James Cunningham, Son & Co. completes its final funeral cars.

1937: Henney secures an exclusivity agreement with Packard, offers "Leveldraulic" side-to-side leveling on its Nu-3-Way hearses. Eureka introduces a "Western-style" open-well flower car on a LaSalle chassis. Superior discontinues its Studebakers in favor of the professional Pontiacs it launched as 1936 models.

1938: S&S Victoria popularizes the landau-style hearse. Superior introduces the first welded all-steel professional car bodies. Henney debuts a mechanically air-conditioned ambulance and an "Eastern-style" casket-carrying flower car with a height-adjustable stainless steel deck.

1942: Civilian professional car production suspended "for the duration" in favor of defense materiel. Sayers & Scovill sold to long-time employees Willard Hess and Charles A. Eisenhardt.

1945-50: Firms like Guy Barnette, Economy Coach, and Weller Brothers make Memphis a center of low-cost professional car manufacture.

1947: S&S Cadillac Macedonian is the last carved panel-style hearse from a major coachbuilder.

1949: Cadillac Commercial Chassis adopts full-fendered "postwar" styling and high-compression V-8 engine.

1950: The Miller First Aider and S&S Professional Kensington spark interest in high-headroom ambulances capable of carrying four patients.

1951: Arbib-styled Henney-Packards are the first hearses and ambulances with wrap-around rear quarter windows.

1952: Flxible suspends Buick professional car production for a 7-year period to focus on busses.

1953: Superior begins building Pontiacs at its "Southern Division" plant in Kosciusko, Mississippi.

1954: Henney builds its last Packard professional cars. Superior debuts its Beau Monde hardtop floral coach. Wayne Works purchases the Meteor Motor Car Company of Piqua, Ohio.

1956: Wayne Works acquires the A. J. Miller Co. of Bellefontaine, Ohio, and merges its operations with Meteor.

1957: First Eureka professional cars with all-steel bodies. First Miller-Meteor brand professional cars.

1959: Cadillac Commercial Chassis flamboyantly restyled. Flxible resumes Buick professional car production, introduces removable landau panels for combination coaches.

1960: High-top, standard-wheelbase Flxible Buick Flxette goes on sale. Conceptually similar Superior Pontiac Consort, Cotner-Bevington Oldsmobile Seville, debut as 1961 and 1963 models, respectively.

1963: Springfield Equipment Company of Ohio introduces a spacious, relatively inexpensive raised-roof Interne ambulance based on the International Travelall.

1964: Eureka and Flxible depart the professional car field.

1966: National Research Council's landmark study "Accidental Death and Disability: The Neglected Disease of Modern Society," details deficiencies in ambulances, attendant training, and equipment.

1968: Second-generation Ford Econoline, with less-intrusive engine and more interior space, sets new standard for van-based ambulance platforms.

1969: Superior absorbed by Sheller-Globe conglomerate, initiating an era of cost cutting and smaller model ranges.

1970s: Federal grant money and KKK specifications encourages transition to roomier, better-equipped ambulances based on box-bodied trucks and vans.

1972: Paramedic movement jump-started by NBC-TV series *Emergency!*

1975: Cotner-Bevington builds its last Oldsmobile professional cars. Superior discontinues its Pontiacs.

1977: Cadillac Commercial Chassis downsized from a 157.5- to a 144.3-inch wheelbase, curtailing the demand for car-based ambulances and combinations.

1978: Toronto-area builder AHA debuts the first traditionally sized Lincoln funeral cars in more than 40 years.

1980: Miller-Meteor shutters its Piqua, Ohio, plant. Superior delivers the last U.S. passenger car ambulance, built on a 1979 Cadillac Commercial Chassis. Eureka name revived for AHA's Buick funeral cars.

1981: Superior sold to Armbruster-Stageway President Thomas P. Earnhart, who moves production to a smaller plant in Lima, Ohio, and acquires S&S funeral coach division from Hess & Eisenhardt. Eagle Coach established by former S&S employees in Cincinnati.

1984: Last model year for factory-produced, long-wheelbase Cadillac Commercial Chassis. Superior builds the last series-produced three-way hearses.

1985: First-generation front-wheel-drive Cadillac funeral cars, built from a cut-and-stretched coachbuilder platform, face a chilly customer reception.

1986: Miller-Meteor name applied to funeral coaches built by Collins Industries of Hutchinson, Kansas.

1987: Front-wheel-drive minivans become popular for first calls after Chrysler adds longer-wheelbase Dodge Grand Caravan and Plymouth Grand Voyager models with V-6 engines.

1989: Rescue squads embrace diesel engines after a rash of gasoline-powered Ford ambulance fires. Lincoln, launching an all-new 1990 Town Car, starts to certify coachbuilders through its Qualified Vehicle Modifier (QVM) program. Pennsylvania dealer Heritage Coach acquires Eureka after Concord, Ontario, plant shuts down, resuming production in Norwalk, Ohio. Federal Coach of Fort Smith, Arkansas, enters the funeral market.

1991: S&S/Superior crash tests a funeral coach to demonstrate compliance with Federal safety standards.

1992: CCE consolidates Miller-Meteor, Eureka professional car production in Norwalk, Ohio. Cadillac Master Coachbuilder program established in concert with the rollout of the first completely restyled rear-wheel-drive Fleetwood since 1980.

1996: Rear-wheel-drive Cadillac and Buick professional cars discontinued.

1999: Miller-Meteor, Eureka professional car production moves to Lima, Ohio, after brands acquired by S&S/Superior, which changes its name to Accubuilt.

This 1978 Dodge Medicruiser built by the Wayne Works of Richmond, Indiana, incorporated the design changes called for by the U.S. Department of Transportation's 1973 specification KKK-A-1822. These standards became de facto for all ambulances manufactured nationwide since most of the funds used by fire departments, rescue squads, and ambulance services to purchase new equipment in this period came from Federal grants. Notable equipment fitted in response included high visibility Omaha Orange striping, backwards "AMBULANCE" lettering across the hood of the vehicle and a blue six-pointed "Star of Life." A raised-roof van like this also became known as a Type II Ambulance under KKK-A-1822 criteria, while a box-bodied ambulance with a pickup cab was classified as a Type I and a cutaway van chassis with an aisle between the driver and patient compartments was termed a Type III.

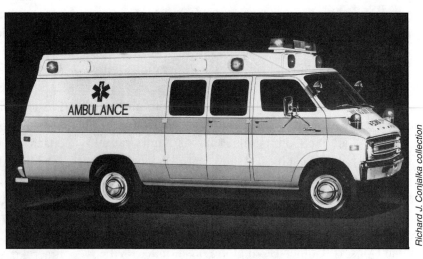

In 1989, following a rash of widely reported fatal accidents involving stretch limousines, the National Highway Traffic Safety Administration (NHTSA) commenced a 3-year inquiry investigating whether coachbuilders were complying with Federal standards for occupant protection and fuel system integrity. On April 24, 1991, S&S/Superior accordingly became the first firm to crash test a funeral coach, putting one of its commercial glass Sovereigns through a 30.5-mph fixed barrier frontal impact at the Transportation Research Center in East Liberty, Ohio. These tests are now a standard part of the coachbuilders' development process.

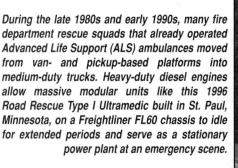

During the late 1980s and early 1990s, many fire department rescue squads that already operated Advanced Life Support (ALS) ambulances moved from van- and pickup-based platforms into medium-duty trucks. Heavy-duty diesel engines allow massive modular units like this 1996 Road Rescue Type I Ultramedic built in St. Paul, Minnesota, on a Freightliner FL60 chassis to idle for extended periods and serve as a stationary power plant at an emergency scene.

While nearly every funeral coach sold in America today is constructed from a heavy-duty Cadillac DeVille or Lincoln Town Car, professional cars based on luxury imports may have a bigger market presence in the future as a means of courting Baby Boomer customers. One firm exploring this possibility is Pilato U.S.A. of North Palm Beach, Florida, which recently commenced U.S. deliveries of this European-style glass-sided funeral coach built in Nervesa Della Battaglia, Italy, on a Mercedes E-Class platform.

Chapter 2

Buick

Combining quality, smoothness, riding comfort, and mechanical stamina with a dignified, upscale image, the cars from Flint have consistently delivered everything that is most desired in a funeral coach or ambulance platform. Along with Cadillac, Ford, and Oldsmobile, Buick is one of just a handful of U.S. makes that has been in production for a century or more, and the No. 1 sales position it achieved in the industry in 1908 (when the company became the cornerstone for Billy Durant's founding of General Motors) has been followed by a number of years where it has been both America's most popular premium car and the country's fourth-, third-, or second-best seller overall.

As it went from one success to another, Buick also schooled such future industry titans as Charles W. Nash and Walter P. Chrysler in the ways of the auto business and emerged as one of the American makes most likely to be found on foreign shores. The first car to cross South America in 1912 was a Buick, while journalist-adventurer Lowell Thomas used another for his 1923 trip from India to Afghanistan. The same London dealer that delivered a Canadian-built McLaughlin Buick limousine to King Edward VIII in 1936 also counted his "special friend" and future wife, Wallis Warfield Simpson, as a customer. Further east, Buicks chauffeured the cabinet of General Chiang Kai-shek, earning a repuration that would, 60 years later, see Shanghai-built Buicks spearhead GM's current initiatives in China. In a strange twist of fate, Buicks commandeered in occupied territories and used by officers of the Japanese Imperial Army during World War II.

Given the company's sterling global reputation, it is certainly not surprising that Buick-based ambulances and funeral coaches were in service by the World War I era. The six-cylinder passenger car chassis debuted in 1915 proved particularly popular for a number of one-

The Hoover Wagon Company, in the business of building caskets and commercial vehicle bodies between 1892 and 1957, constructed this imposing and spacious-looking Buick ambulance for its hometown of York, Pennsylvania, in 1926. The town seal was incorporated into the design of the beveled, leaded-glass windows.

off hearses (many of them utilizing used horse-drawn bodies) from such firms as A. Geissel of Philadelphia, August Schubert of Oneida, New York, the Hoover Wagon Company of York, Pennsylvania, Owen Brothers of Lima, Ohio, and J. Paul Bateman of Bridgeton, New Jersey, while the four-cylinder C-4 and D-4 truck chassis could be found beneath a number of ambulances attached to the British forces on the Western front. During the 1920s, the Eureka Company of Rock Falls, Illinois, and the Silver family's Knightstown Body Company of Knightstown, Indiana, were among the builders demonstrating what could be accomplished by combining a Buick chassis with an up-to-date limousine-style funeral coach body, while The Great Depression of the 1930s found the Meteor Motor Car Company of Piqua, Ohio, and Cincinnati's Sayers & Scovill turning to Buick frames and valve-in-head "straight-eight" engines after they abandoned the practice of assembling their own chassis.

The funeral coach and ambulance builder most inevitably associated with Buick, however, is the Flxible Company of Loudonville, Ohio. The company got its start in 1912 after a Mansfield, Ohio, Harley-Davidson dealer named Hugo H. Young designed a motorcycle sidecar with a flexible connection that allowed the third wheel to tilt and stay securely planted on the road. After dropping one "e" from his company's name so that "Flxible" could be trademarked in 1913, Young and his partner, Carl F. Dudte, leased a factory to manufacture his invention in Loudonville in early 1914. The venture proved a great success since motorcycles were often seen as "poor man's automobiles" in the days before the price of a Ford Model T fell to the point where the masses could afford one. Charles F. Kettering, a Loudonville area native who invented the electric self-starter for General Motors in 1911 and served as the company's director of research until 1947, invested more than $183,000 in Flxible in the form of loans and stock, in return for which he was appointed the firm's president while Young maintained day-to-day control as vice president and general manager. This endowed the company with enough capital to dedicate its own factory across the tracks from Loudonville's railway depot (which would certainly prove convenient for customers taking delivery) in January, 1917. It was not long afterwards that the company received a huge government contract to supply sidecars for the Allied forces' Excelsior motorcycles that were painted regulation olive drab, equipped with machine gun mounts and shipped to Europe in knocked-down form. By 1919 the company could claim to be the largest exclusive manufacturer of motorcycle sidecars in the world, with 60 workers shipping more than 300 units a month on average to customers as distant as Australia and New Zealand.

After U.S. motorcycle sales began to weaken with the 1920-21 recession and the increasing availability of inexpensive, mass-produced passenger cars, Flxible sought out other uses for its existing plant machinery and prototyped its first motor bus on a Studebaker chassis in late 1924. Thanks to Kettering's influence, most of the busses built after full production was initiated in the summer of 1925 were Buick-based, and by 1927 nearly two-thirds of Buick's factory branches and distributorships were handling Flxible products. Funeral coach and ambulance production at Loudonville, calling on many of the same body-building skills as busses, increased rapidly, from just 11 units during their initial year on sale in 1925, to 264 in 1929—by which time motorcycle sidecars constituted just 1.5 percent of the company's sales. They would become an even more important contributor to Flxible's financial health after The Depression sparked a big drop in bus output and a wave of repossessions.

While the bus business eventually recovered, Flxible's professional car output also increased to the point where it reached a prewar peak of 542 units in 1940 and an all-time record (despite a devastating January 2, 1947, fire that destroyed large portions of the Loudonville plant and much of the tooling used to build professional cars) of 646 units in 1948.

Though it's true that Flxible also produced Cadillac funeral cars and ambulances from 1932 to 1942, Pontiacs from 1933 to 1936, LaSalles from 1938 through 1940, and a few Chevrolet Panel Truck service coaches in 1938 and 1939, Buick was always the firm's favorite platform and the only make of chassis that it used for building professional cars after World War II. Flxible was one of the few coachbuilders for which complete production figures are available. According to automotive hsitorian Robert R. Ebert, who researched figures for his book on the history of the company, Buicks accounted for 6,808 units, or an incredible 92.1 percent, of the 7,393 Flxible professional cars built in Loudonville between 1925 and 1965 (with a hiatus spanning the 1953 through 1958 models). While the 234 LaSalles completed constituted 3.2 percent of the total, the 177 Cadillacs and 134 Pontiacs built amounted to 2.4 percent and 2.1 percent, respectively. The 20 Chevrolets constructed in 1938 and 1939 accounted for the 0.3 percent remaining balance.

Following Flxible's decision to focus on its fast-growing municipal bus business in 1965, the tooling used to manufacture its Buicks was sold to National Coaches of Knightstown, Indiana, where it was also used to create Chevrolet, Chrysler, and Mercury professional cars, among other makes. Buicks were also offered by the Trinity Coach Company of Duncanville, Texas, during the 1967 and 1968 model years. Starting in 1976, Buicks were also offered by the Armbruster-Stageway firm that had already forged a fine reputation by building six- and eight-door limousines in Fort Smith, Arkansas, for nearly half a century.

The costly 1977 downsizing of the Cadillac Commercial Chassis spurred the funeral profession's interest in less-expensive alternatives. Full-sized Buick LeSabre and Electra station wagons, touting a body shell that endured without major alterations all the way from 1977 through 1990, quickly proved themselves amenable to wheelbase, roof, and quarter panel extensions that converted them into reasonably elegant and spacious funeral coaches and "first-call" vehicles. The impressively long list of companies performing such alterations included the newly combined S&S/Superior operation in Lima, Cincinnati's Eagle Coach, Alberter Coach in Johnstown,

Pennsylvania, Marquis Custom Coach of Canoga Park, California, B&B Custom Coachworks of Waxahachie, Texas, Collins Industries of Hutchinson, Kansas, and the Wolfington and Heritage Coach concerns located in the Philadelphia area. A resurrected Eureka company in Toronto particularly impressed industry observers by assembling the components needed to reintroduce traditional commercial glass Buick hearses in 1980, and the Chevrolet Corvette-derived 260-horsepower LT-1 V-8 added to the aerodynamic Roadmaster in the 1994 model year encouraged the coachbuilders to create some of the most muscular hearses that funeral directors had ever driven.

Though the manufacture of heavy-duty, rear-wheel-drive Buick station wagons suitable for funeral coach conversions ceased in 1996, it is likely that the division will soon return into mortuary duty in "first-call" and other utility-related capacities. For the 2005 model year, General Motors will build a Buick version of its front-wheel-drive minivan platform for the first time, giving it the Terraza nameplate and updating its exterior with a more-imposing front end design inspired by sport-utility vehicles.

Buick Motor Division

The successful use of motor ambulances in World War I accelerated their adoption by industries and communities on the home front. This open-cab, six-cylinder 1916-18 Buick from an unknown body builder, fitted with ceiling-level vents and vertically split double rear doors, took part in a first-aid drill at Buick's massive plant in Flint, Michigan.

In 1925, with his hand on the rear door handle, Flxible founder and president Hugo Young prepares to show off the interior of one of his first Buick hearses, which he was delivering to Charles Hehr (left) and Charles Bringman of Bringman & Company of Upper Sandusky, Ohio.

American Funeral Director

While 1926 was a banner year for Buick, which built a then-record 266,753 cars, Flxible completed only 21 professional cars on the Series 50 Master Six chassis. This was, nevertheless, nearly double the 11 cars completed when the former motorcycle sidecar maker entered the field in 1925. As word spread about the company's coachbuilding skill, production would double again to 40 units in 1927, and bodies would also be offered on the cheaper Series 47 Standard Six chassis.

Moby's Eureka Autos

Floyd Miller's 1930 Eureka Buick hearse posed in front of the mausoleum in St. Paul, Minnesota's Forest Lawn Cemetery during the Professional Car Society's 1996 International Meet. It featured interlocking side doors and a three-way table that allowed caskets to be loaded from the sidewalk and the street. Arch-shaped side windows and a slightly sloped windshield distinguished Eureka's DeLuxe Model 29 funeral car body from the less-expensive model 30. Both were also fitted to Cadillac, Lincoln, Hudson, Hupmobile, Studebaker, Reo, Franklin, Packard, Pierce-Arrow, Graham, Nash, and even Chevrolet chassis.

These 1929 and 1930 Buicks, based on Flxible's sedan-style 12-passenger bus, were used by the Goodyear Tire & Rubber Company to tow its 3,900-lb. Airwheels around the country on promotional tours. Flxible also built several Goodyear blimp tenders with ground crew seating and folding mooring masts attached to the vehicles' roofs.

NAHC, Detroit Public Library

Built for the Schooler Brothers mortuary in Missouri, this 1931 Flxible Buick combination features wicker flower trays and pull-down window shades. Leaded-glass inserts could also be placed into brackets behind the quarter windows to further the transition from funeral coach to ambulance. This was a great model year for Buick, given the introduction of valve-in-head "straight eight" engines in 220-, 272- and 344-cubic inch variants, and synchromesh transmissions on all but the cheapest Series 50.

Moby's Eureka Autos

Owned by John Kellam of Pickering, Ontario, since 1998, this Oshawa-built 1933 McLaughlin Buick combination was bodied by the Mitchell Hearse Company of Ingersoll, Ontario, which emulated English coachbuilding tradition by attaching aluminum panels to a hardwood frame. Also featuring a fold-down wash basin, the car's career began in northeast Ontario with the Blair Funeral Home in Perth, after which it served the Zummach Funeral Home in Killaloe from 1944-55. Kellam found the 42,000-mile vehicle in fine shape in 1997, despite 43 years' storage in a dirt-floored shed. The biggest task entailed replacing the original black paint with a tasteful silver/charcoal two-tone scheme.

National Automotive History Collection, Detroit Public Library

Soon after the 1934 model year began, Flxible's '34 Buicks received restyled bodies with "beavertail" rear ends. Other improvements included Knee Action independent front suspension, a rear anti-sway bar, and a combined starter and accelerator pedal. This base model Series 40 Sentinel, identified as such by its single windshield wiper, was used by Schaefer's Ambulance of Los Angeles and was motivated by a new 233-cubic inch straight eight motor making 93 horsepower at 3200 rpm.

The 1935 model year was the first time Flxible-bodied Buicks had one-piece stamped steel roofs, no-draft ventilation systems with pivoting front vent windows, and raised hoods. The hoods, much more evident on Flxible's 1935 Pontiacs, would become more pronounced when raised headlight pedestals were added in 1936. This stylish Series 60 Sterling was built for the Morris-Leiman Funeral Home of Miller, Missiouri.

By 1936, Sayers & Scovill used heavy grille bars, special badging, and a custom radiator shell to mask its switch to Buick sheet metal and soften the effect of Harley Earl's annual styling changes. Similar hood trim pieces are still a no-cost option on S&S funeral cars today.

THE DISTINCTIVE S&S
· FRONTAL ASSEMBLY ·
No "Year-marks" to Date It!

Flxible's raised hood and cowl is plainly evident on a 1936 Buick ambulance that was operated by the Greenbelt, Maryland, Rescue Squad. Squared-off upper window corners identify this vehicle as a Flxible Sentinel built from a Series 40 Special, or a Sterling sharing the Series 60 Century's powerful 320-cubic inch straight eight. Top-of-the-line Flxible Premiers, which had curved upper window corners, were based on the Limited.

Diagonal grille bars distinguished 1937 model S&S professional cars, which also switched from Buick mechanicals mounted in the firm's own frame to a Buick-built long-wheelbase commercial chassis. The Cincinnati company's most ornate offering that year was the Byzantine, epitomized by this two-owner example belonging to Mifflinburg, Pennsylvania, funeral director James L. Schwartz. This 21,285-mile coach is basically original, except for some re-chroming. Its casket compartment is as elaborate as the exterior with its maroon mohair fabric and carved rosewood trim.

Moby's Eureka Autos

While 1938 and 1939 were the only years that Superior offered Buicks before the mid-1970s, the Lima, Ohio, firm scored an important industry first by introducing welded all-steel bodies on its 1938 models. This method of construction promised fewer squeaks and rattles than the glued-together joints used in competitors' composite wood frames. Extremely long #2 side doors were another feature of this Series 40 Special-based Superior Fairhaven limousine style hearse.

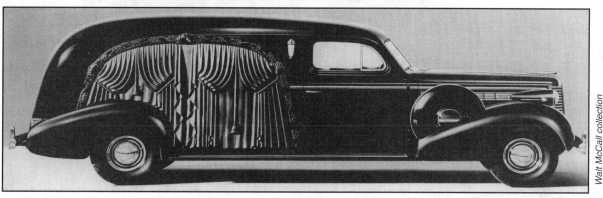

Walt McCall collection

In 1938, the incredibly intricate side panels of this Eureka Buick Chieftain funeral coach were still handcrafted the old-fashioned way from seasoned yellow poplar. Cast-aluminum carvings, satin finished to simulate real draperies, would not appear on the Rock Falls, Illinois, company's hearses until 1940.

Moby's Eureka Autos

Flxible joined in the carved funeral coach revival by launching the "Classic A" at the October, 1937, NFDA convention in Minneapolis. Sold through 1941 and shown here on a 1939 Buick chassis, this model featured two elaborately trimmed semi-circular arches surrounding carved drape or (in the case of the Classic AA) beveled glass inserts. Trailing Superior by just one year, Flxible offered all-steel bodies for the first time in 1939.

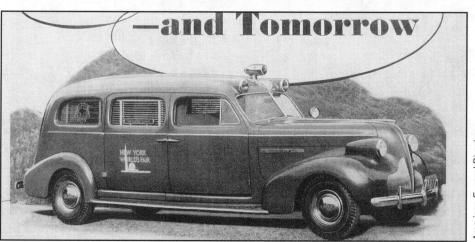

American Funeral Director

Named the official ambulance supplier to the New York World's Fair, Flxible constructed a number of specially trimmed Buicks, Cadillacs, and LaSalles for the event during the 1938-40 model years. In addition to dark blue paint and orange letters overlaying the Fair's Trylon and Perisphere logo, this 1939 model Buick Premier featured faired-in tunnel lights, a Federal 78 Traffic King siren, Venetian window blinds, and an inlaid walnut medicine cabinet with the Flxible script on an inscribed plaque.

Displayed alongside a 1956 A.J. Miller Cadillac at the 1999 PCS International Meet in Lancaster, Pennsylvania, is a 1940 Flxible Buick Series 60 Premier owned by New Jersey ambulance dealer Paul Vickery. It saw service at the New York World's Fair before being sold to the fire company in Bethel, Connecticut. From the time it was retired in 1955 until the early 1970s, the vehicle saw only about two weeks' use each year when the track was open at the Danbury Fairgrounds. It was mostly dismantled by the time Vickery purchased it in 1976.

WHEN BETTER AUTOMOBILES ARE BUILT BUICK WILL BUILD THEM

American Funeral Director

While 1940 saw Flxible set a prewar output record with 542 professional cars emerging from its Loudonville, Ohio, plant, 1941 wasn't far behind with 403 Buicks and 100 Cadillacs completed. Hidden door hinges were a notable improvement in 1941, but few buyers opted for the new air conditioning option since its $299 cost entailed a big boost over the $2,870 and $2,995 respective starting prices of the Series 50 Sterling and Series 70 Premier Buick ambulances.

Walt McCall collection

One of only three Buick flower cars built by Flxible in 1941, this example stands out by retaining a stock height hood and cowl assembly. The barrel-vaulted flower deck is also unusual for not having a convertible-style rear boot.

It's safe to assume that only a small number of the 183 Buick-based professional cars built by Flxible in the war-truncated 1942 model year were service cars like this B72-8 based on the more powerful Roadmaster chassis (the same car as a Super chassis was designated Model B52-8). A beltline-level rack allowed the interior to carry flowers above the casket or first call cot. It cost $62.80 extra to paint the body white, cream, or ivory.

Moby's Eureka Autos

Flxible added landau-style hearses in 1941, but at the time it was considered a $175 trim option as opposed to a separate model. America's entry into World War II slashed Flxible's 1942 professional car output to just 207 units, but the company's Buicks were pleasingly restyled with an even-higher hood (raised 5 5/8 inches, versus 4 inches in 1941) and "airfoil" front fenders flowing into the doors.

Moby's Eureka Autos

After World War II, Flxible dropped its Cadillac professional cars and concentrated on Buicks. The starting price of a base Sterling funeral car had exploded from $2,620 in 1941 to $3,590 in 1946, but there was no shortage of eager buyers after a 3 1/2-year new car drought. Touting a relatively modern look, thanks to 1942's extensive styling changes, the 164 3/8-inch-wheelbase Buick commercial chassis remained a fine foundation for a visually imposing funeral coach or ambulance.

American Funeral Director

Flxible dropped its Super-based Sterlings for 1947 and focused on its Premier models, which used the 165-horsepower Roadmaster 711-X chassis. Output increased 116 units over 1946 to 357, in spite of a gigantic January 2 fire that destroyed large portions of the Loudonville, Ohio, plant, 55 partially completed professional cars and much of the tooling used to build them.

American Funeral Director

PCS members Gene and Steve Lichtman bought this used 1947 Flxible Buick ambulance when production staffers for the 1987 Barry Levinson movie *Avalon* needed a period ambulance. This car has also appeared in the TV miniseries *A Woman Named Jackie* and *Liberty Heights*.

Dropping the raised hood for good, the 1949 Flxible-Buicks marked the firm's most-radical change from one model year to the next. Dynaflow and front-hinged #2 side doors were now standard, with the side-loading hearses getting interlocking rear doors that omitted the outside handle. Showing just 22,000 original miles when Bob Behr of Sellersville, Pennsylvania, purchased it in 1984, this 1949 Premier ambulance originally served at an Ingersoll-Rand air compressor plant in Phillipsburg, New Jersey, and was subsequently donated to the Forks Township VFD near Berwick, Pennsylvania.

This one-off 1949 Buick flower car was created by the Joseph Wildanger Company of Red Bank, New Jersey. The company was best known as a builder of wooden station wagon bodies. Interesting features included wrap-around rear quarter windows and a slide-out flower tray made from arched wood slats similar to those used in 1920s hearses. Originally owned by the John Flock Funeral Home in Long Branch, New Jersey, this vehicle was purchased by James Smallwood of Fort Wayne, Indiana, in 1991.

Developed and supplied by Eureka, the Heise three-way casket table fitted to this 1950 Flxible Buick Premier funeral car could be manually operated or power-assisted. The former model cost $7,040, while the latter listed for $7,513. This represented a significant premium over an end-loading Premier priced at $5,864, but a side-to-side Flxible Leveler was standard in both variants.

The toothy grille and bumper assembly on 1950 Buicks was toned down considerably for 1951—the year that Flxible completed this fleet of five Super-based Sterling ambulances. They are distinguished from the Roadmaster Premiers by having three front fender VentiPorts instead of four.

The 1950 model year was the first year since 1946 that Flxible Buicks were offered on the Series 50 Super as well as the Series 70 Roadmaster chassis, with the former sold again as Sterlings and the latter still designated Premiers. This limousine-style Premier combination coach is now owned by Neil Elliott of Mt. Brydges, Ontario.

The same hardware that allowed the hoods on 1941-53 Buicks to hinge open from either side also allowed them to be easily removed, prompting Flexible to offer a special ambulance hood that could be attached to a combination coach in a matter of seconds. By mid-1951, the emergency lighting was faired into the hood for a more graceful appearance.

This is what a 1952 Flxible Buick Sterling combination coach interior looked like when configured for funeral service. Once the casket was loaded onto the easily removable roller racks, it was secured at each end using the rubber-cushioned bier pins seen here stored on the inner rail of the right side rack. When the vehicle was used as an ambulance, the cot hook at left was slid into anchors on the wheelhouse and a pair of attendant seats folded out of the linoleum-surfaced floor. The elaborate window drapes were also removed in favor of sliding shades with stainless steel guides.

Buick had a great year in 1954, with across-the-board V-8 power and Panoramic windshields propelling it past Plymouth to the third place industry position. The National Body Manufacturing Company of Knightstown, Indiana, demonstrated good timing in debuting Buick-based professional cars as a step up from its Chevrolet and Pontiac offerings.

National would build a funeral car or ambulance on almost any chassis requested, but its generally budget-conscious customer base rarely opted for costly platforms like this 1957 Buick. Bigger bumper bombs, twin spotlights and distinctive body side molding extensions enhanced the presence of the Ott-Laughlin Funeral Home's limousine-style combination, while a new 364-cubic inch V-8 afforded suitable performance.

After a 7-year absence from the field, Flxible resumed professional car production with the 1959 models. The 48 funeral cars and ambulances they built that year by stretching an Electra 4730 stripped chassis stretched 23.2 inches to create a 149.5-inch wheelbase. The quarter window decoration on this ambulance, delivered to the Hinton-Turner Funeral Home of Paris, Kentucky, was not a decal, but a sandblasted pattern with gold-painted horizontal striping and a mirrored cross.

In addition to building 48 extended-wheelbase Buicks in 1959, Flxible constructed a single standard-length Flxette from a model 4490 LeSabre stripped convertible frame. Offering a 103.5-inch-long rear floor, this prototype garnered considerable customer enthusiasm and 110 were made the first year that the concept entered full production in 1960.

Unrestored, aside from a repaint in its original tan-over-red-two-tone, Steve and Gene Lichtman's 1960 Flxible Buick Premier ambulance was purchased new by Allegheny Ludlum Steel for its West Leechburg works outside New Kensington, Pennsylvania. Used until 1985, it had accumulated only 9,000 miles by the time it was traded in to Terry Pfund's Superior Sales in Lower Burrell, Pennsylvania. The odometer shows less than 15,000 miles today.

Though its $6,520 factory price promised big savings over the $8,615 Flxible quoted for an equivalent long-wheelbase Premier, Pittsburgh enthusiast John Ehmer's 1960 Buick Flxette service car is very likely a one-off. Ordered by the long-established Tickner Funeral Home in Baltimore, the car ended up in the basement of a mortuary that paid a junkman $50 to haul it away and crush it. Fortunately, an airplane mechanic spotted the car on the junkman's truck, bought it for another $50 and got it running before selling it to Ehmer for $300 in 1993. Aside from a new exhaust system, this largely original car has required surprisingly little work since.

Recalling the raised hoods used from 1935 to 1948, Flxible's 1962 models added a raised cowl that, while retaining the stock Buick vent windows and windshield, allowed better-balanced proportions and a "hidden 2 1/2 inches" of extra headroom for the driver and ambulance attendants. The Flxible script behind the side mirror of this Flxette landau hearse highlights where sheet metal was added to cant the windshield slightly forward. A delicate chamfer line above the landau bow, meanwhile, adds definition to the quarter panels.

This 1962 Flxible Buick Flxette combination interior reveals several refinements, including a split front seatback from a LeSabre two-door sedan, rectangular bier pin pads, an under-floor storage area inside the rear door threshold, and thumbscrew anchors for securing the removable roller racks. A partition with sliding window glass, standard on the extended-wheelbase Premiers, was a $200 option on Flxettes.

Flxible delivered this1962 Buick Premier ambulance to the Goodwill Fire Company of Pottstown, Pennsylvania. In concert with the new raised cowl, the more formal-looking roofline offered 42 inches of headroom in the patient compartment. A 46-inch-high headroom ambulance with a fiberglass cap was also listed on Flxible's price sheets through 1964, but none were apparently built beyond a single prototype in 1960.

Richard J. Conjalka collection

Celebrating its 50th anniversary in 1963, Flxible saw its professional car sales grow by 53 units over 1962 to a post-1952 record of 199. Of that number, 111 were standard wheelbase Flxettes, like this landau hearse. It is interesting to note that the exterior combines Electra front fender trim with LeSabre Estate Wagon taillight housings.

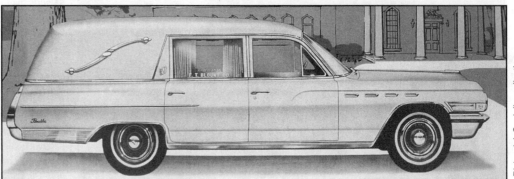

Richard J. Conjalka collection

Seemingly inspired by an Alexander Calder sculpture, boomerang-like trim accented the front emergency lights of 1963 Flxible Buick ambulances. New features for the model year included front fender cornering lamps and a seven-position tilt steering wheel.

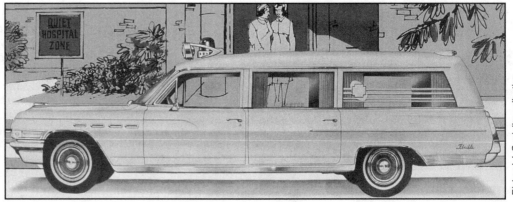

Richard J. Conjalka collection

Richard J. Conjalka collection

National Coaches of Knightstown, Indiana, created this attractive and unusual hardtop limousine from a 1964 Buick Electra 225. There is the similarly rare 1965 National Ford ambulance parked in the adjacent garage opening.

Recalling the last year that National Coaches of Knightstown, Indiana, used its distinctive "two-step" window line, this 1964 Buick high-top ambulance was built from a LeSabre sedan as a community donation from a Montana Elks lodge. 1963 Chevrolet taillights, a Federal "Q" siren flanked by faired-in tunnel lights, and an exceptionally long whip antenna for reliable communication in the Big Sky Country were notable design elements. John Ehmer learned of the car's existence from an Internet classified and brought it home to Pittsburgh in 2001.

Richard J. Conjalka collection

In January, 1965, Flxible sold its professional car tooling, plus the trade names "Flxette" and "Premier," to Vernon Perry's National Coaches of Knightstown, Indiana. The 1965 Buicks produced with Flxible fixtures touted numerous changes, including the new Cadillac commercial cowl assembly with its wider, higher windshield and reduced-angle pillars.

Tim A. Fantin photo

This limousine-style 1965 National combination coach with Wildcat trim, used by Mueller's Greenlee funeral home in Pasco, Washington, until the early 1990s, is now owned by Larry R. Freels of North Manchester, Indiana.

Richard J. Conjalka collection

This 1966 National Buick Premier combination sports the concave grille and stacked fender portholes of a Wildcat, along with removable landau panels to complete the transition from ambulance to funeral duty. The tooling that National acquired from Flxible in 1965 was also used to build coaches on Chevrolet, Ford, Mercury, and Chrysler chassis.

Joe W. Summers, a former Flxible dealer in Duncanville, Texas, who also distributed S&S and Superior, founded the Trinity Coach Company with Dallas businessman G.M. Fulgham and produced a number of Buick-based professional cars in 1967 and 1968. This was its 1966 model prototype.

Showing off its generous rear door opening, this Electra-based National made good use of the reverse-curve body sculpturing and more pronounced Coke bottle quarter panels on 1967 Buicks. Mechanical changes included a bigger 430-cubic inch V-8 and the option of power front disc brakes.

Measuring 243 inches end to end, extended-wheelbase Buick Electras from Trinity Coach were called Royals, while the Triune name was given to factory-length Wildcats and Electras. Both models featured all-steel construction with roof bow reinforcements, but Plexiglas quarter windows were a questionable cost-saving measure.

Bristling with lights and sirens, this orange-and-white 1968 Trinity Buick high-top was owned for many years by Littlerock, California, ambulance buff Bobb Kosoff. The original owner was Harry Snyder of the Snyder Ambulance Company in Van Nuys, California, who specified a four-patient interior with dual A/C and heat.

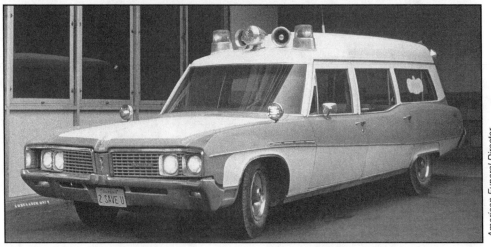

Tim A. Fantin photo

Armbruster/Stageway of Fort Smith, Arkansas, best known for its six- and eight-door limousines, made the industry's first commitment to Buick funeral cars in five years by building this Precision Crown for Superior Coach of Lima, Ohio starting in 1976. These cars had a 12-inch chassis stretch between the rear doors and rear wheels, while the less-costly Custom (prototyped as a 1975 model) and Custom Crown had their wheelbases extended between the front and rear doors.

Accubuilt

Given the significant price increases imposed on downsized 1977 Superior Cadillacs, the company's Armbruster-built Buicks received more attention from the funeral trade, and 58 were constructed during the model year. The hearse-style rear window added to the Precision Crown for 1977 certainly afforded a more traditional look to the coachwork.

Tim A. Fantin photo

The 1977 Superior Buick Customs continued to use a between-the-doors wheelbase stretch with a widened B-pillar. This Custom Crown model with a wrapover tiara band was owned by the Sheets-Love Funeral Home of Lowell, Indiana.

While the Iranian revolution-induced recession saw Superior Buick production fall slightly from 63 units in 1978 to 53 in 1979, these cars remained promising replacements for the Pontiac professional cars that Superior had discontinued after the 1975 model year.

Accubuilt

Richard J. Conjalka collection

Reviving a great name in funeral coaches that had last been used in 1964, this 1979 Electra was one of the first "Eureka" Buicks built by AHA's professional car division. The "halo" vinyl roof was an especially elegant design element. The company, which built only Buicks and Lincolns until Cadillacs were added in the spring of 1981, had been established in Toronto by author Thomas A. McPherson and Vancouver coach dealer Howard Carter.

Thomas A. McPherson collection

Seeking better fuel efficiency and looks, GM's 1980 fullsize cars added aerodynamic sheet metal with lower hoods and higher trunk decks. In Toronto, the new Eureka Coach Company Ltd. responded to the sleek new styling with the first commercial glass Buick hearses seen in more than a decade. In addition to this Electra-based Centurion with a half-vinyl roof and wrap-over tiara band, Eureka also offered a Premier with a full-length padded roof and a price-leading Sterling landau.

In 1982, Eureka asserted that its Buicks were the only medium-priced funeral cars with an optional ExTend table, which facilitated casket loading by sliding up to 40 inches beyond the rear door opening. The inner door panel bears a 1971-73 Buick Centurion medallion.

Thomas A. McPherson collection

American Funeral Director

Having already purchased Superior Coach from the Sheller-Globe conglomerate in January, 1981, Armbruster/Stageway CEO Tom Earnhart acquired the S&S funeral car division from Hess & Eisenhardt the following September and started building both brands under one roof in Lima, Ohio. S&S Buicks, adding raised roofs, hearse-style rear doors, and 16-inch wheelbase extensions with one-piece driveshafts to the Estate Wagon, were introduced as a less-costly alternative to the company's Cadillac coaches in December 1981.

Thomas A. McPherson collection

To match its Buick hearses, the Eureka Coach Company Limited also built Empire Electra limousines in both four- and six-door versions. The Empire IV had a 152.9-inch wheelbase and 256.1-inch overall length. The Empire VI was 6 inches longer.

Thomas A. McPherson collection

Inspired by his huge collection of professional car literature, Tom McPherson encouraged Eureka to revive limousine-style funeral coaches with rear quarter windows. This Buick Premier limousine also features the wraparound Oldsmobile Ciera taillights added to 1984 models, which were more visible than the bumper-mounted lamps used previously.

Tim A. Fantin photo

Employing veteran craftsmen from the famed Hess & Eisenhardt shops in nearby Cincinnati, Eagle Coach was founded in Amelia, Ohio, in the autumn of 1981. One of the company's typical early products is this 1984 Buick Americana, endowing a LeSabre Estate Wagon with an all-steel, 10-inch quarter panel extension and a custom designed rear door hinge, allowing a 110-degree opening. This car is still in service with the Leggett Funeral Home in Hopkins Park, Illinois.

Accubuilt

Buick's deep-dish aluminum wheels were an appealing addition to this mid-1980s Superior Sovereign long-door, whose 16-inch chassis stretch afforded space for a 102-inch-long casket floor and a one-piece steel partition with sliding glass panels. These coaches were strong sellers, thanks to a $28,928 starting price in 1985 that made them nearly $20,000 less expensive than the new front-wheel-drive Cadillac hearses.

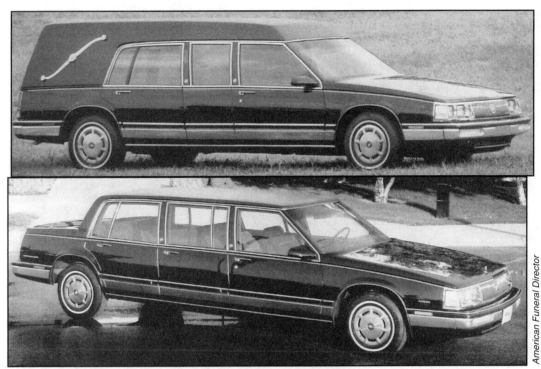

Collins Professional Cars of Hutchinson, Kansas, acquired the rights to apply the venerable Miller-Meteor name to its hearses in 1985. The new front-wheel-drive Buick Electra served as the foundation for the company's Savoy funeral coach, which was joined on sale by a matching Roadmaster six-door limousine.

American Funeral Director

Two-door versions of the front-drive Electra were available from 1985 to 1987, facilitating Eureka's offering of a four-door Empire limousine as a companion to its so-called "New Generation" Buick funeral coaches. With its big, new, 100,000-square-foot Concord, Ontario, plant producing 600 vehicles a year by the mid-1980s, Eureka regularly-vied with S&S/Superior for the title of North America's largest builder of hearses and funeral limousines.

American Funeral Director

Ken Earnest

Eureka built this attention-getting cutaway trimmed as a Buick Premier Landau to highlight the engineering features on its "New Generation" front-drive hearses at funeral directors' conventions. Notable componentry included commercial-height door and windshield glass, a space-efficient trailing arm rear suspension derived from a design developed from a cancelled Buick station wagon program and 16-gauge, one-piece stamped steel C-pillars with 11-gauge reinforcements; four-wheel disc brakes were optional on New Generation Buicks and Oldsmobiles and standard on the Cadillacs. Cincinnati funeral coach dealer Carl Woerner owns this one-of-a-kind car today.

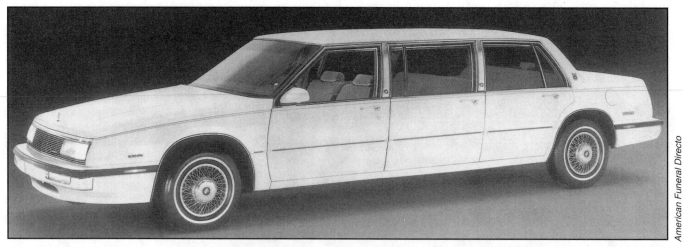

American Funeral Directo

One year after the Electra, the Buick LeSabre became a transverse-engine front-wheel-drive car in 1986, setting it on a path that would eventually make it America's most popular six-passenger sedan. This six-door limousine conversion by Armbruster/Stageway of Fort Smith, Arkansas, wears the front-end styling used on 1987-89 models, combining one-piece rectangular headlamps with a full-width grille.

Tim A. Fantin photo

The 1988-90 Superior Buick Sovereigns added commercial-glass windshields and side windows with reduced-tumblehome roof pillars. With its 141.9-inch wheelbase, the body was 10 inches longer and 5.5 inches higher than Superior's previous Buick model, which continued in production as the Precision. The S&S Buick Victoria was similarly upgraded, and this basic body design was also used for the Chevrolet Caprice-based Superior Concept sold in 1989 and 1990.

The Buick Roadmaster sedan debuted a year after the Estate Wagon as a 1992 model, but it offered the incentive of a standard 5.7-liter V-8 in place of the wagon's 5.0-liter block. With its horizontal taillights complimenting the stainless-steel boot, it proved a fine foundation for this flower car conversion from Specialty Vehicles of Plainview, Long Island, New York.

Richard J. Conjalka collection

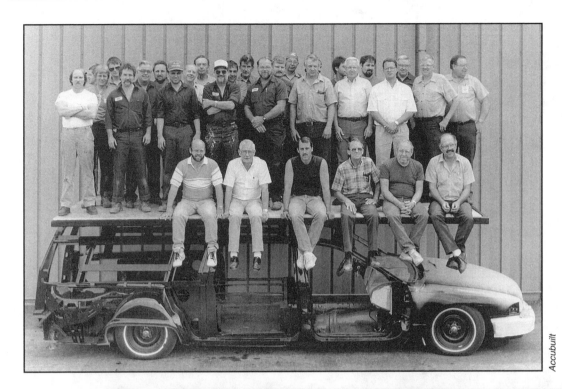

Accubuilt

While the springs were sorely taxed, S&S/Superior of Lima, Ohio confirmed the strength of its jig-built, all-steel superstructure by posing 31 employees on the roof of one of its commercial glass 1992 Buick Roadmasters.

Eagle Coach Company

Built from a Roadmaster equipped with the V90 heavy-duty trailering package and load-leveling suspension, Eagle's 1992 Buick hearse had a substantial 140.9-inch wheelbase and 244-inch overall length, allowing a 110-inch-long casket floor with 46 1/2 inches of clearance between the wheelhouses. The church truck compartments had swing out doors, while the options list included a flush-mounted extension table, a Ferno Washington cot fastener and a Federal #184 roof-mounted Beacon Ray with an amber housing.

Mike McKiernan

Given a relatively small price difference between the $42,360 Precision and $49,336 Sovereign, it was not surprising that the smaller coach was replaced within a year by the Superior Buick Regent, which shared the Sovereign's 141.9-inch wheelbase but not its commercial glass roofline. This is how the model looked after mild styling revisions in mid-1992.

Limousine Werks of Schaumberg, Illinois, targeted this Buick Grand Estate Wagon toward the hospitality and funeral trades. It shared a 44-inch wheelbase extension with the Roadmaster six-door limousine in the background.

Priced at $32,900 as a Buick Roadmaster, or $30,900 as a Chevrolet Caprice, the Pittsburgh-built Imperial GL mini-hearse typified the relatively inexpensive conversions several companies offered on full-sized General Motors station wagons in 1993. Modifications included a squared-off rear roof with a padded vinyl covering, and a 130-degree rear door opening, custom velour draperies, and an 89-inch-long black laminated casket table with bier pins, and eight rubber rollers.

Richard Shelly

Image Coaches of Warsaw, Indiana, sold a budget-priced Buick Roadmaster conversion called the CS, shown here with the company's Plymouth Grand Voyager minivan.

Image Coaches

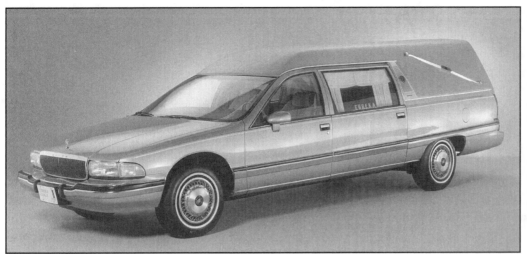

Borrowing a more powerful LT-1 V-8 from the Chevrolet Corvette, the 1994-96 Buick Roadmasters assumed the "Banker's Hot Rod" allure of their 1950s ancestors. While displacement was unchanged at 5.7 litres, the addition of sequential fuel injection at each cylinder boosted horsepower from 180 to 260. This 1994 Eureka Encore Brougham also added an electronically governed four-speed automatic overdrive transmission, ozone-friendly air conditioning, and a passenger-side airbag.

The commercial glass Sovereign became the sole Superior Buick model in 1994-96, and the Lima, Ohio, coachbuilder stressed that it was priced to compete against the standard glass Roadmasters sold by rival firms. This Sovereign was photographed outside S&S/ Superior's East Wayne Street plant in February 1994, three months before the company broke ground on its new Central Point Parkway production facility.

Tim A. Fantin photo

Cadillac taillights spruced up the ceremonial end of the 1995-96 model Eureka Buick Brougham—most of which were sold to funeral homes affiliated with the Service Corporation International (SCI) chain. This slate-colored "Buillac" belonged to the Blake-Lamb Funeral Home in Chicago.

Chapter 3

Cadillac

No make of automobile has had greater influence on the professional vehicle industry than Cadillac. More funeral coaches, flower cars, funeral-style six-door limousines, and passenger car-based ambulances have been built from Cadillacs than any other vehicle, and the "Standard of the World" still enjoys a 75 to 80 percent share of the American hearse market in spite of Lincoln's recent overtures toward mortuary customers. After recalling how some coachbuilders were driven out of business by the redesign costs incurred after Cadillac downsized its Commercial Chassis in 1977 and the further turmoil such firms experienced after the division's even-smaller front-drive hearse platform debuted in 1985, it could even be asserted that it is the only supplier of professional car

platforms with the power to make or break the entire industry. As far as the rest of the planet is concerned, Mercedes-Benz is probably the only make that can begin to rival Cadillac when it comes time for people to express their first choice for a last ride.

This position of dominance is all the more intriguing when one considers that Cadillac was a relative latecomer to professional car circles. Its sturdy, precision-manufactured passenger cars, given an important competitive edge through the addition of the auto industry's first mass-produced V-8 engine in 1915, were employed by a number of hearse and ambulance builders mounting new or used horse-drawn bodies on both new and owner-furnished used chassis. But it was not until 1926 that Cadillac truly entered the

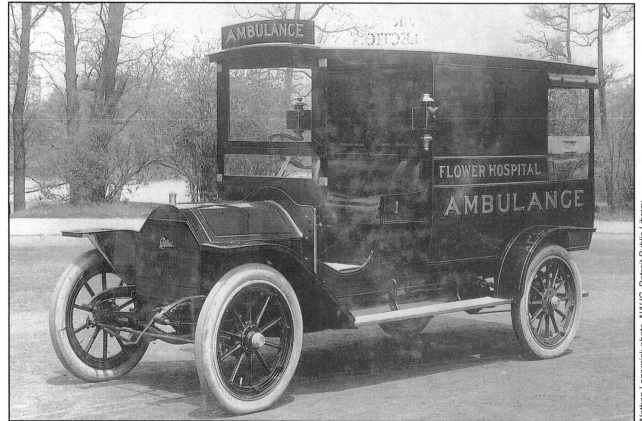

Nathan Lazernick photo, NAHC, Detroit Public Library

Combining the precision construction, modest purchase price, and low running costs of its first single-cylinder cars with the robust four-cylinder engine, sliding-gear transmission, and shaft drive of its 1907 Model G, Cadillac really hit its stride when the Model Thirty debuted in August, 1908. With a $1,350 selling price including fenders, hood, and dashboard, not to mention 112 components made to tolerances of 1/1000 inch, the bare chassis proved a fine foundation for this ambulance created by an unknown builder for the Flower Hospital located on Central Park West in New York City.

funeral market with a line of "Custom-Built" hearses and ambulances constructed on its behalf by the Meteor Motor Car Company. Winton, Velie, Studebaker, Lincoln, and Buick, among the best-remembered makes, offered factory-built, longer-length chassis suitable for funeral coach or ambulance bodywork. The 160-inch-wheelbase Commercial Chassis Cadillac evidently debuted in 1935 arrived just in time to take on the 158-inch-wheelbase frame that Packard included in its new, volume-boosting One-Twenty series.

Even then, the 1938 model year is the earliest for which a separate production total for the Cadillac Commercial Chassis is available, and the numbers initially paled against Packard's in the wake of Packard's 1937 exclusivity agreement with the Henney Motor Company. Only 101 units were built as a 159-inch-wheelbase Cadillac Series 61 variant, plus another 11 examples of a Series 75 version using a 161-inch wheelbase, compared to an estimated 800 Henney-Packards and an overall U.S. funeral coach and ambulance production output figure of 2,529 units (this overall statistic, along with other annual counts listed in Thomas A. McPherson's 1973 book *American Funeral Cars and Ambulances Since 1900,* is likely a calendar-year total, but it is still useful for comparison purposes).

As far as the 1930s transition from coachbuilder-constructed to automaker-supplied chassis was concerned, it was Cadillac's companion make LaSalle that received the most initial attention from body builders and their customers. In 1934, coinciding with its successful initiatives to trim prices and increase sales by adopting an Oldsmobile straight-eight engine and attractive, Art Deco-detailed styling, LaSalle officially catalogued its own Commercial Chassis in the Series 50 range. The ten units built that year (six of which went to A.J. Miller in Bellefontaine, Ohio) used a 119-inch wheelbase that had to be extended for funeral coach or ambulance duty. After the 121-inch-wheelbase 1935 version garnered 53 orders (50 from Meteor, two from Miller and one from the Silver family-owned Knightstown Body Company of Knightstown, Indiana), the 120-inch wheelbase 1936 Commercial Chassis chalked up an even more-encouraging shipment total of 498, with 381 units going to Meteor, 104 to A.J. Miller, six to the Eureka Company of Rock Falls, Illinois, two to Superior's plant in Lima, Ohio, and one each to Cadillac agencies in Pittsburgh and Indianapolis. The adoption of a factory-furnished 160-inch wheelbase for the 1937 model year kicked LaSalle Series 50 Commercial Chassis production into high gear, with a total of 949 units shipped to various

coachbuilders. The long-established Cincinnati builder Sayers & Scovill became the platform's number one buyer by purchasing 222 of the 900 units produced during 1938. Flxible of Loudonville, Ohio, traditionally pre-disposed to Buicks, was another big new LaSalle customer that year, with the 81 coaches it constructed on the chassis being distinguished by the company's raised hoods and cowl assemblies.

1939 results remained strong with 874 Commercial Chassis LaSalles constructed on a 156-inch wheelbase, enough for a 32-percent share of the 2,702 funeral cars and ambulances reportedly built in the U.S. that year. LaSalle's last year on the market in 1940 witnessed the assembly of 1,030 Series 50 Commercial Chassis using 159-inch wheelbases. Of this final tally, 235 units went to A.J. Miller, 234 to Meteor, 210 to Superior, 160 to S&S, 80 to Flxible, 60 to Eureka, 45 to Knightstown, two to General Motors Canada in Oshawa, Ontario, and one each to GM Detroit, GM Switzerland, the Mitchell Hearse Company of Ingersoll, Ontario, and the Jones Motor Co. of Richmond, Virginia. By this time, the Cadillac Commercial Chassis had achieved a solid 10-percent share of the professional car market with 265 units produced in 1939 and 327 (out of an industry total of 3,118 units) in 1940, and the LaSalle's replacement by a new entry-level Cadillac Series 61 saw the division's 1941 Commercial Chassis output soar to 1,625 units in a 3,801-unit market, equating to a 42 percent share—10 points greater than that constituted by Henney-Packard.

Cadillac became the undisputed master of the American funeral coach and ambulance market soon after World War II, ironically elevated to that status by the Henney-Packard exclusivity pact that had garnered so much admiration from competitors just a decade earlier. In 1946, there were five major U.S. coachbuilders creating vehicles on Cadillac's 163-inch-wheelbase Series 75 Commercial Chassis—the S&S division of Hess & Eisenhardt in Cincinnati, Superior Coach of Lima, Ohio, the A.J. Miller Company of Bellefontaine, Ohio, Meteor Motor Car in Piqua, Ohio, and the Eureka Company of Rock Falls, Illinois.

Prevailing shortages of steel and other essential components compelled Henney to postpone production of its postwar professional cars until the bathtub-themed Twenty-Second Series Packards bowed in mid-1947 as 1948 models. As imposing as those first production "postwar" Henney-Packards were, with an extra row of grille bars accentuating their overall heights, Cadillac accounted for 65 percent, or 2,423 units, of the 3,746 funeral cars and ambulances built by U.S. coachbuilders during 1947. With a 4,727-unit professional car production record that would not be broken until 1965, the 1948 model year was the final one where the Cadillac Commercial Chassis and the equivalent Packard platform were built in similar numbers, with Cadillac's production totaling 2,067 versus Packard's 1,941.

The 1949 debut of an all-new "postwar" Cadillac professional car chassis featuring tail-finned, full front fender styling, a new Series 86 designation and a modern, high-compression overhead-valve V-8 engine consigned Henney-Packard's smooth but antiquated straight eights to also-ran status. The comparative model-year commercial platform totals: 1,861 Cadillacs versus 380 Packards in 1949; 2,052 to 244 in 1950; 2,960 to 401 in 1951; 1,694 to 322 in 1952; 2,005 to 544 in 1953; and 1,635 to 325 during the final model year of Henney-bodied Packards in 1954.

With its greatest rival in the high-end funeral coach and ambulance field gone forever, Cadillac's total share of U.S. professional car production increased from 61 percent, or 1,756 units out of 2,880 built, in the 1954 calendar year to 77 percent (2,040 out of 2,661) in 1955, 79 percent (1,799 out of 2,281) in 1956, 75 percent (2,182 out of 2,917) in 1957, and 79 percent again (1,943 out of 2,452) in 1958.

More-spirited competition from the 1959-64 Flxible-Buicks, the Oldsmobiles sold by Cotner-Bevington of Blytheville, Arkansas, and the Pontiacs built in Kosciusko, Mississippi, by Superior attracted enough customers to keep Cadillac's share of the overall professional car market in the high 50 to high 60-percent range from the end of the 1950s through the early 1970s. Still, the Cadillacs constructed during this era by S&S, Superior, and the merged Miller-Meteor company are among the most coveted and collectible ambulances and hearses of all time, with their dynamism and desirability epitomized by the razor-shaped, rocket-tipped, 42.4-inch-tall tailfins found on the 1959 models.

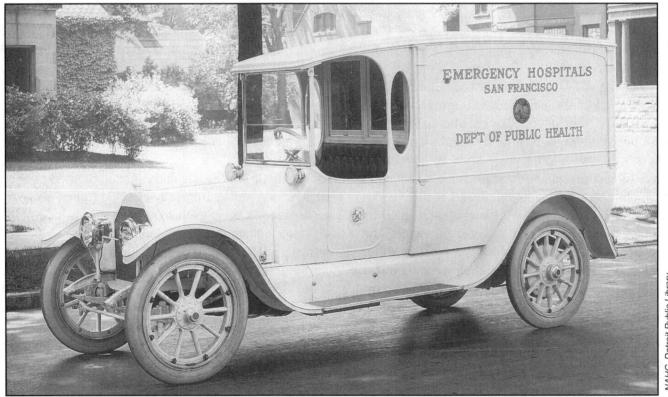

NAHC, Detroit Public Library

Henry M. Leland's uncompromising standards on the Model Thirty earned admiration from no less an authority than Pierce-Arrow Chief Engineer David Fergusson, who once wrote that "Cadillac for years had the reputation of producing the best medium-priced car in the world." The Seaman Body Company of Milwaukee is believed to be the builder of this all-white or light gray 1914 Cadillac ambulance operated by the San Francisco Department of Public Health. It was attractively detailed with an arching roof, a sliding glass partition, and oval opera windows for the driver's compartment.

The driver may have had an old-fashioned open seat on the right side of the body—the steering wheel, at least, was hinged at the top for easier entrances and exits—but this 1914 Cadillac built for the City of Detroit Receiving Hospital by the Seaman Body Company of Milwaukee touted such up-to-date amenities as a wash basin with running water, a folding rear step and a second stretcher suspended from the ceiling; patients would have certainly appreciated how the large side windows and light-colored interior panels (apparently made of steel) fostered a feeling of airiness and cleanliness.

NAHC, Detroit Public Library

David E. Wolfe collection

Announced as a 1915 model, the 70-horsepower Cadillac Type 51 earned a place in automotive history as the first mass-produced V-8 car. After outlasting legions of less carefully engineered imitators, its basic three-piece design, comprised of two blocks of four cylinders bolted to an aluminum/copper alloy crankcase, would remain in production through 1935. This elaborately carved funeral coach version, either a first-year model or a 1916 Type 53, was still being used by Kalkaska, Michigan, mortician Lowell M. Clapp as late as 1925. The body builder is unknown.

Richard J. Conjalka collection

Destined to become America's largest-volume coachbuilder, the Superior Body Company of Lima, Ohio, sold its first funeral cars and ambulances in 1925, two years after the firm was founded to build bus bodies for the locally produced Garford chassis. Though most of its early coaches were based on the Studebaker Big Six, this modern-looking "Landau Back" hearse was mounted on a Cadillac V-63 chassis. Notice there are no window drapes to obscure the flower tray.

The Professional Car

Cadillac's first direct initiative towards the funeral market took place from 1926 to 1928, when it marketed "Custom-Built" hearses and ambulances constructed on its behalf by the Meteor Motor Car Company of Piqua, Ohio. The 150-inch wheelbases on 1926-27 models were 18 inches longer than the standard 314 and 314A chassis. This 1928 model operated in Rochester, New York, by the Monroe County Morgue, used a 152-inch wheelbase that was 10 inches longer than stock. Funeral coach interiors fitted walnut, mahogany or carpet-covered floors, 12-inch-wide rubber casket rollers, a nickel-trimmed slide-out flower tray with 29 inches of casket clearance and the customer's choice of hard or rubber-covered, non-rattling bier pins mounted in bronze sockets.

Tim Cenowa collection

Founded in 1838 and incorporated in 1882, James Cunningham, Son & Co. of Rochester, New York, had earned an impressive reputation as a premier hearse and carriage maker by the time it launched America's first commercially produced, gasoline-powered auto ambulance in 1909. The company was still building its own high-quality V-8 chassis in 1930, but St. Louis funeral director Robert Armbruster opted for the new Cadillac V-16 when he commissioned this eight-column, carved panel town car hearse.

As more funeral coach and ambulance builders moved away from assembling their own chassis in the early 1930s, Cadillac emerged as one of their top choices. Using the 1932 V-8 chassis, the Superior Body Company constructed this classy town car hearse for A.E. Kingsley of Spencer, Massachusetts. A hard cover could be fitted over the driver's seat in case of inclement weather.

Craig Zwiebel

Bernie Weis collection

Confirming that a second-hand chassis could inspire awe, James Cunningham, Son & Company turned a 1933 Cadillac V-12 into this magnificent town car hearse for Math. Hermann & Son of St. Louis, Missouri in 1935. With a natural walnut mound, a cathedral interior, and dull-finished carvings that simulated cloth draperies, this body (designated style 337-A) cost $4,250 plus tax—enough to buy nine new Chevrolets, but still a bargain considering how much craftsmanship went into the coachwork.

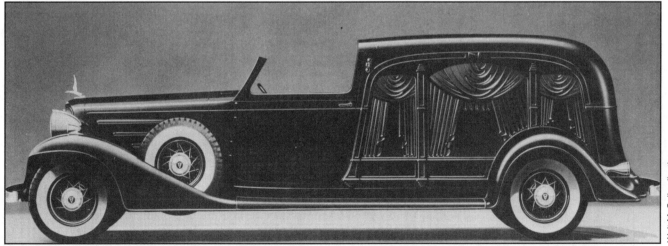

Walt McCall collection

Carved panel hearses with Art Deco overtones began to interest funeral directors as a way to stand apart from their competition as the Depression deepened, so the Eureka Company of Rock Falls, Illinois, rendered this sleek-looking "beavertail" town car on a 1933 Cadillac combining V-8 hubcaps and V-16 hood louvers. This style, apparently, was not actually built until the following model year, but the attention lavished on each car was still a great source of pride to Eureka employees. The side carvings were constructed from the finest seasoned yellow poplar, while the rear door frame could be sloped at several different angles according to individual customer taste.

Once the 1934 Cadillacs took their bow, the wheels, now independently suspended at the front by "Knee Action" coils, were the only chassis components not concealed by streamlined sheet metal. Cadillac's new "biplane" bumpers, mounted on telescoping springs that recoiled two inches in an impact, looked sensational on this Cunningham-bodied hearse, but were dropped for 1935 after they proved to be easily damaged and expensive to repair.

Honoring a heritage of superb hand-craftsmanship sustained since 1838, this intricately carved style 374 hearse on a 1936 Cadillac V-8 chassis was one of the last, if not the last, funeral cars built by James Cunningham, Son & Company of Rochester, New York .

The three-piece flathead V-8 had served Cadillac extremely well with only two displacement increases since 1915, but the 1936 model year marked the introduction of a modern "monobloc" engine with down-draft carburetion. The new low-priced Series 60 models offered 125 horsepower from 322 cubic inches, while the 156-inch wheelbase Series 75 Commercial Chassis used for this Eureka Chieftain Side-way funeral coach shared a 346-cubic inch block making 135 hp with the Series 70.

Walt McCall collection

While the Eureka Company of Rock Falls, Illinois, is generally credited with prototyping the industry's first purpose-designed flower car on a 1936 LaSalle Series 50 chassis, factory shipping records recently uncovered by Ron Van Gelderen and Matt Larson indicate that the six of these production 1937 models, assigned the special style number 37-5067F, were created by the Meteor Motor Car Company from stock two-passenger convertible coupes sent to its Piqua, Ohio, plant. These open-well models were dubbed "Western" or "Chicago" flower cars because livery services in the Windy City were among the first to use them in quantity, while "Eastern" style flower cars had stainless-steel bed covers.

Walt McCall and Tim Cenowa collections

While 2,887 Cadillac V-16s were sold during the model's first year on the market in 1930, the Depression-era bias against flaunting one's wealth saw production quickly plummet to 364 in 1931, 296 in 1932, 125 in 1933 and just 56 units in 1934, 50 in 1935 and 52 in 1936. Only two of the 49 Cadillac V-16s built in 1937 were produced as bare chassis, one of which went to the Meteor Motor Car Company of Piqua, Ohio, to create this gigantic six-window limousine ambulance for the Detroit Fire Department. It was the second of three completely custom-built ambulances (the first being a 1927 Packard and the third a Gerstenslager-bodied 1969 GMC) donated by Fire Commissioner Paxton Mendelssohn, a lifelong fire buff whose family made its fortune as early investors in the Fisher Body Company. In 1951, Mendelssohn arranged, at a cost of $22,000, to have the vehicle completely rebuilt with a new Cadillac OHV V-8, a one-piece windshield and up-to-date lower body sheet metal.

Featuring some of the biggest cast-aluminum panels ever seen on any funeral coach, this 1938 Meteor LaSalle was purchased in Kentucky by the Joseph Pray Funeral Home of Charlotte, Michigan, and given a full restoration by vintage hearse specialist Rance Bennett of Lowell, Michigan. Bennett cleverly integrated a modern pull-out casket table into the interior fittings. The 159-inch wheelbase Series 50 Commercial Chassis gave coachbuilders 35 extra inches to devote to the driver's and casket compartments without having to alter the factory-furnished driveline.

Tim Cenowa collection

Though the Flxible Company was better-known for its Buick funeral cars and ambulances, the company did body 20 of the 101 Cadillac Series 61 Commercial Chassis produced during the 1938 model year. This was especially impressive considering that this was the first time since 1932 that Flxible offered Cadillacs, but this full carved panel funeral hearse (as opposed to the twin arch Classic "A" and "AA" covered in the Buick chapter) appears to be the only one the company ever built.

Jerry W. Kayser

One of only 237 Cadillacs constructed on the 156-inch-wheelbase 61-S Commercial Chassis during the1939 model year, this spectacular Sayers & Scovill Model 916 Imperial Carved Panel Hearse earned Moses Lake, Washington, funeral director Jerry Kayser the Best-of-Show at both the 1998 and 2001 PCS International Meets. Its detail-emphasizing two-tone gray paintwork, satin-finished cast aluminum draperies, bumper-mounted "Silent Siren" and identity-disguising S&S "date marks" are dramatically complemented by a casket compartment trimmed with Gothic-motif walnut paneling and sunburst-pattern partition glass. Reportedly owned at one time by a Calgary, Alberta, area construction company, the car was purchased from Lowell, Michigan, vintage funeral coach specialist W.R. Bennett in 1994 and comprehensively restored by Glenn Vaughn Restoration Services of Post Falls, Idaho.

Fifty-five-inch-wide side doors were a distinguishing feature on this Superior-built 1939 LaSalle Devonshire used in Pennsylvania. The model's $2,625 starting price made it $300 cheaper than an equivalent Cadillac Cambridge ambulance. The combination of an old-fashioned bumper bell and a Buck Rogers-flavored Federal Traffic-Master rooftop siren gave the emergency equipment on this rig a Janus-like quality.

Steve Loftin collection

American Funeral Director

The "landau" look most people automatically associate with hearses, defined by a padded roof with S-shaped bows on the quarter panels, was introduced on a 1931 Eureka body, but was not imitated by other builders until the S&S Victoria appeared in 1938. Its appeal lay in the fact that, while it was more dignified and less passenger car-like than a limousine-style funeral coach, it was not much more expensive or difficult to produce. Note how, on this 1940 model Victoria, the Cincinnati coachbuilder continued to disguise the Cadillac grille with diagonal trim pieces topped by heavy castings on the front of the hood.

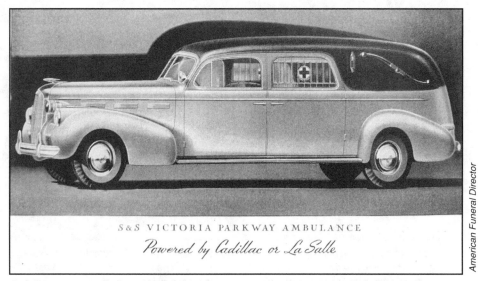

S&S VICTORIA PARKWAY AMBULANCE
Powered by Cadillac or LaSalle

American Funeral Director

S&S did not restrict the landau trend it started to funeral coaches alone, suggesting that this Victoria Parkway ambulance on a 159-inch-wheelbase LaSalle chassis would deliver "More distinguished invalid car service." While 1940 would end up being the LaSalle's last year on sale, a record 1,030 Series 50 Commercial Chassis were produced.

The Series 72 Commercial Chassis' extra-long 165-inch wheelbase allowed the welded all-steel body on this 1940 Meteor Model 630 Cadillac Funeral Car to contain a 103-inch-long casket compartment. It had 50 inches of clearance between the rear wheelhouses or 60 inches between the 42-inch-wide side doors. A particularly novel design detail on the Piqua, Ohio, firm's Cadillacs since the previous year were front doors combining coupe-style window openings with Gothic coach lamps.

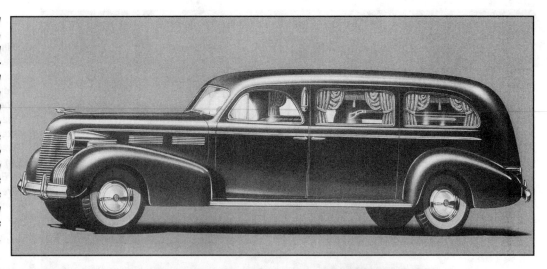

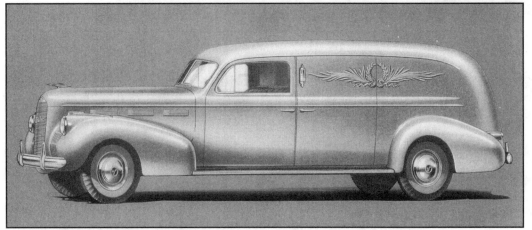

"Although its purpose is chiefly utility," Meteor conceded when promoting its 1940 Model 532 Service Car on the 159-inch-wheelbase LaSalle Commercial Chassis, "it is also out on the streets carrying your name, and must make the same good public impression." Elaborate cast-aluminum wreaths accented by elegant coach lamps attended to the issue of appearances, while the interior emphasized durability over dazzle with a linoleum-surfaced floor and artificial leather trim that would resist scarring from folding chairs or a casket packing crate. Designating it Model 632, Meteor also offered this body style on a Cadillac chassis.

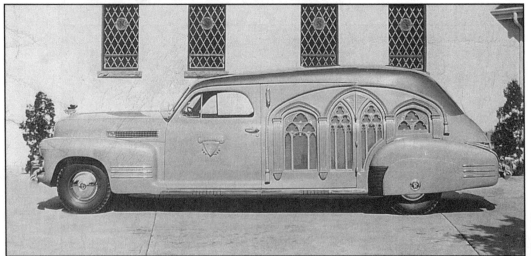

Mary Little

After 18 years as a foreman for the Mitchell Hearse Company, John James Collins Little established his own coachbuilding shop in a small Shell station on the west end of Ingersoll, Ontario in 1940. His first and most famous creation was this Gothic panel carved hearse with blue stained-glass windows, a lift-up rear door, and a Henney side-service casket table that was created in just four months from a 1941 Cadillac 6127 Sedanette for Russel Needham, a former Mitchell customer who operated funeral homes in Chatham and London, Ontario.

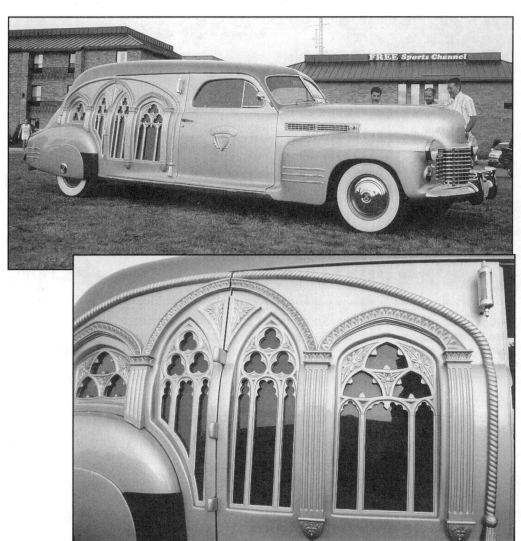

After its retirement in 1963, the cathedral-style 1941 Cadillac hearse created by John J.C. Little of Ingersoll, Ontario, spent the next two decades deteriorating in a succession of service station lots, salvage yards, and open fields in Essex County. In 1985, Chatham, Ontario, funeral director Lloyd Needham, whose father Russel had commissioned the car 44 years earlier, rescued what was left from a field outside Kingsville and commenced a full restoration under the supervision of Stan Uher at RM Restorations in Chatham.

William N. Schwartz photo, Rich Litton collection

One of the more confusing chapters in professional car history concerns two similarly named coachbuilders in Knightstown, Indiana. The companies became rivals when the original partners of the Knightstown Buggy Company founded in 1900 had an apparent falling out in 1922. The Knightstown Body Company advertised its products as Silver-Knightstowns since the concern was controlled by the Silver family, while the Walters family at the rival Knightstown Funeral Car Company used the Knightstown Galahad name. This imposing 1941 Cadillac ambulance used by the Ocean Grove, New Jersey, Fire Department First Aid Squad is a Silver-Knightstown, and it appears to have a raised hood like Flxible-built coaches from the same time period.

Thomas A. McPherson collection

Launched to great acclaim at the NFDA Convention in St. Louis in October, 1941, the 1942 Flxible Innovation might have spawned more imitators had World War II not intervened. Carved side panels made of natural finish walnut were combined with a coupe-style cab resembling a flower car's, though there was no provision for carrying floral tributes on the smooth rear deck atop the casket compartment. Three examples, with the latter two having curtain-themed side inserts, were constructed on the Cadillac Commercial Chassis. Flxible also completed two Series 70-based Buick Innovations with all-steel flanks and a second pair of side doors.

Catalogued though 1947, the Sayers & Scovill Cadillac Macedonian was the last carved-style hearse offered by a major coachbuilder. This extremely rare 1942 model with 41,000 miles was purchased in New Jersey by Bessemer, Alabama, funeral director Howard Johnson in December 1990.

Johnson Memorial Funeral Directors

American Funeral Director

During World War II, Eureka manufactured many different types of vehicles. When peace returned, landau and limousine-style coaches were the company's only offerings, as carved models demanded too many scarce resources.

Steve Lichtman collection

There was little motivation to make changes to the 1947 Cadillacs beyond a new grille with three stamped crossbars in place of the four die-cast ones used before. Taking up residence with a 1937 Seagrave Sentry pumper, this Superior-bodied 1947 ambulance was purchased second-hand by the Chillum-Adelphi Volunteer Fire Department in Adelphi, Maryland, in the fall of 1952.

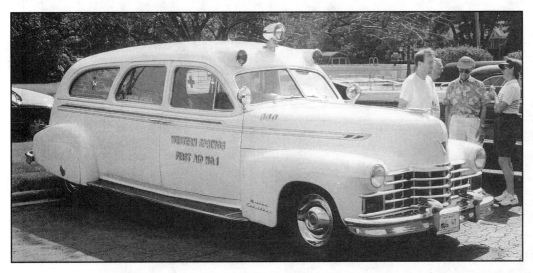

Original except for a new clutch installed the week before, one of the finest unrestored vehicles at the Professional Car Society's 1998 International Meet outside Chicago was this 11,000-mile 1947 A.J. Miller Cadillac ambulance that the Western Springs Fire Department purchased new with its World War II scrap drive proceeds and kept in service until the early 1970s.

American Funeral Director

In 1942, Sayers & Scovill of Cincinnati was sold to Emil Hess and Charles A. Eisenhardt Sr., who had joined the company as office boys in 1891. The company then became the last major firm to offer carved-style funeral cars. With the last full-panel Macedonian built in 1947, however, such craftsmanship was limited to the window openings of the Arlington service car by 1948.

While the Cadillac Series 61, 62, and Fleetwood Sixty Special got full-fendered bodies featuring tailfins in February 1948, the newly designated Series 76 Commercial Chassis and Series 75 limousines soldiered on with prewar styling until the 1949 and 1950 model years, respectively. Fitted with the distinctive hood trim that Hess & Eisenhardt of Cincinnati offered at no extra cost, this S&S DeLuxe Florentine was a fine choice for general funeral service duties or the transportation of flowers.

Retaining a theme that first appeared on its 1939 models, Meteor's postwar Cadillacs continued to combine trapezoidal front windows with door-mounted coach lamps. This 1948 combination coach is owned by Bill Wages of Stone Mountain, Georgia.

With their new full-fendered bodies and high-compression overhead-valve V-8s, S&S asserted that its "Stylasized" 1949 models were "As Modern as Supersonic Flying." This limousine-style Knickerbocker, which could be ordered as a straight hearse or a part-time ambulance combination, was available as an extra-plush "Superline" or a less-lavish "400" lacking rain gutter and rocker panel trim. Other S&S Cadillacs for '49 included the Londonderry limousine ambulance, the Florentine flower car, a service coach with carved drapery panels in the window openings and landau-style Victorias in funeral coach, ambulance, and combination variants.

Paul Cichon

Paul Cichon of Hampton, Connecticut, purchased this 1949 Superior Cadillac end-loading landau funeral coach from a Harley-Davidson repair shop in St. Petersburg, Florida, in February 1990. Equipped with a column-shifted three-speed manual transmission, it is basically unrestored except for an exterior and dashboard repaint, some re-chroming and new driver's compartment carpets.

Steve Loftin collection

Advertising it was "Not a Compromise with (the) Hearse Body Design," S&S launched its first standard production Professional Kensington high-top ambulance in 1950. For rescue squads with the means to afford them, roomier rigs like these would become the standard to aspire to during the ensuing decade.

Walt McCall collection

Acting a decade after most of its competitors, Superior debuted its first Cadillac flower cars for 1949. Ironically, the company would become the body style's biggest-volume maker in the years to come. The 1950 version, officially dubbed the Coupe de Fleur, touted more than 50 improvements, including concealed side door hinges, a one-piece windshield, and a wraparound rear window for a completely modern look .

American Funeral Director

Proposing a cheaper alternative to purpose-built Cadillac flower cars, John V. Morris of Wilkes-Barre, Pennsylvania, marketed this clever "Converto-Coupe" unit featuring stainless-steel trim, lightweight aluminum flower trays, and a "naugahide leather" weather cab.

Bernie Weis photo

Cadillac ambulances built for the U.S. military during the 1950s conformed to unique specifications. The side doors and their windows were deleted, and the interiors were much simpler with fold-down cots and no driver's compartment partition. The ambulance on the left was built by Superior. The taller unit to the right is a Meteor.

Tim A. Fantin photos

In 1951, S&S proudly celebrated the 75th anniversary of its founding by William Sayers and A.R. Scovill. Originally purchased by the Gill Funeral Home in Ponca City, Oklahoma, this stately limousine-style Kensington ambulance passed through the hands of the Anderson Funeral Home in Garber, Oklahoma, and Port Arthur, Texas, PCS member Steve Diamond, who sold it to the Easton, Pennsylvania, Emergency Squad as a parade vehicle in 1995. Its odometer showed just 38,000 miles by the time Tim A. Fantin of Merrillville, Indiana, became its owner in 2000.

In addition to building S&S funeral cars and ambulances, Hess & Eisenhardt of Cincinnati was renowned for the armored and custom limousines it created for governments and heads-of-state. Equipped with one-way windows (including the partition) and air conditioning, this 1951 Cadillac six-door was one of 20 built for transporting the wives of King Ibn Saud of Saudi Arabia. The fleet cost $250,000 and was presented to the king as a gift from the Arabian-American Oil Company.

Purchased new and operated until 1971 by the Morgan H. Dawkins Funeral Home in Newport News, Virginia, this 1952 Sayers & Scovill Cadillac Florentine model 52420 flower car earned the prestigious "Funeral Director's Choice" Award at both the 1997 and 2003 national meets. Though it ended up as a delivery vehicle for a clothing shop before being parked inside a chicken coop, current owner Eddie Moore of Orange, Virginia, found the car in reasonably good shape and commenced his three-year restoration in 1995. The Tudor-style door nameplates are another distinctive S&S detail.

Meteor used a Coupe DeVille-style hardtop roofline on its 1952 flower car. The customer could choose between a "Western" or "Chicago" type open flower trough, or the "Eastern" model shown here, which could carry a casket when its stainless-steel deck was left in the horizontal position.

The 1953 Cadillac funeral cars featured the first significant front-end restyling since 1950, with subtly hooded headlights and bigger bumper bullets that were soon nicknamed "Dagmars" after a well-endowed actress of the day. Stylish as it was with its newly added one-piece wraparound rear window, Robert F. Parsons' Eureka flower car (recently sold to Tom Hoczyk of Fort Wayne, Indiana) used a body frame assembled from seasoned ash the old-fashioned way.

Richard J. Conjalka collection

In mid-1952, Superior's ambulance lineup was expanded with a raised-roof Super Rescuer touting 52 inches of rear compartment headroom. Up to four patients could be transported when the overhead stretcher hooks were used. This fire engine red example dates from Superior's 30th anniversary season in 1953.

Spitler, Inc.

Harking back to the first purpose-built flower cars debuted in the 1930s, the S&S Florentine adopted a simulated convertible top in the 1954 model year. Fitted with a Chicago-style open flower trough and no #2 side doors, this example does not appear capable of carrying a casket.

With their wrap-around windshields and finer grille textures, the 1954 models were the most-changed Cadillacs since 1950. The Series 86 commercial chassis featured a 1-inch wheelbase increase to 158 inches and a wider front tread that promised easier handling, even though power steering was still optional. 1954 also marked the year that Eureka, who built this electric three-way landau owned by Tom Hoczyk of Fort Wayne, Indiana, became the last U.S. coachbuilder to begin phasing-out composite wood bodies by switching to all-steel doors.

American Funeral Director

In Bellefontaine, Ohio, A.J. Miller marked the start of its second century in business with airy new bodies featuring front-hinged second doors and extruded aluminum window frames. The look hinted strongly at the "colonnade" styling used on GM's mid-sized sedans from 1973-77. The landau hearse continued to use the oval opera windows that had first appeared in 1949.

Craig Stewart collection

Addressing the long waits endured for ambulances by residents of the Ironbound section of Newark, New Jersey, several area tavern owners banded together and raised funds for the founding of a local volunteer squad in 1952. Three years later, the company's original 1952 Miller Cadillac was proudly posed alongside its brand new 1955 Miller First Aider high-headroom ambulance.

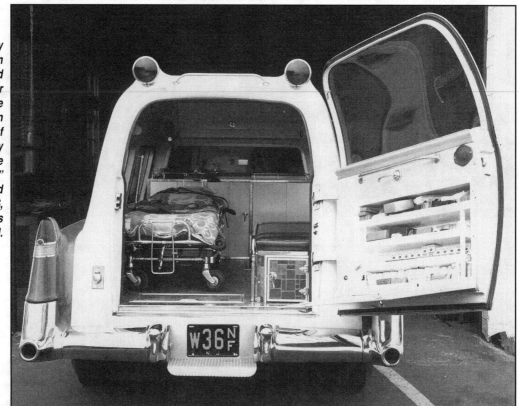

While today's EMT's would likely feel confined, the high-headroom interior of the Ironbound Ambulance Squad's 1955 Miller First Aider offered much more work and storage space than earlier vehicles. Being one of the first patterns offered by Armstrong after World War II, the brick-style "Colonial Classic" linoleum on the floor and squad bench is also seen on S&S, Superior, and other ambulances from the period.

Craig Stewart collection

Adding a raised roof with enlarged rear door openings, extra-tall side glass and a prominent brow above the windshield, Derham of Rosemont, Pennsylvania, custom-crafted this incredible invalid car from a 1955 Cadillac Series Seventy-Five limousine.

Bill Harris photo, Noel Thompson Library, CCCA Museum

During 1955 and 1956, the prestigious Broadmoor resort in Colorado Springs, Colorado, commissioned about a dozen "SkyView" sightseeing coaches from Hess & Eisenhardt of Cincinnati. Needing little more than a repaint in its original Mandan Red and Pecos Beige two-tone, this 1955 model is owned by David Bennett of Manitou Springs, Colorado.

Richard J. Conjalka collection

After Packard and Henney left the field at the end of 1954, Cadillac enjoyed a virtual monopoly in the high-end funeral coach and ambulance market starting in 1955. With its expanded factory, Superior Coach was particularly well positioned to exploit the void that year. On the basic Cadillac funeral car, the 22 1/2-inch-high rear door threshold was claimed to be the lowest on the market, while the top-of-the-line Super Rescuer ambulance touted 51 inches of headroom in the patient compartment.

Flower cars reached their peak of popularity in the 1950s, and it is plain to see why when taking in the imposing proportions, brushed stainless-steel deck, and matching casket compartment of Pittsburgh funeral director Dan D'Allessandro's 1955 Miller Cadillac.

Old Cars Weekly

With its flattop roof and nylon blend airline draperies nicely augmenting the fine aluminum grille and "Slipstream" exhaust fairings that Cadillac added for 1956, this limousine-style S&S Superline Knickerbocker was a stately last ride by any standard.

Prepared for any contingency that the scenic seaside town of Ocean Grove, New Jersey, might face, this 1956 S&S Cadillac Professional Kensington would have looked good in a Fourth of July parade. Its red-and-white exterior was accented by a blue Plexiglas skylight for the front of the patient compartment. Another interesting detail on the two-step roof is that the Federal C-Series siren was recessed into the top of the driver's compartment.

Cadillac's 1957 changes were nothing less than revolutionary, with razor-edge tail fins and an all-new Tubular Center "X" Member Type frame that allowed overall height to drop an average of 3 inches. Even with the wheelbase on the Series 86 Commercial Chassis shortened by 2 inches to 156 inches, the longer, lower look allowed was plainly evident on this 1957 S&S Superline Knickerbocker, especially since the hood was no longer higher than the front fenders.

S&S officially called its 1957 styling theme "The Sculptured Look," which was appropriately promoted in initial advertising with this plaster model.

S&S asserted that "The Sculptured Look" of its 1957 Superline Victoria landau hearse was backed by "Unitized Engineering." In his capacity as Hess & Eisenhardt's manufacturing chief, Willard C. Hess told American Funeral Director *that this principle provided "a body and a chassis with exactly the same stress characteristics—a unit that is entirely one automobile. The result is the most perfect handling feel of any professional car ever built."*

After purchasing the A.J. Miller Company in March 1956 and merging it with the Meteor assets it had owned since 1954, the Wayne Works launched its first "Miller-Meteor" Cadillacs as 1957 models. Owned by Fred and Joanne Vanderlaan of Hudsonville, Michigan, this M-M Landau Panoramic Combination touted sleeker styling to take full advantage of Cadillac's new x-layout frame design.

Spitler, Inc.

Publicly unveiled in June 1957, the awe-inspiring S&S Park Place (called the Florentine in early concept sketches) was basically a Victoria hearse with the rear roof replaced with a manually folding top. It was based on the design Hess & Eisenhardt developed for the U.S. Secret Service's 1956 Cadillac parade vehicles "Queen Mary II" (which was following John F. Kennedy's 1961 Lincoln X-100 limousine, also built by H&E, during that fateful day in Dallas) and "Queen Elizabeth II."

While the 1957 S&S Cadillac Park Place seems, in retrospect, much too special and elaborate to have handled everyday utility duties for its owners at the Spitler Funeral Home in Montoursville, Pennsylvania, roller racks could be placed in its rear compartment to accommodate a casket shipping box when the canvas top was raised.

Spitler, Inc.

Indianapolis Motor Speedway Hall of Fame Museum

Emphasizing how far Eureka had evolved since its founding as a manufacturer of school desks and church pews in 1871, the 1957 model year marked the completion of the firm's transition from composite wood-framed to all-steel bodies for its Cadillac professional cars. Sporting two-tone paint and checkered flags on its front fenders, this limousine-style Eureka ambulance was operated by the Conkle Funeral Home at the Indianapolis Motor Speedway.

With his funeral home located just a stone's throw from the Brickyard, John Conkle was an avid race fan who provided ambulance service at the Indianapolis 500 from the 1950s through the 1970s. This fleet of 1957 Eureka Cadillacs attended to the 1959 event. Typically, there were two ambulances standing by on practice days, and four on race days.

Indianapolis Motor Speedway Hall of Fame Museum

NAHC, Detroit Public Library

For 1957, the Superior Cadillac Coupe de Fleur flower had a reverse-angle roofline with a recessed rear window and small quarter windows behind the front doors. This basic design would prove contemporary enough to serve through the 1964 model year.

Richard J. Conjalka collection

While Superior's sleek Criterion Styling was essentially unchanged for 1958, all models added quad 5 3/4-inch headlamp systems with separate high beams that promised more precise aiming. Given that it was photographed at the Allen County Fairgrounds east of Lima, Ohio, in 1961, it is very likely that this limousine style Beau Monde funeral car was a trade-in at one of Superior's used coach shows.

Cadillac tailfins reached their giddy, 42 2/5-inch climax in 1959, and professional car makers celebrated by consuming 2,102 Commercial Chassis (now designated Series 6890) during the model year. Decatur, Illinois, funeral director Dan Brintliger owned this 1959 Eureka combination when the Professional Car Society convoyed to the Auburn Cord Duesenberg Museum during its 1995 International Meet.

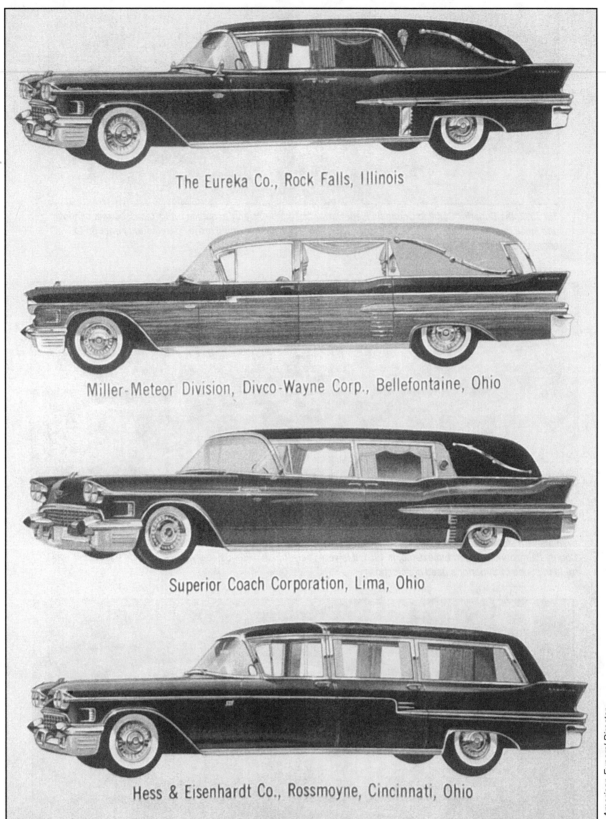

The Eureka Co., Rock Falls, Illinois

Miller-Meteor Division, Divco-Wayne Corp., Bellefontaine, Ohio

Superior Coach Corporation, Lima, Ohio

Hess & Eisenhardt Co., Rossmoyne, Cincinnati, Ohio

American Funeral Director

Cadillac was well aware of the halo effect that high-visibility funeral cars had on its sales, and made a point to publicize the coachbuilders that purchased 1,915 of its Series 8680S Commercial Chassis during the otherwise-slow 1958 model year. Interestingly, the image representing Miller-Meteor depicts a Crestwood model with wood-grain bodyside appliqués.

When the 1959 Cadillac professional cars debuted at the NFDA's October 1958 convention in Cleveland, their stylistic possibilities were explored by Superior's new Crown Royale limousine and landau models. This series featured forward-leaning C-pillars that, in concert with a wrap-over tiara band, backward-sloping D-pillars and nearly straight landau irons, created a sleek wedge effect.

Richard J. Conjalka collection

Identified by its vertical "C" pillars, the Superior Royale offered 1959 Cadillac customers a slightly more conservative alternative. Lyle Steadman's three-way loading version hails from Brigden, Ontario.

Becoming the most-famous movie procar since a Jaguar XK-E was turned into a hearse for *Harold and Maude*, a limousine-style 1959 Miller-Meteor Cadillac Futura became the basis for the ECTO-1 used in the hit comedy *Ghostbusters*. This replica was parked at Universal Studios in Orlando, Florida.

Lisa Lachover-Merksamer photo

Richard J. Conjalka collection

For 1960, more-triangular corner windows were employed for the Full Vision Styling option on Eureka professional cars. Superior and Miller-Meteor Cadillacs may have been even sleeker looking, but the innate elegance of this two-tone, three-way, limousine-style hearse is indisputable.

Whether a funeral director ordered Miller-Meteor's 1960 limousine as a straight hearse or a combination ambulance, the company's literature promised that its "low-sweeping lines, elegant simplicity, and deep encircling glass will compliment your taste for years to come." This still rang true when Rick Stockellburg drove this car 1,182 miles from Lincoln, Rhode Island, to the PCS 1993 International Meet in Chatham, Ontario.

Richard J. Conjalka collection

Even with the slightly smaller fins, the 1960 style taillight pods gave the impression that Cadillac had gone from two rocket engines to four. This was reinforced by the canted pillars and ribbed-aluminum quarter panels on this Superior Crown Royale limousine-type combination.

Richard J. Conjalka collection

Superior constructed 977 professional cars on the Cadillac Commercial Chassis during the 1960 model year, and out of these only 10 were Coupe de Fleur flower cars. This even represented a valley between the 1959 and 1961 sales volumes, when output totaled 23 and 37 units, respectively. Still, the reverse-angle roofline launched on 1957 models was wearing just as well as the durable, stainless-steel rear deck.

Richard J. Conjalka collection

All-white paint must have been a great boon towards increasing visibility and reducing interior temperatures in this mid-level, 48-inch headroom Superior Cadillac Royale Rescuer ambulance. The B&M Super Chief siren mounted above the driver's seat also did its part in making sure this rig was heard as well as seen.

Owned for many years by Pittsburgh area firefighter John Schmidt, this sleek 1961 Eureka Cadillac combination currently belongs to Virgle and Karen Onnen of Sterling, Illinois.

Conservative S&S coachwork complemented Cadillac's flamboyant 1961 styling surprisingly well, judging from this noble Victoria that earned Nanticoke, Pennsylvania, funeral director Jonathan Stegura a class first in the 1970-and-earlier hearse category at the 1999 PCS International Meet. Stanley Sipko of Dupont, Pennsylvania, owns this coach today.

Stanley Sipko

Topping a range that also included the 42-inch-headroom Royale and 48-inch-headroom Rescuer, Superior's ultimate Cadillac ambulance in 1961 was this 54-inch Super Rescuer. A fiberglass roof cap reinforced with U-section steel bows allowed lots of working space without excess weight and top-heaviness.

Accubuilt

This three-way 1961 Cadillac Crown Royale Landaulet had metal-threaded sliding draperies, diamond-tufted upholstery, and flush-mounted floor bearings, which allowed the casket table to glide out easily. The two-tone headliner also featured a wrap-over molding that echoed the exterior trim.

Accubuilt

Richard J. Conjalka collection

Responding to Cadillac's design changes, Eureka gave its 1963 models more angular roof and window lines. Rear-hinged side doors identify this stately landau with Full Vision styling as a three-way loading funeral coach, priced at $12,847 with a manually operated casket table or $13,664 with electric servicing. "Floating" landau bars with barbed ends, added in the 1960 model year, were an attractive Eureka trademark.

Hess & Eisenhardt's simple, dignified detailing worked particularly well with the more-conservative exteriors on 1963 Cadillacs, and the Cincinnati builder's premium pricing promised extra exclusivity. Mike Barruzza's baby blue S&S Superline Park Row combination would have started at $12,550 when it was new, making it $1,968 more expensive than the similarly configured Superior Sovereign.

Joseph P. McDonald

After 93 years in business, the Eureka Company of Rock Falls, Illinois, closed its doors on June 6, 1964. This awe-inspiring 54-inch headroom Highboy, originally used by the Papillion, Nebraska, FD and recently restored by Rock Falls funeral director Joseph P. McDonald, is believed to be the last ambulance the company ever built.

From 1963 to 1969, funeral directors who had a hard time deciding between limousine and landau-style coaches could get the best of both worlds with the Miller-Meteor Paramount. Until October 1995, this 1964 Paramount combination owned by Larry and Michelle Allan of Grand Rapids, Michigan, worked a dragstrip in Marion, South Dakota, where it was once timed at almost 98 mph in the quarter mile!

A raceway grandstand offered an ideal venue for assessing the basic styling differences among Superior's 1964 Cadillacs. Clockwise from the lower left are a limousine-style Sovereign, a Crown Sovereign Landau, a Crown Royale Limousine and a Royale Limousine.

With its removable "Ambulance" signs installed between the airline drapes, this 1964 Superior Cadillac Royale combination still looked ready for a few more years of action when it was traded in to the factory on July 6, 1967. This photo was taken at the Allen County Fairgrounds just east of Lima, Ohio, where Superior staged many used coach sales.

Accubuilt

This side-servicing 1964 Superior Cadillac Crown Royale featured elaborate brocade upholstery with sunburst-pattern quarter panel tufting. After the casket was glided into place using the swing-out table's rubber rollers, the table was slid into driving position using the recessed rails and floor bearings, after which the casket was secured by inserting rubber-faced bier pins into the optimal holes at each end of the table.

Robert and Georgia Parsons have earned numerous accolades with this 1965 Superior Cadillac Royale low-top ambulance. In addition to air conditioning, it has fender-mounted Mars warning lights with lenses that wobble in a figure-8 pattern.

Richard J. Conjalka collection

Cadillac's 1965 models were the most thoroughly revised in a decade, with an all-new frame where the X-layout used from 1957-64 was replaced with a much stiffer box-section perimeter design. The 156-inch-wheelbase Series 69890 Commercial Chassis had shorter sill sections that encouraged taller "commercial glass" windshields, and side windows flanked by reduced angle roof pillars. The elegant proportions that resulted are entirely clear on this 1965 Miller-Meteor Classic Duplex combination, which wears removable landau panels over the side windows.

Tim A. Fantin photo

Equipped with a three-way electric casket table and a painted metal roof that cost $1,000 more than a vinyl covering, this all-white 1966 S&S Cadillac Victoria was reputedly the most expensive car that Uniontown, Pennsylvania, coach dealer Dick Conaway sold during the entire 1960s. Originally purchased by the Vaughan Funeral Home of Parkersburg, West Virginia, at a cost of more than $18,000, it has been owned since December 1999 by Tim A. Fantin of Merrillville, Indiana.

Accubuilt

Coming off record sales season where an all-new Cadillac Commercial Chassis was introduced, it was no surprise that 1966 was a relatively quiet year for funeral coach and ambulance builders. With its new rear door trim and revised roof badging, this Superior Crown Sovereign still had plenty of stage presence, and Cadillac again offered matching Fleetwood limousines after carrying over the 1964 styling into 1965.

Looking sleek but delivering little visibility past the tall, stainless-steel deck, Superior's flower cars used an A-shaped fastback roofline from 1965 to 1970. Wilkes-Barre, Pennsylvania, funeral director Ted Collins' exquisite 1966 example is a frequent prize winner.

In 1967, Miller-Meteor built only six Embassy Flower Cars to special order, making Carlton Ham's Inverness Green example from Franklin, New Haven, even more awe inspiring.

Accubuilt

While Miller-Meteor advocated all-metal ambulance roofs, Superior asserted that its one-piece fiber glass cap, which was reinforced by several U-section steel bows, offered a 300-lb. weight saving that delivered a lower center of gravity, better handling, and improved fuel economy. This elevated view of a 1967 Superior Rescuer emphasizes Cadillac's new forward-lunging fenders.

95

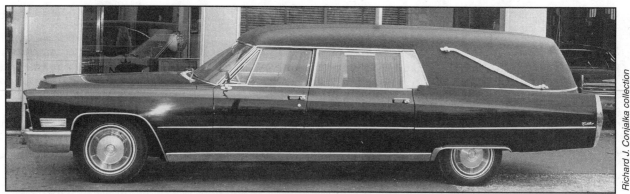

Richard J. Conjalka collection

This extremely rare photo provides another example of what National Coaches could create without relying on the Cadillac Commercial Chassis. To construct this long-wheelbase landau hearse, the Knightstown, Indiana, builder started with a 1967 Calais sedan.

Hinting stylistically at the Miller-Meteor Olympian that would bow as a 1970 model, the Brownlie-Maxwell funeral home in Melbourne, Florida, ordered its Emperor Blue 1968 M-M Citation three-way with a white half-vinyl roof and matching side curtains. Ellisville, Missouri, resident Dennis Goethe purchased this unique coach after its 1997 retirement.

Tim A. Fantin photo

Elaborately trimmed with brushed aluminum quarter panel moldings and a contrasting color roof with a wrapover tiara, this 1968 Superior Crown Royale was the company's top-of-the-line limousine style funeral coach; Sovereign series models omitted the rear corner windows for a more formal appearance.

Accubuilt

Best known for the open-well, standard-wheelbase flower cars it created from Cadillac Coupe DeVilles, the McClain Sales and Leasing Company of Anderson, Indiana, coverted nearly 400 vehicles between 1959 and 1997. Accented by a matching boot, the flower well on this 1969 model is lined with sturdy stainless-steel sheeting.

Richard J. Conjalka collection

Photographed outside the Road Rescue ambulance factory in St. Paul, Joe Klein's 1969 Miller-Meteor Volunteer boasted loads of emergency paraphernalia. This 48-inch-headroom rig touted a Federal Q2B siren flanked by electronic speaker/sirens, 360-degree "Ful-Vu" corner beacons, a rear door spotlight, a rooftop fracture board compartment with a flat top Beacon Ray, and fender-mounted Mars lights.

Accubuilt

Options such as illuminated roof signs, fender-mounted flashers, and twin Federal CP-26 electronic sirens, as well as a "West Coast" mirror on the driver's door, would have pushed the final tab for this imposing 1970 Superior Super Rescuer 54-inch-headroom ambulance far beyond its $14,769 starting price.

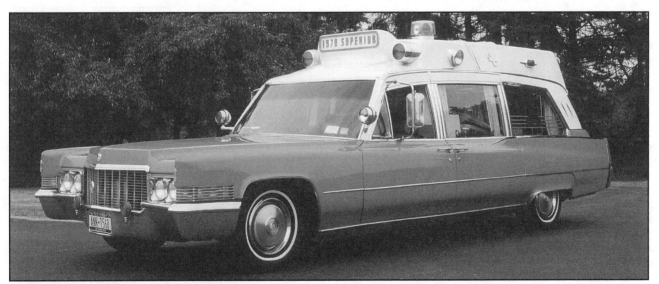

This big 1970 Superior Royale 51-inch-headroom Rescuer ambulance is now owned by Rev. Daniel K. Herrick of Chatham, New York. It originally served the Pine Plains, New York, Fire Department Rescue Squad before seeing action with the Beacon, New York, Fire Department.

The padded cabinets in the back of this Superior Cadillac Super Rescuer confirm that safety was being taken seriously by 1970. The tall cabinet in the center houses an oxygen cylinder, while lighter linens and bandages were generally stored overhead. Note that roll-up doors are used to increase working space in the stretcher area and the passenger side footwell. The squad bench has a fold-up rail that allows it to be used for a second patient.

Accubuilt

Tim A. Fantin photos

Miller-Meteor's already-angular bodies did not need many modifications to mate attractively with Cadillac's much-revised 1971 Commercial Chassis. But it was still an exciting year for the Piqua, Ohio, firm as it recalled the completion of its very first horsedrawn funeral coaches 100 years before. This light green Landau Traditional end-loader, originally the pride of the Parker Funeral Home in Lakeview, Ohio, is now owned by Harold Loyd of LaPorte, Indiana.

While their sales were diminished by a three-month strike at General Motors, Superior's 1971 Cadillacs were all-new for the first time since 1965. Design cues included ventless front door glass and squared-off quarter panels that dispensed with rear corner windows. The funeral coach line was now topped by this three-way loading Crown Limited Landau.

This 1971 S&S Medic Mark I, built by Hess & Eisenhardt of Cincinnati for the Myerstown, Pennsylvania, First Aid Unit, has earned numerous best-in-class and "Medic's Choice" awards at Professional Car Society events since Evan Butchers purchased it in February, 1994. In addition to its original Grecian White upper, Kensington Green middle, and Lexington Green lower color scheme, this three-stretcher unit touts two Federal Twin Sonic electronic "Interceptor" sirens and a grand total of 24 emergency lights.

Posed outside Hess & Eisenhardt's Blue Ash Road facility in the Cincinnati suburb of Rossmoyne, this S&S flower car is thought to be the only one produced in 1971. A standard Cadillac windshield and side windows were used to emphasize its low, sleek lines, taking full advantage of the 1971 Cadillac Commercial Chassis' 157 1/2-inch wheelbase.

Richard J. Conjalka collection

After a 1971 model changeover that took more than two years to prepare for, Superior was the only coachbuilder that officially catalogued a Commercial Chassis Cadillac flower car. Styling was more formal than S&S' one-off creation, but these were still extreme rarities with only fifteen examples constructed during the model year.

Promising a smoother ride than its van-based rivals, this top-of-the-line 1972 Superior Model 626 touted 54 inches of headroom under its steel-reinforced fiber glass roof cap, which could be fitted with illuminated signs at extra cost. The energy-absorbing front bumper presaged the battering rams that would appear on 1973 Cadillacs, while the oversized cross on this unit's quarter panel would be superseded by the six-pointed "Star of Life" under the Federal government's new KKK guidelines.

Richard J. Conjalka collection

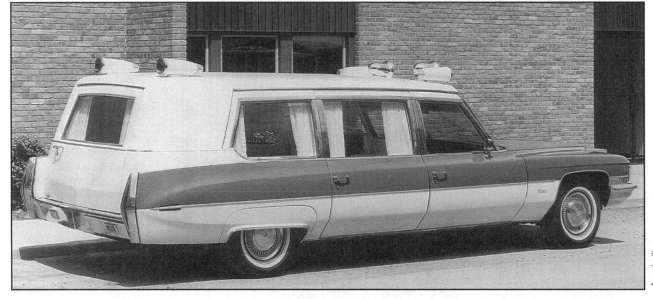

Accubuilt

By 1972, it was fairly unusual to see a Superior Cadillac as a straight ambulance with the shortest 42-inch-headroom passenger compartment. Unless the car was finished as a combination coach, most customers opted for the 51- or 54-inch-headroom models.

Steve Lichtman photo

Among the nicest ambulances out of 222 constructed on the Cadillac Commercial Chassis by Superior in 1973 was this 54-inch high-top originally delivered to the Reeb Funeral Home in Bueyrus, Ohio. It had metallic gold paint, three rooftop Beacon-Rays, two Federal CP-25 electronic sirens, twin Mars 888s flanking the Federal Q2B siren and a padded rear roof with a wrap-over tiara band.

Chuck Madderom photo, courtesy Mike McDonald

Mike McDonald of Escondido, California, has garnered admiration with this virtually mint 1973 S&S Cadillac Medic Mark I ambulance. This rig was originally owned by the "Life Squad" in Fort Wright, Kentucky, after which, McDonald recalls, it ended up at a Manitoba speedway "getting used one night a month for another eight years."

Mary Little

On October 15, 1973, the National Funeral Directors Association opened its annual convention in Hess & Eisenhardt's home town of Cincinnati, Ohio. Here are three of the company's 1974 S&S Victoria funeral coaches, which added wrap-around cornering lamps and a slimmer-looking rear bumper with vertical rub strips and side reflectors. The taillights had been relocated under the elegantly V-shaped rear door.

Distinguished by shield-like medallions on the D-pillars, this white-and-black 1974 Superior Cadillac Sovereign Chateau Baronet combination was bought new by the Wise Funeral Home (later Defenbaugh-Wise) of Circleville, Ohio. Sold in 2001, this coach is still in active service at a Tennessee mortuary.

Tim A. Fantin photo

Tony Karsnia photo

With its blanked-out side panels and rooftop fracture board freeing up additional cabinet space, this 1974 Miller-Meteor Criterion "walk-through" ambulance was one of two owned by PCS Archivist Tony Karsnia of St. Paul. Painted Cotillion White over Dynasty Red, it was originally used on Long Island by the Stony Brook, New York Fire Department. Karsinia's other Criterion, finished in white and Omaha Orange, came from the Garfield County Ambulance Service in Jordan, Montana.

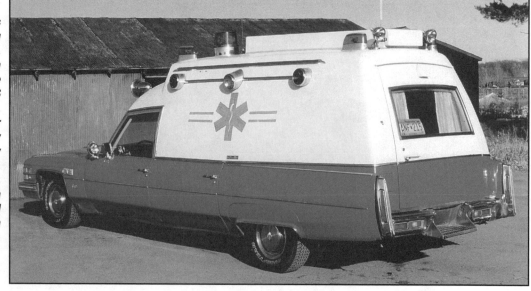

Mike Barruzza's 1974 Superior Cadillac Coupe de Fleur has a rear-hinged stainless-steel flower deck, which could be inclined electrically to accommodate different-sized tributes, as well as the hearse-style rear door for admitting a casket when the deck is horizontal. This example was owned and operated by the M.W. Murphy Funeral Home of Trenton, New Jersey, from December 1978 through March 1993.

Superior climbed onboard the opera window craze with the 1975-6 Sovereign Regal. This Firethorn-colored 1975 model, identified as a combination by the rear compartment air vent, was operated by the Jackson Funeral Service of Demotte, Indiana.

Tim A. Fantin photos

In the mid-1970s, limousine-style professional cars became less common as the duties of funeral home-operated combinations were increasingly assumed by truck-based ambulances run by community rescue squads. Nevertheless, this 1976 Miller-Meteor Cadillac Eterna was one of the most attractive coaches in the genre with its vinyl-padded or crinkle-painted D-pillars accented by color-keyed landau bows and a wrap-over tiara molding.

103

Completed September 24, 1976, this Miller-Meteor Lifeliner owned until recently by Craig and Roseanne Stewart was the last ambulance the company delivered to New Jersey. Its $26,258.62 original price included twin sirens (one mechanical, one electronic) behind the bumper, Ful-Vu corner beacons, a Federal 184 rooftop Beacon Ray, and a Mars 888 light above the windshield that wobbled to clear traffic. Twin Delco batteries handled the electrical load.

Craig Stewart

Tim A. Fantin photo

General Motors began to pare excess size and weight from its cars starting with the 1977 model year. No exception was made for the low-volume funeral coach market as the wheelbase of the Cadillac Commercial Chassis shrank from 157.5 inches in 1976 to 144.3 inches for 1977 and was shared for the first time with the factory-built Fleetwood limousines. The Superior Coach Division of Sheller-Globe still managed to produce 516 Cadillacs using the new platform, with the most-popular model continuing to be the end-loading Sovereign landau hearse. This Commodore Blue example was purchased new by the Jones funeral home in Appleton, Wisconsin.

Richard J. Conjalka collection

While extended-wheelbase Cadillac flower cars went on hiatus when the downsized 1977s debuted, the McClain Sales and Leasing Company of Anderson, Indiana, completed numerous Coupe DeVille conversions.

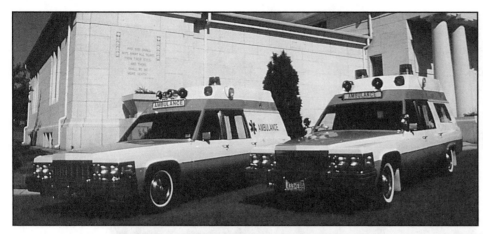

Celebrated as the first and last of only 30 ambulances constructed by Superior on Cadillac's downsized Commercial Chassis, Mike Barruzza's 1977 and Dr. Roger White's 1979 models were memorably posed in front of the mausoleum at Forest Lawn Cemetery during the Professional Car Society's 1996 International Meet in St. Paul, Minnesota.

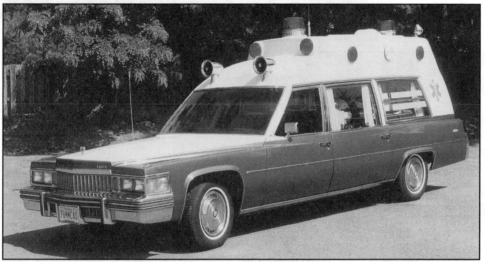

Craig Stewart photos

Out of 348 professional cars produced by Miller-Meteor in 1978, only four were straight ambulances like this three-patient capable unit, originally used by the Omaha Ambulance Service in Nebraska and subsequently owned by Craig Stewart of Wood Ridge, New Jersey, and Martin Schmeisser of Tampa, Florida. Completed April 20, 1978, it would become the last ambulance produced at the Piqua, Ohio, plant before the doors closed the following year.

Tim A. Fantin photo

As the smallest of the "Big Three" coachbuilders, Cincinnati-based Hess & Eisenhardt was hit hard by the costly 1977 changeover. S&S ambulances were discontinued, and the sole remaining funeral coach was the landau-style Victoria. This 1978 model, once owned by Huber's funeral home in East Chicago, Indiana, now belongs to Bob Baldwin of Ann Arbor, Michigan.

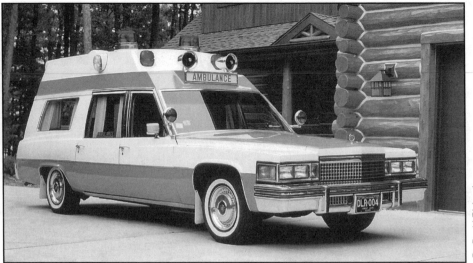

On February 19, 1980, Dr. Roger D. White of Rochester, Minnesota, a Mayo Clinic anesthesiologist and advocate of passenger car ambulances, came to Superior's East Kibby Street plant in Lima, Ohio, to take delivery of the last Cadillac ambulance ever built. This historic 1979 model is now owned by Dr. David Richards of Bloomfield Hills, Michigan.

Dr. David Richards

Richard J. Conjalka collection

Wolfington Body Company of Exton, Pennsylvania, was a prominent Philadelphia area coach and ambulance dealer and also a big converter of Cadillac Coupe DeVilles into standard-wheelbase flower cars. This 1980 model features the more crisply chiseled sheet metal that would stay in use through 1992. The mechanics under the skin were generally unchanged aside from a smaller V-8 displacing 368 cubic inches, instead of 425.

A limousine-style roofline with large quarter windows remained the look of choice for a Superior Cadillac outfitted as a combination coach, but only five such cars were completed during the 1980 model year, compared to 396 end-loading and 57 three-way hearses. Quite simply, the part-time funeral home ambulance had been replaced by truck-based rigs operated by rescue squads, and this was crippling the old-line coachbuilders' production volumes. At year's end the Sheller-Globe Corporation, racked with losses from its Transportation Group and other divisions, shut down Superior's 55-year-old plant on East Kibby Street in Lima, Ohio.

In 1979 Armbruster/Stageway of Fort Smith, Arkansas, which had been producing Buick hearses for Superior since 1975, introduced a standard-glass Royale built from a Sedan DeVille that was stretched 16 inches between the rear doors and the rear wheels. Renamed the Envoy for 1980-81, this model was positioned as a budget alternative to the Superior Sovereigns based on Cadillac's 144.5-inch wheelbase Commercial Chassis. This 1981 example was attractively styled with Coupe DeVille quarter windows, a wrapover tiara band, and squared-off rear doors without the "dogleg" seen on earlier versions. The fender badging reveals that the donor sedan was powered by the problematic new V-8-6-4 variable-displacement 368 engine.

After Sheller-Globe shuttered its Superior Coach Division in late 1980, Armbruster/Stageway President Thomas P. Earnhart (who built six-door limousines and Superior-Buick hearses in Fort Smith, Arkansas) purchased the company's name, inventory, and tooling on January 6, 1981, and moved production to a new, smaller plant in Lima, Ohio. The 62 former Kibby Street employees involved in the enterprise rolled their first car off the line on February 2, completed 30 more by month's end and ended the year selling 332 Cadillacs and 32 Buicks. This stately Sovereign Landau, distinguished from the 1981 model by a vertical bar grille with two horizontal dividers, was one of 450 Superior Cadillacs completed in 1982.

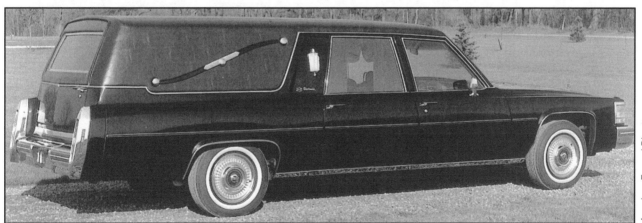

Now built alongside Superior funeral coaches in Lima, Ohio, this 1982 S&S Cadillac Victoria maintained the styling cues and craftsmanship of its Cincinnati-built predecessors, with a chamfered roofline, ornate coach lamps set into a recess behind the commercial glass side windows, and multiple-coat, hand-rubbed, wet-sanded paint finish. Special S&S wheel cover centers continued to be used as a distinguishing touch.

Superior discontinued its Cadillac flower car after building 18 examples during the 1976 model year, after which the company prototyped a body for the downsized 1977 model that was never mounted on a chassis. Volumes remained minimal after the Coupe de Fleur reappeared at the October 1981, NFDA convention in Boston, with the single prototype produced that year (later sold to the Harrison and Ross Mortuary in Los Angeles) followed by just nine units in 1982, three in 1983 and just two in 1984.

The Eureka Coach Company Ltd. of Toronto, having previously offered Lincoln and Buick hearses, launched a Cadillac Concours series in the spring of 1981. What made them revolutionary was that they were built the way all funeral coaches would be built in the future, by cutting a sedan in two, stretching the wheelbase to 147.5 inches (three more than the Cadillac Commercial Chassis) and adding commercial glass, reduced angle roof pillars, heavy-duty suspension components and D-rated tires. It's not easy to tell one year of early 1980s Cadillac from another, but this example is confirmed to be a 1983 by the Cadillac script within the vertical grille pattern.

At the 1981 NFDA convention, Eureka introduced a long-wheelbase Cadillac flower car called the Concours Classic, which was produced for a longer time and in greater numbers than the Superior Coupe de Fleur. The roof and deck were noticeably taller and flatter than Lima's entry, with a prominent lip overhanging the rear window, and triangular, stainless-steel trim pieces bearing ornamental wreaths for the pillars behind the driver's compartment.

Richard J. Conjalka collection

After Miller-Meteor shut down its Piqua, Ohio, plant on May 16, 1980, Jack Hardesty's Barron Corporation in Lima, Ohio acquired the rights to the name and applied it to this cathedral-style landau hearse created from a 1983 Cadillac Eldorado coupe. The front-drive power train put the rear floor within 24 inches of ground level, while the coachwork featured interior flower wells underneath the three-pane side windows, and an etched wreath for the three-piece rear door window. The 32-inch chassis stretch yielded a 146-inch wheelbase and 93.5 inches of casket space between the front and rear bier pins.

American Funeral Director

With a front-drive DeVille and Fleetwood set to bow as 1985 models, 1984 was the last year that Cadillac offered a Commercial Chassis combining the 144.5-inch factory long wheelbase with a big 368-cubic inch (6.0-liter) V-8 engine without the variable displacement feature. 1984 was also the last year that Superior funeral coaches could be ordered with three-way casket table using rear-hinged #2 side doors, and only 29 manually operated and 18 power-operated examples left the plant. The $51,800 price tag on this range-topping Crown Sovereign electric three-way represented a $5,237 premium over an end-loading version.

Gregg D. Merksamer collection

The October 1984 National Funeral Directors Convention in Dallas witnessed the debut of an all-new front-wheel drive S&S Victoria (shown) and Superior Sovereign, which were built from Cadillac's all-new 6CZ90 Commercial Body Package; this was basically a standard-wheelbase Coupe DeVille stripped of its doors, trunk lid, window glass and interior, and fitted with heavy-duty suspension components, alloy wheels, and wiring.

Stressing that its new front-wheel-drive 1985 Victoria was more practical and space efficient than the previous rear-drive version, S&S noted that the height of the rear door threshold had been reduced from 27.44 to 24 inches. It was also pointed out that the 105.12-inch casket floor had lost only 2.48 inches, even though the exterior was 13.86 inches shorter, and the rear door width and interior height were unchanged. The rear struts, however, were significantly more intrusive than the coil springs used previously, creating a 36-inch bottleneck between the wheelhouses.

Inspired by a Lincoln that the first Eureka Company had constructed in 1925, the Eureka Coach Company Ltd. used the 1984 NFDA Convention to debut the 1984 Cadillac Concours Town Car hearse with a lift-off panel over the driver's compartment. Though it proved difficult to seal the roof from leaks and Eureka had originally planned to build only one or two for show purposes, firm orders came in and more than a dozen examples eventually emerged from the firm's plant in Concord, Ontario.

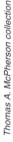

Thomas A. McPherson collection

Cadillac's rear-wheel-drive sedan, originally slated to be dropped in 1985, continued in production as the Fleetwood Brougham, and this was pure deliverance to coachbuilders grappling with the poor reception given to the new front-drive hearses. S&S/Superior promptly launched new rear-wheel drive Victorias and Sovereigns, adding a 16-inch-longer wheelbase using the cut-and-stretch method. These models were not, however, given commercial-height glass like their front-drive siblings.

Thomas A. McPherson collection

Announced almost a year before companion funeral coaches debuted at the October 1985 National Funeral Directors Association Convention in Minneapolis, the four-door Concours Talisman and six-door Concours Calais were the first front-wheel drive Eureka Cadillacs to actually go on sale. In addition to Coupe DeVille quarter panel sheet metal for a traditional limousine look, the Talisman continued to offer a full nine-passenger interior with comfortably padded, forward-facing folding jump seats.

In 1984, the nearly 20-year-old firm of Paul Demers & Sons of Beloeil, Quebec, took advantage of prevailing exchange rates and entered the U.S. hearse market with all-steel, standard-wheelbase Cadillac and Lincoln conversions that were given 90-inch-long casket floors by extending the quarter panels. This silver 1985 model, snapped outside Sacred Heart Church in Monroe, New York, in 2001, seemed to be holding up well.

Centerpieced by the new Concours Classic Flower Car, Eureka's all-white exhibit at the 1986 NFDA Convention in Orlando, Florida, emphasized the incredible array of body styles offered by the Concord, Ontario, builder on both front and rear-wheel-drive GM chassis.

Ken Earnest

Though its longer exterior increased the casket floor length by only 3 1/2 inches compared to the New Generation Cadillacs, Eureka's rear-wheel drive Concours stayed in production and remained popular with tradition-minded funeral professionals. This Eureka Concours Brougham d'Elegance, featuring a half-vinyl roof with wreath-etched formal windows, is a 1987 model combining the 1981-style egg-crate grille with the larger bumper rub strips added in 1986.

Thomas A. McPherson collection

Filled with orchids, the front-wheel-drive Eureka Concours Classic Flower Car attracted plenty of attention during its debut at the NFDA's 1986 convention in Orlando, Florida. Its stainless-steel, pushbutton-operated Elecdraulic flower deck (a fixed-position tray was a no-cost option) was essentially identical to the rear-drive version launched five years before.

Ken Earnest

In 1986 S&S/Superior, still the only builder given use of Cadillac's heavy-duty 6CZ90 front-wheel funeral coach platform, introduced a Superior Sovereign Elite with a 5-inch taller roof that allowed the floral spray to remain on top of the casket during the procession to the cemetery. In the long run its traditional profile made it a stronger seller than the low-roof Sovereign, Crown Sovereign and Contache models. This 1987-88 model looked even more imposing with its one-piece composite headlights and extended taillight housings.

Mike McKiernan

In honor of company founder Howard G. Carter, a Vancouver coach dealer who had died in July 1988, Eureka named its new 1989 premium front-wheel drive Cadillac the "HGC Signature Series." But the Ontario-based company, which exported nearly 80 percent of its output to the U.S., closed in February 1989. Pennsylvania Eureka dealer Heritage Coach acquired control of the company and resumed production at a new facility in Norwalk, Ohio.

Ken Earnest

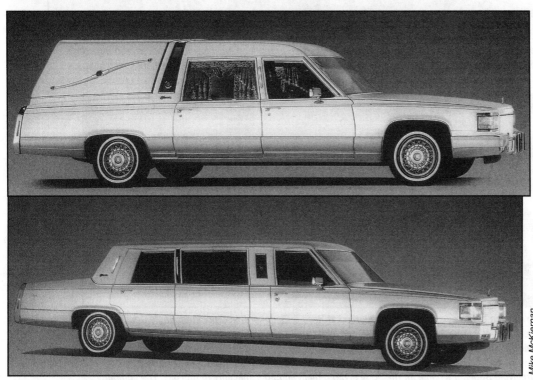

Since it was still the car of choice among conservative funeral customers, Superior steadily expanded the variety and increased the size of its body-on-frame, rear-wheel-drive Cadillac offerings throughout the late 1980s and early 1990s. By 1991, the 16-inch extended standard glass Sovereign funeral coach launched in 1985 had evolved into a Statesman with a 20-inch chassis stretch and a 66-inch overall height, while a revived commercial glass Sovereign (top) had a 24-inch wheelbase extension and 71-inch height. To handle proms, weddings, and business affairs as effectively as funerals, the limousines (bottom) could be equipped with reversible center seats, solenoid-released center doors, and concealed beverage and TV consoles.

Mike McKiernan

Mike McKiernan

The 1993 Cadillac Fleetwood, still called the Brougham when it was publicly unveiled at the 1992 New York auto show, retained the 121 1/2-inch wheelbase used since 1977, but added an all-new, more aerodynamic body with dual air bags, nickel chrome bumpers, improved sound insulation, snap-on fender skirts and a radically raked, flush-mounted windshield for reduced wind noise. Being 4.3 inches longer than the 1980-92 models at 225.3 inches overall, it was proudly billed as the longest regular production car in America. This dark red Superior Crown Sovereign prototype, sporting a painted front roof and a stainless steel tiara band with specially minted C-pillar medallions, was used by the author for daily transportation when he freelanced at S&S/Superior for two weeks writing the company's new owners' manuals in February 1994.

Mike McKiernan

Though its 31-inch chassis stretch, 255.9-inch overall length, and Lima, Ohio production facilities were shared with Superior's funeral cars, the 1993 S&S Masterpiece looked entirely unique with its squared-off door frames and trademark coach lamps.

Eagle Coach

Though more than a dozen of its key employees had worked at Hess & Eisenhardt in Cincinnati, Eagle Coach of Amelia, Ohio started modestly in 1981, stretching Buick and Oldsmobile station wagons in various directions and fitting them with wide-angle rear door hinges for funeral coach duty. By 1992, it was the only volume coachbuilder offering extended-wheelbase, casket-carrying Cadillac flower cars on a regular basis, and these interesting Coupe de Fleurs (reviving Superior's name for the body style) remain an Eagle specialty to this day. The company nevertheless built only one example on the all-new Fleetwood chassis in 1993.

Eagle Coach

The 1993 Eagle Cadillac Ultimate was promoted as the largest funeral coach on the market with its 152.5-inch wheelbase, 256.3-inch overall length and 115-inch casket floor, which was accessed through a 46-inch-wide and 40.5-inch-tall rear door made of corrosion-proof composite. Other selling points included a steel roll cage partition, insulated galvanized steel floors, lowered spring cradles to reduce loading height, and a raised exhaust system for improved ground clearance.

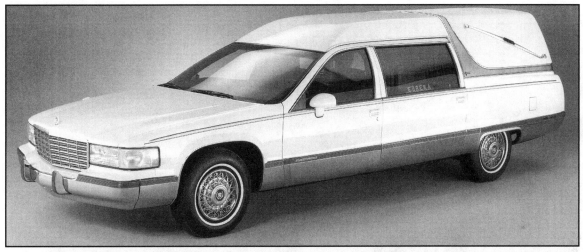

As Eureka Buick hearses had employed the "aerodynamic look" for a year, funeral directors were prepared when the Cadillacs took up similar styling for 1993; the top-of-line Signature Series was especially pleasing with its L-shaped tiara band wrapping around the rear door as well as the roof.

Starting in the early 1990s, Miller-Meteor and Eureka professional cars were built side by side in Norwalk, Ohio, under the CCE corporate umbrella. In addition to the double-bar landau bows that generally identified a Miller-Meteor, this 28-inch extended LeClassic also sports the new heavy-duty aluminum wheels added to 1994 Cadillac B9Q Funeral Coach and V4U Limousine conversion vehicles to reduce unsprung weight, sharpen steering response and make tire changing easier. More momentous changes took place under the hood, where the previous 180-horsepower, throttle body fuel-injected 5.7-liter V-8 was replaced with a port-injected "Gen II" LT-1 V-8 making 260 horsepower.

There were still a few buyers yearning for the traditional elegance of the old factory-built Cadillac limousines in 1994, so Limousine Werks of Schaumburg, Illinois, used the Fleetwood to create this 31-inch "corporate formal" with squared-off rear doors and rearward-facing folding jump seats.

Terry O'Neill

Specialty Vehicles Manufacturing, a division of Specialty Hearse & Limousine Sales Corporation in Plainview, New York, used a new or customer-supplied Fleetwood to build this standard-wheelbase Metropolitan Flower Car at its Long Island Facility. The base conversion consisted of a 72-inch stainless steel bed mounted in a tubular-steel framework, chrome tie rails and a hydro-finished stainless-steel rear boot, which could be hinged in order to carry "first call" cots or body pouches underneath a heavy-duty vinyl tonneau cover.

The Gordon F. Tompkins Funeral Home of Kingston, Ontario, came to the 2000 PCS National Meet with a 1994 Cadillac Sedan DeVille bearing a "Hearsette" cremation urn carrier developed by the Victoriaville Casket Company of Quebec.

When he took customers through S&S/Superior's Wayne Street plant in Lima, Ohio, marketing manager Mike McKiernan liked to demonstrate the strength of the company's solid steel superstructures by grabbing any part of a Masterpiece-in-progress and shaking the entire car with it. He would also draw attention to the "beefy working end of the hearse," with its steel back door frame supported by diagonal braces welded directly to the chassis. Ninety percent of this structure, subsequently skinned in space age composite panels, was built from scratch in S&S/Superior's own press and stamping rooms using corrosion-resistant galvanized steel.

Krystal Koach

Krystal Koach, a large manufacturer of VIP stretch limousines based in Anaheim, California, entered the funeral coach market in 1994. One-hundred twenty hearses were completed the first year. This stately pair of Krystal Cadillac Waterford hearses, readily identified as 1995 models by the new hinged side mirrors relocated to the junction of the beltline and A-pillar, featured 52-inch-long #2 side doors, power glass dividers, and limousine-style overhead control panels.

While it still featured a 28-inch wheelbase extension and a one-piece composite roof /quarter panel cap to ensure rigidity and finish quality, the Miller-Meteor LeClassic was substantially revised for 1995. It had wider, squarer side doors, and redesigned rear quarters for increased interior space.

S&S revived the concept of commercial-height glass combined with a contemporary-looking low-profile roofline on the Fleetwood-based Victoria launched in 1994 (to reduce confusion, the standard-glass S&S Cadillac Victorian was renamed the Medalist soon afterwards). In addition to hinged side mirrors faired into the base of the windshield pillars, this 1995 model featured a restyled interior with pewter-finished trim and smaller ledge boards for increased casket floor and flower space.

Despite the strong sales coachbuilders had enjoyed with the platform, General Motors announced in the spring of 1995 that it would discontinue the rear-wheel-drive Cadillac Fleetwood, Buick Roadmaster, and Chevrolet Caprice at end of the 1996 model year. Up in Norwalk, Ohio, CCE opted for a grand finale by debuting a commercial glass Cadillac Eureka Monticello (shown) and Miller-Meteor Olympian for 1996. This Monticello was finished with a Signature exterior trim package adding a painted front section and a wide stainless steel band wrapping around the top and rear of the 70-inch-tall roof.

Anticipating the end of Fleetwood production, Eureka displayed a prototype of its new generation front-wheel-drive Cadillac hearse at the Professional Car Society's 1996 International Meet in St. Paul. It featured a 32-inch wheelbase stretch and extended quarter panels, with the small fillers behind the rear wheels revealing that the composite body shell had been adapted from the outgoing Fleetwood hearse. The prototype was retrofitted with 1997-style sheet metal and open rear wheels. The car is now owned by John Hadley, a funeral director from Marietta, Ohio.

Richard J. Conjalka collection

One of the last, and most spectacular, 1996 Fleetwoods completed during S&S' 120th anniversary year was this commercial glass Masterpiece with limousine-style quarter windows, a gold trim package and a highly polished rosewood casket extension table built for the Archambault Funeral Home of Lowell, Massachusetts. The firm also took delivery of a matching S&S six-door limousine with a commercial glass high headroom roofline, formal window treatment, and a wrap-over tiara molding.

Mike McKiernan

Recalling how the first-generation front-wheel-drive Cadillacs launched in 1985 never clicked with conservative funeral customers, S&S went to great lengths to make sure its 1997 Masterpiece was as spacious and imposing as the Fleetwood it succeeded. Overall height, at 69.25 inches, was equivalent to the rear-drive model and the roof still incorporated more than 400 specially made components, including an oversized windshield, reduced-angle pillars and squared-off commercial glass side windows.

In addition to this Crown Ultimate with a 35-inch wheelbase extension and a half-padded, half-painted roof treatment, Eagle's 1997 front-drive Cadillac funeral coach lineup also included a 25-inch Tradition intended for smaller garages or overseas customers, and a value-priced 35-inch Kingsley.

Eagle Coach Company

With its stainless-steel deck, matching casket compartment, and skylight-like rear window, Eagle's 1997-99 Coupe de Fleur flower car maintained a useful "family" resemblance to the 1993-96 Fleetwood version.

Eagle Coach Company

Author's collection

Between 1997 and 1999, the front-drive Cadillac funeral coaches built at CCE's plant in Norwalk, Ohio, were offered in two basic sizes to target different customers and budgets. The value-priced Miller-Meteor LeSalle and Eureka Onyx (top) had 30-inch wheelbase extensions and 109.9-inch-long casket floors, while the plus-sized Miller-Meteor LeClassic and Eureka Brougham (bottom) added 6-inch quarter panel stretches and widened rear cross-sections to create a 116-inch-long casket floor with 47 inches of clearance between the wheelhouses.

Mike McKiernan

Shot from the same angle for Superior's 75th anniversary year in 1998, these photos show the many subtle differences between the standard glass Statesman (top) and its commercial glass Sovereign sibling (bottom). The Statesman stressed modern styling and a modest purchase price, while the Sovereign touted reduced-angle roof pillars and squared-off quarter panels for a more traditional appearance (especially when being followed from behind) and a deluxe interior with dual front bier pins, dramatically backlit embroidered shadowboxes, and clear partition corner panels for enhanced driver visibility.

Accubuilt

Eureka and Miller-Meteor's move to Lima, Ohio, coincided with the launch of all-new Cadillac funeral coaches for the 2000 model year, which incorporated such fundamental functional improvements as bigger door openings, increased suspension travel and a second-generation Northstar 32-valve V-8 producing 275 horsepower.

Accubuilt

After a year's absence, high-headroom Cadillac limousines with commercial glass windshields and side windows returned to the Superior and 125th-anniversary S&S model lineups for 2001. One of the most interesting options was a patent-pending spare tire delivery system where the tire raised from an extra-deep well in the specially lowered trunk floor.

Federal Coach is a major player in the both the V.I.P. and funeral livery markets, and an industry pioneer of "24-hour" cars that could handle funerals in the morning, corporate clients in the afternoon, and recreational excursions in the evening. The company's Cadillac limousine range encompasses this five-door 85 JLP fitted with a curbside center door, 41- and 46-inch Ambassador six-doors, a four-door Windsor, and a six-door 24-E with 64-inch center stretches, and a giant 130-inch Silverstone with J-seat and a 245.3-inch wheelbase.

Federal Coach

Eagle's current generation Cadillac Ultimate (top) and Crown Ultimate (bottom) emphasize designed-in simplicity for trouble-free operation and premium materials such as galvanized steel floors and frame extensions, stainless steel door lock rods, and exterior body panels that are constructed entirely in-house from advanced composites carrying a lifetime warranty against rust-through and finish defects. Dimension-wise, both cars feature 37-inch wheelbase extensions, 49-inch-long side doors for the easiest possible access to the church truck storage area, and 116-inch-long rear floors.

Dwight Luna, Service Printers, Elkhart, IN, courtesy Eagle Coach

Even if the small, high-mounted rear window may only be useful for admitting light into the driver's compartment, the hand-crafted, polished stainless-steel deck on Eagle's current generation Coupe de Fleur is a magnificent sight by any measure. This remains the only extended-wheelbase, casket-carrying flower car available from a Cadillac-certified Master Coachbuilder.

Dwight Luna, Service Printers, courtesy Eagle Coach

For 2002, Eagle Coach announced a standard-wheelbase, open-bed Le Escort for customers in search of a less-expensive flower car. It was only offered for one year, in spite of such attractive details as a Crown Ultimate-style roof band and fender-mounted funeral flagholders.

Krystal Koach

In 1996, two years after Krystal Koach began producing funeral coaches, the firm's manufacturing operations moved from six separate buildings in Anaheim to an all-new, self-contained structure at the corner of Imperial Highway and Kraemer Boulevard in Brea, California. The company's current generation Cadillac features a high-strength composite rear door with a misalignment-resistant one-piece steel hinge, dual batteries, and high-durability BASF paintwork.

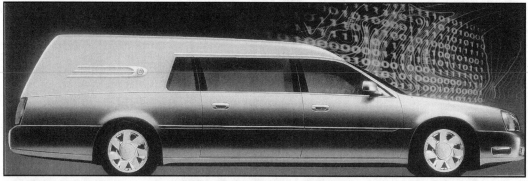

PGAM Professional Vehicles

At the 2001 NFDA convention in Orlando, former S&S/Superior engineering chief Ron Benedict presented a bold alternative to padded vinyl tops and S-shaped landau bars with a radical-looking Cadillac funeral coach (ultimately named the PPV Omega) with a painted carbon fiber roof and an oversized rear window. The small windows blending into the #2 doors recalled the half-limousine, half-landau Paramount sold by Miller-Meteor in the 1960s, while the quarter panels were trimmed with comet-like streaks to give an impression of motion.

Robert Logan, LCW Automotive

In recent years Ken Boyar's LCW Automotive (originally Laredo Coach Works) of San Antonio, Texas, has increased its presence in the funeral market by offering six-door Kingsley, Ultimate, and Ultimate Elite limousines trimmed to match the identically named hearses built by Eagle Coach in Amelia, Ohio. Having already provided limousines for the TV series "Law & Order" and "Sex and the City," LCW scored an even bigger coup when GM's public relations department commissioned it to build a pair of raised roof Cadillac Presidential limousine replicas for NBC's "The West Wing."

Federal Coach

Offering a full view of the casket and flowers, Federal Coach of Fort Smith, Arkansas added limousine-style quarter windows as a new option on its 2003 funeral cars. While the company's traditional winged-motif coach lamps can also be specified, the slim-line coach lamps seen on this car are ideally suited to the DeVille's contemporary character and match those seen on Federal's 64-, 85- and 130-inch Cadillac stretch limousines.

Chapter 4

Chevrolet

Fifteen years after building its first production cars in 1912, Chevrolet became the No. 1 U.S. carmaker by promising budget-conscious buyers better comfort, classier styling, and easier driving than was possible with Henry Ford's Tin Lizzie. Since 1927 there have just been a few years where more Fords than Chevys have emerged from American factories. In spite of this enviable sales streak and the affection earned by millions of Bel Airs, Biscaynes, Impalas, Novas, Suburbans, Silverados, Corvettes, Corvairs, Chevelles, and possibly even Chevettes, inexpensive brands like Chevrolet have always been considerably rarer than expensive brands when it comes to the prestige-focused funeral business. And, for many years, when it came to lower-priced platforms that might be suitable for use as an ambulance, hearse, or combination of the two, Chevrolet's unquestionably sturdy Stovebolt six was simply not as compelling performance-wise as a Flathead V-8 Ford or a Pontiac straight eight. Under the circumstances, Chevy enthusiasts should consider themselves extremely lucky to spot one or two Chevrolets for every 50 Cadillacs, 15 Buicks, or half-dozen Packards that show up at a Professional Car Society International Meet, but this state of affairs assures, at least, that any Chevrolet that does appear will certainly attract a crowd.

There were certainly a number of instances in the 1920s and 1930s where Chevrolet cars and trucks became the basis for lower-priced professional vehicles, though the quantities were always small in comparison to the Studebakers bodied by Superior of Lima, Ohio, or the "assembled" coaches built around Continental engines by the Meteor Motor Car Company of Piqua, Ohio. In 1928, the year before Chevrolet went to six cylinders, the Henney Motor Company of Freeport, Illinois, used a stretched National Series AB Light Delivery to create a "landau-back" coach priced at $1,500 as a hearse or $1,600 as an ambulance, and the

Thomas A. McPherson collection

Recalling the town car sedan deliveries used by high-class flower shops, this open front 1930 Chevrolet Universal Series AD "first call" car built by the Eureka Company of Rock Falls, Illinois, would have certainly gotten the funeral director's relationship with a bereaved family off to a good start. This body, built on any chassis supplied by the buyer, would have cost $1,250 complete, including an opening windshield with automatic wiper, electric coach lamps, and hand-crafted solid ash structural framework with mortised joints, metal reinforcements, and a 20-gauge sheet metal exterior with aluminum drip moldings.

Lagerquist Auto Company in Des Moines, Iowa, sold at least one limousine-style 1929 Chevrolet funeral coach with an arched flower tray and gracefully curved quarter window openings. The Eureka Company, whose policy of building bodies on any chassis new or used also saw Dodges, Reos, Hupmobiles, Marmons, Franklins, Lincolns, and Pierce-Arrows emerge from its Rock Falls, Illinois, facility, constructed a few Chevrolet hearses, combination coaches, and "first-call" service cars to individual order in the 1930-34 period. The A.J. Miller Company of Bellefontaine, Ohio, similarly better known for its Packards, Nashes, and LaSalles, was another confirmed builder of Chevrolets in 1933 and 1934, while Eureka, Meteor, and the Flxible Company of Loudonville, Ohio, all launched wreath- and scrollwork-decorated service coaches built from half-ton Chevrolet panel trucks in 1938. Meteor also catalogued extended-wheelbase Chevrolet passenger car-based combination and service coaches in the 1940 and 1941 model years.

Post-World War II inflation and the concurrent shortage of luxury car chassis considerably increased the funeral director's interest in the simple, sometimes cut-and-stretched Chevrolet sedan delivery conversions launched by a half dozen different firms that had been established in Memphis, Tennessee While most of these companies, including Guy Barnette, Economy Coach, and Comet, were founded between 1945 and 1960, the Weller Brothers enterprise could trace its origins to 1922 and might have been building hearses and ambulances as early as 1936. After completing a fleet of Chevrolet ambulances in 1939, Weller raised its industry profile with the 1947 debut of a so called "4 Purpose" Unit based on a standard-wheelbase Chevy Stylemaster Model 1508 Sedan Delivery, which could be used as a child's hearse, emergency ambulance, closed-roof flower car, or general utility vehicle. These cars were itted with a HYTEX leatherette interior with Battleship Linoleum floor covering, a fold-down attendant's seat, two front-facing warning lights, two roof-mounted rear marker lights, and roller shade-equipped quarter panel windows made of "any color Plexiglas" desired. "We have traveled a rugged road to get the funeral director to see that by using these economical units he is able to preserve high-price equipment," Weller Brothers proclaimed in a 1948 advertisement obviously aimed at rural prospects facing rudimentary dirt or gravel highways. The company claimed that a 4 Purpose Unit operated by the Parker Funeral Home of Carbondale, Illinois, had saved its new owners $177 on gasoline alone in one month.

Judging from the number of surviving cars, and the number of photographs that have surfaced to chronicle the cars that did not survive, it is likely that the National Body Manufacturing Company of Knightstown, Indiana, built more Chevrolet professional vehicles than any other coachbuilder. This firm, later known as National Coaches, was founded by Vernon Z. Perry from the remnants of two prewar rival, and nearly identically named (Knightstown Body Company and the Knightstown Funeral Car Company) coachbuilders situated 30 miles east of Indianapolis. Since Knightstown Body was controlled post-breakup by members of the Silver family (father Robert, son Ralph, and daughter Jessie), the company's funeral cars and ambulances were sold as Silver-Knightstowns, while the bodies built by their one-time partners, Charles and Martha Walters at the Knightstown Funeral Car Company, were known as Knightstown Galahads.

Both firms created an incredible variety of coaches from donor cars that were usually supplied by their customers, with Galahad bodies appearing on Auburn and front-wheel-drive Cord L 29 chassis, while Silver-Knightstown built a fleet of four Springfield Rolls Royce Phantom I hearses (plus a matching service car) for the prestigious New York City funeral firm Walter B. Cooke and a side-loading 1934 DeSoto Airflow that was used for Walter P. Chrysler's 1940 funeral. After both firms were dissolved during World War II, Perry sought out loans from local banks, purchased Knightstown Funeral Car's old production facilities along the U.S. 40 National Road in January, 1945, and put a number of his old Silver-Knightstown colleagues to work converting six-cylinder Chevrolet sedan deliveries that were soon joined by straight eight-powered Pontiacs.

By 1952, National's increasingly comprehensive product range included standard-wheelbase "Ambulette" ambulances and "Servette" service cars, a "Midway" series lengthened by 18 inches, and an "Imperial" line with a 30-inch chassis stretch that was even offered as a flower car, with the $2,640 charged for a six-cylinder Chevrolet Ambulette representing an even better buy than the $4,750 price of a top-of-the-line Pontiac Imperial funeral coach/ambulance combination. A memorable new "Minute Man" designation was bestowed upon the ambulance models in 1954, the same year National took a step up by advertising Buick coaches for the first time. 1955 witnessed a further expansion of the model line through the addition of four-, six- and eight-door limousines seating seven, nine, or 12 passengers. Having started life as two-door sedans, National's four-door limousines featured rear-hinged back doors and removable center pillars that allowed funeral homes to use them as sedan ambulances, while the longer six- and eight-door cars derived from four-door sedans proved ideal for resorts, church groups, college sports teams and airport livery services. Even with the majority of coaches based on the medium-priced Two Ten series, Chevrolet's up-to-date "Turbo Fire" V-8 became National's power train of choice just as soon as it hit the streets in 1955, and its spirited performance was especially appreciated in the ambulances fitted with high-headroom or four-stretcher capable two-stage roofs.

In addition to a line of funeral coaches, combinations, service cars, and airport limousines built from Pontiac, Oldsmobile, Buick, Chrysler, Mercury and other passenger cars besides Chevrolet, National also offered municipal customers a similarly-wide variety of truck-based rescue-type ambulances on Ford, Dodge, GMC, and, of course, Chevrolet chassis. In 1968, three years after purchasing Flxible's body tooling to freshen his car lines with commercial glass windshields and side windows, Vernon Perry sold his company to Warren Morris, a New Castle, Indiana, businessman whose other ventures included a firm that manufactured metal barn door fixtures. Changing the corporate name for a second time, this time to National Custom Coaches, Morris emerged as an early pioneer when it came to ambulances created from the sturdy Chevrolet Suburban and the all-new, more-spacious Chevy-Van launched in 1970.

While Knightstown ceased to be an ambulance manufacturing center after Steve Fribley, who had purchased National Custom Coaches from Morris in 1975, resold the firm and its equipment to Tec Coach of Goshen, Indiana in 1978, new equipment specifications and subsidies from the federal government encouraged dozens of other firms to raise the roofs on Chevrolet vans or mount modular box bodies on the division's chassis/cab pickups. With the ever-higher prices asked for Cadillac and Lincoln hearses, the last two decades also witnessed an interesting proliferation of straight funeral cars built from the Chevrolet Caprice—the most-ambitious of which were the extended-wheelbase, commercial-glass Eureka Régence and Superior Concept launched in 1987 and 1989, respectively.

After the Caprice adopted more aerodynamic sheet metal in 1991, companies like Imperial Coach of Pittsburgh fitted squared-off tailgate areas to their standard wheelbase station wagon conversions to insure adequate casket clearance, while Eagle Coach added a raised-roof, extended-tail Alternative to its lineup in 1993. This Amelia, Ohio, builder continues to offer a Chevrolet Alternative touting stretched quarter panels and a hearse-style rear door, though the base vehicle is now a front-drive Venture minivan after the rear-drive Caprice was discontinued in 1996.

In 1931, the Superior Body Company of Lima, Ohio, used the Chevrolet Series AE half-ton truck chassis to construct a fleet of heavy-duty ambulances for the U.S. Navy. The view through the quarter window suggests that one-piece instead of panel truck style rear doors were used for these vehicles. The C-section steel beam bumper could not have been more simple, but Chevrolet truck styling was otherwise updated for 1931 with more hood louvers and a new radiator shell shared with the passenger car models. The division's two-year-old, 194-cubic inch overhead-valve six-cylinder motor, rated at 50 hp since 1930, was also improved with a strengthened block and a crankshaft vibration dampener.

Thomas A. McPherson collection

While The Depression was at its worst in 1933, Chevrolet sales increased nearly 60 percent to 486,000 cars thanks to all-new "Airstream" styling with skirted fenders and a V-shaped grille complemented by a slanting radiator shell and hood shutters. Given the extensive changes, a top-of-the-line Master Eagle Series CA six made a fine foundation for this extended-wheelbase Eureka Princess ambulance built for the Department of Health in Cicero, Illinois.

Thomas A. McPherson collection

Owned by John Andrews of Burlington, West Virginia, this limousine-style 1934 Chevrolet hearse was created by an unknown builder. The original owner might well have done the work himself, given that many rural morticians constructed carriages and furniture, as well as coffins. The starting point appears to be a standard half-ton DB Series panel truck (factory price $560) on which the original 112-inch wheelbase was extended.

Steve Lichtman photo

Thomas A. McPherson collection

1937 marked the 50th anniversary of the Eureka Company of Rock Falls, Illinois, and even budget-minded funeral coach buyers could partake in the celebration by choosing a Chevrolet-chassied Chieftain whose wheelbase had been extended from 113 to 161 inches. In the case of ambulance models, rear compartment access was enhanced with a fold-down step between the bumperettes and a pull-out platform built into the rear door threshold.

Thomas A. McPherson collection

Adding coach lamps, wreaths and scrollwork to the upper body panels, Flxible, Eureka (shown) and Meteor all launched service cars based on half-ton Chevrolet panel trucks in 1938. Despite a low price and sturdy demeanor, these lightly modified vehicles were not unique enough to interest image-focused funeral directors. Flxible sold only 18 examples in 1938 and just two in 1939.

NAHC, Detroit Public Library

Awaiting shipment from a Staten Island pier aboard the Greek freighter *Georges I. Potmanios* in a *Wide World* photo dated May 21st, 1940, this utilitarian fleet of ambulances based on Chevrolet KF Series 1-ton panel trucks would have been a welcome sight on the European war front — if a German U-boat didn't cancel the delivery.

American Funeral Director

Combining the remnants of two prewar companies in Knightstown, Indiana, Vernon Z. Perry (formerly the wood shop foreman at the "Silver" Knightstown Body Company) founded the National Body Manufacturing Company in 1945. The first vehicles to emerge from his manufacturing operations at the old Knightstown Funeral Car Company factory were 1946 Chevrolet sedan deliveries converted into standard and extended-wheelbase ambulances, funeral coaches, and "first-call" service cars.

In spite of the federal grant money and KKK specifications encouraging rescue squads to purchase modern truck, van, and modular-type ambulances in the late 1970s and early 1980s, this quaint little 1948 Chevrolet woody wagon remained in service with the Grand Valley, Colorado, Volunteer Fire Department until 1991.

Steve Lichtman collection

Often required by insurers but rarely used, plant ambulances are extremely tempting propositions for professional car collectors. Owned by the Glen Burn Colliery near Frackville, Pennsylvania, this 1948 Barnette Chevrolet ambulance showed just 6,000 miles when it was put on sale in November 1994.

Steve Lichtman collection

A stretched Chevrolet chassis served as the foundation for what is thought to be the last carved-drape hearse built in Canada, which John J.C. Little completed for the McLaughlin Funeral Home of Listowel, Ontario, in September 1948. This coach is one of many constructed to individual order at Little's Ingersoll, Ontario, Shell service station and body shop between 1940 and 1958.

Mary Little

The National Body Manufacturing Company created this service car from a 1950 Chevrolet sedan delivery by stretching the wheelbase 30 inches, fitting a sliding glass partition, adding a second door on each side, and ornamenting the body with chrome-plated wreaths and scrollwork. Cedar Bluff, Virginia, funeral director Jim Singleton purchased it from a Pennsylvania mortuary with only 7,000 miles on the odometer.

The Professional Car

Participating in a mid-1950s parade, this 1951 Barnette Chevrolet "short stretch" sedan delivery ambulance used by the Clinton, Maryland, Rescue Squad has several interesting touches, including a Packard Cormorant attached to the stock hood ornament, and fender-mounted Trippe beacons where the mirror rotated around the bulb.

Steve Lichtman collection

Shown by Edward Sasser of Richmond, Virginia, this 49,000-mile 1951 National Chevrolet ambulance attracted many admirers at the Professional Car Society's 1994 International Meet in Pittsburgh. In addition to this 30-inch stretch "Imperial," Knightstown also offered an 18-inch extended "Midway" series and standard-wheelbase "Ambulette" ambulances and "Servette" first-call cars; being not much more expensive, most were built on Pontiac chassis.

A standard-wheelbase Chevrolet Ambulette from National started at just $2,640 in 1952, though this 30-inch extended chassis model likely cost the Vincentown, New Jersey, Emergency First Aid Squad at least another $1,000.

Steve Lichtman collection

131

Headquartered in Memphis, the Economy Coach Company courted budget-conscious communities with this standard-wheelbase 1953 Chevrolet ambulance constructed from a 150 Special Series sedan delivery. A one-piece curved windshield was a notable enhancement for 1953.

Hitchings-Newman photo, courtesy Walt McCall collection

Lloyd & Karen Ray

Lloyd & Karen Ray of Council Bluffs, Iowa, once owned this nice-looking 1954 National Chevrolet Minute Man ambulance that came from the Hastings, Nebraska area. It appeared in the Sean Penn-directed movie *Indian Runner*, starring Charles Bronson.

Richard J. Conjalka collection

Most likely built by National of Knightstown, Indiana, this 1955 Chevrolet 3800 panel truck ambulance was targeted at Spanish-speaking export markets. This body styling was new after the first of the calendar year, with the most noticeable changes being a Panoramic windshield, hooded headlights, and a 12-volt ignition system.

With its movements signaled to fellow motorists by a massive Federal Q-Series siren, this extended-wheelbase 1957 National Chevrolet ambulance served the Burtonsville, Maryland, Volunteer Fire Department.

Steve Loftin collection

Photographed by Larry Blesch of Evansville, Illinois, this 1957 Chevrolet Landau hearse with 210 Series trim was built by National. Note the unusual placement of the dip in the beltline trim.

The Professional Car

In 1955, Economy renamed itself the Memphis Coach Company and referred to its products as the "Memphian" professional car line. The 1957 Memphian Chevrolet service car was available as a 24-inch chassis extension variant with a 139-inch wheelbase and a 92-inch-long rear compartment floor, or a partition-equipped 32-inch model with a 103-inch rear floor and 147-inch wheelbase. Either version could be ordered with three, four or five doors flanked by reinforced center posts. The sturdy linoleum floor could be outfitted with inset casket rollers or a two-piece removable table.

Walt McCall collection

Richard J. Conjalka collection

Resting on an all-new X-member frame, 1958 model Chevrolets were 9 inches longer and much more elaborately adorned. Neither seemed a negative factor in the case of this Memphian funeral coach/ambulance combination, especially when Bel Air side trim and two-tone paint were applied to its 237.1-inch-long exterior. The added bulk was easily handled by a big new 348-cubic inch "Turbo Thrust" V-8 producing 250 horsepower.

With its longer, lower styling accented by oval tunnel light lenses, this 1959 National Chevrolet ambulance looked ready to fly should its attendants at the Cabin John Park, Maryland, Volunteer Fire Department have required it. Thanks to thinner doors and a 2.2-inch-wider body, interiors were 5 inches wider than the 1958 models.

Steve Lichtman collection

By 1960, Vernon Perry had condensed the official name of his Knightstown, Indiana, firm to National Coaches Inc., but this did not prevent his biggest cars from getting longer. Tailor made for airport taxi duty with its full-length luggage rack, this eight-door Bel Air seated 12 passengers.

Richard J. Conjalka collection

Between 1959 and 1975, Cotner-Bevington of Blytheville, Arkansas, was the "go-to" builder for Oldsmobile-based funeral cars and ambulances. The company also built standard-wheelbase Chevrolets and Pontiacs during its first few years, with the arched roof and wrap-around quarter windows endowing the finished coachwork with an egg-like character. This 1960 Cotner-Bevington Chevrolet Biscayne combination was operated in rural Lynchburg, Ohio, by the K.K. Davis Funeral Home.

William Davis photo, Steve Loftin collection

Fred & Dorothy Feiser of New Oxford, Pennsylvania, have earned several conversion class awards at PCS International Meets with this 1960 Chevrolet "first-call" car.

The America Emergency Squad in Mount Holly, New Jersey, operated this heavy-duty 1961 Chevrolet Apache 30 panel truck, which was purchased locally from Kardon Chevrolet in Lumberton and converted into an ambulance by the J.B. Hunt Company (also known as Huntco) of Trenton, New Jersey. This stick shift-equipped rig eventually served as the first ambulance of the Country Lakes Emergency Squad in Pemberton Township, New Jersey, in 1969.

Rich Litton Collection

Having moved from Memphis to Blytheville, Arkansas, by 1959, Cotner-Bevington became best known for Oldsmobile-based professional cars, even though they did build this extremely unusual 1962 Chevrolet standard wheelbase high-top ambulance owned by Lloyd & Karen Ray of Council Bluffs, Iowa. Note how carefully the sheet metal has been shaped between the taillights and the side-hinged rear door.

Fitted with a two-way radio and an almost disproportionately large Federal "Q" siren, this standard-wheelbase 1962 Chevrolet ambulance from Winnipeg, Manitoba, was given a raised roof conversion by National Coaches.

Terry Lange photo

National Coaches created this 1964 Chevrolet limousine from a thoughtful synthesis of two- and four-door sedan sheet metal. Impala trim and spinner-style wire wheel covers yielded an unusually sporty livery vehicle.

Richard J. Conjalka collection

Responding to the growing need for a cost-effective ambulance that was roomier and tougher than a car-based rig, the Challenger Corporation of Memphis built this Centurion from a 1964 Chevrolet C30 panel truck. An extra set of standard Chevrolet truck cab doors improved access to the patient compartment, while the lights above the windshield appear to be 1959 Pontiac taillights.

Steve Lichtman collection

In 1960 Jack W. Pinner, a one-time partner in the Comet Coach Company, established his own firm with offices in Memphis and a factory 10 miles down U.S. 78 in Olive Branch, Mississippi. By the time Pinner constructed this extended-wheelbase 1964 Chevrolet service car from a Biscayne station wagon, manufacturing operations had moved another 15 miles southeast to Victoria, Mississippi. The Fred Herbst & Sons Funeral Home operated this extremely unusual vehicle in Brooklyn, New York.

Walt McCall collection

Full-sized Chevrolets changed considerably for 1965, adding Coke bottle contours attractively accentuated by curved window glass. The factory windshield and front door glass were retained when National converted one into an extended-wheelbase ambulance for the Township of Moorestown, New Jersey.

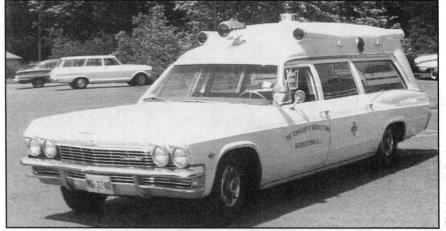

Rich Litton collection

Discontinuing its Buick-based professional cars after building two 1965 model prototypes, Flxible of Loudonville, Ohio, sold its body dies and tooling to National Coaches, which used it to produce vehicles mounted on Chevrolet, Buick, Ford, Mercury, and Chrysler chassis through the end of the decade. Operated by the Marlboro, Maryland, Volunteer Fire Department, this commercial glass 1966 National Impala had a circular flasher in the C-pillar.

Steve Lichtman collection

Roger D. White MD collection

Pinner's Chevrolet portfolio also included this imposing high-top built in 1966. Before closing its doors around 1970, this small Victoria, Mississippi, concern also constructed ambulances on Cadillac, Chrysler, Ford, and Pontiac passenger car chassis.

Steve Lichtman collection

As fans of the old TV series "Emergency!" are well aware, California's Los Angeles County was a national leader in training firefighters to be paramedics. This spacious 1969 Suburban was built for the Whittier Fire Department by Stoner Industries of Santa Fe Springs, California.

Richard J. Conjalka collection

Sold by Adam & Hense of St. Paul, Minnesota, as an inexpensive substitute for traditional funeral coaches, this 1972 Chevrolet mini-hearse had an etched rear window and easily removed Ferno roller rack. While the sliding clamshell tailgate used on GM's 1971-6 full-sized station wagons enhanced cargo access, it didn't leave much clearance for a casket.

Superior responded to the recommendations of the National Ambulance Design Criteria Committee by launching this unusual-looking "61" model in late 1972. Without altering the steering, suspension tread, or drivetrain, the body of a Chevrolet G-30 or Dodge 300 van was sliced down the center and widened 14 inches, yielding a 68.4-inch-wide back door and 84 inches of interior width at beltline level. At 206 inches including the rear step, the Chevrolet 61 was also 4 feet shorter than Superior's Cadillac ambulances.

Accubilt

137

By naming its 1973 Chevrolet G-30 Hi-Cube van ambulance the "Exchangeable," Star-Line Enterprises of Sanford, Florida, emphasized that the Type III body could be transferred to a new chassis when the old one wore out. Standard equipment included a 350-cubic inch V-8, "Junior West Coast" side mirrors, a 120-inch-long patient compartment module with 68 inches of headroom, and a walk-through partition with a 16-inch-wide sliding door and window.

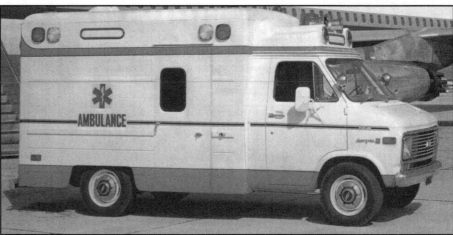

Wisely opting not to modify the driver's cab as Superior had done, Wayne offered its own take on the wide-body theme with this 1974 Care-O-Van ambulance. In addition to 48.5-inch-wide rear and side door openings, and 61 inches of headroom, novel features included a full-length under-floor backboard compartment and a walk-through partition with a sliding door.

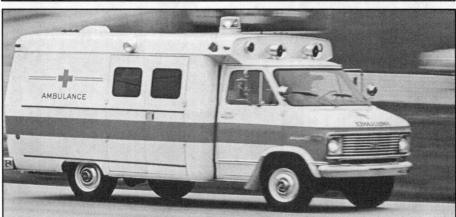

Richard J. Conjalka collection

With no rescue service in the area of Colorado where he lived, race car driver Wally Dallenbach decided to start one by picking up this Chevrolet van from National Custom Coaches after qualifying for the Indianapolis 500. After stopping by the Brickyard for this photo, he drove the ambulance to Colorado and donated it to his hometown, returning to Indianapolis in time to race.

Indianapolis Motor Speedway Hall of Fame Museum

As passenger car-type styling and amenities became available on the Chevrolet Suburban, funeral directors in rural and mountain regions embraced the mix of space and rough road ability. Small coachbuilders such as A.G. Solar of Dallas, Texas, stood ready to fit such requisites as padded roofs and casket racks.

Richard J. Conjalka collection

When the Chevrolet Impala and Caprice were downsized for 1977, the station wagons got squared-off rears with conventional two-way tailgates. This proved far more practical for first calls and back-up hearse duty than the sliding clamshell design used from 1971-76. This 1978 Impala service coach was built by A.G. Solar of Dallas, Texas.

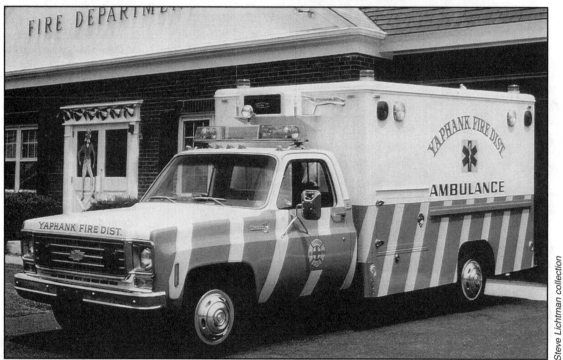

Jarring as it was, Omaha Orange candy striping indisputably enhanced the visibility of this 1975-76 Chevrolet Silverado "Type I" modular ambulance built by Horton Emergency Vehicles of Grove City, Ohio, for the Yaphank Fire District of Long Island, New York.

Converted from a funeral coach to an ambulance, this one-off, raised-roof, extended-wheelbase 1981 Chevrolet combination was built in-house by the Miller Funeral Home of St. Marys, Ohio. The thin rocker panel moldings and the absence of the factory-fitted front fender nameplates appear to confirm reports that this car began life as an Impala station wagon that was retrofitted with a Caprice grille, stand-up hood ornament and locking wire wheel covers.

Quite a few Chevrolet El Caminos entered funeral service as flower cars after a Cadillac-style grille with quad headlights was added in 1982, but few received as much modification as this 1984 model built by a New York mortuary for its own use. Changes included a removable bed cap, a rear quarter panel stretch, and a roller-equipped floor with carpeted wheelhouses, which allowed the vehicle to transport a casket.

Tim A. Fantin photo

In April 1987, Eureka Coach of Concord, Ontario, launched the Chevrolet Caprice Régence as a successor to its 1985-86 Pontiac Parisienne-based Chieftains. With its 30.5-inch wheelbase extension, extra-tall commercial glass and reduced-angle roof pillars, this coach offered the same size and profile as the company's Buicks and Cadillacs. The top-of-the-line version, known initially as the Versailles and later as the Viceroy d'Elegance, featured a half-padded vinyl roof with a wrap-over tiara band.

Ken Earnest

A procession with a Chevrolet Caprice funeral coach would not be complete without a matching limousine, so Eureka also sold the six-door Régence Ambassador as well as a four-door formal with coupe-style rear quarters called the Sceptre.

Tim A. Fantin photo

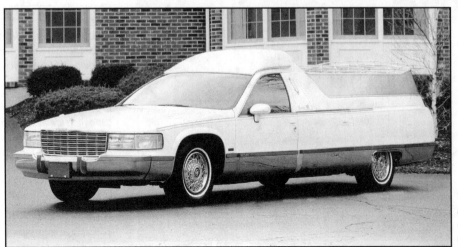

Though more than a dozen of its key employees had worked at Hess & Eisenhardt in Cincinnati, Eagle Coach of Amelia, Ohio started modestly in 1981, stretching Buick and Oldsmobile station wagons in various directions and fitting them with wide-angle rear door hinges for funeral coach duty. By 1992, it was the only volume coachbuilder offering extended-wheelbase, casket-carrying Cadillac flower cars on a regular basis, and these interesting Coupe de Fleurs (reviving Superior's name for the body style) remain an Eagle specialty to this day. The company nevertheless built only one example on the all-new Fleetwood chassis in 1993.

Eagle Coach

Mike McKiernan

Positioning it as a sensible step up from squared-off station wagon conversions, Superior Coaches targeted the moderately priced funeral coach market with the 1995-96 Chevrolet Chancellor Caprice Landau. In addition to extra-length side and hearse-style rear doors made from solid steel, it featured a 15-inch wheelbase extension. Retaining the standard Caprice windshield and front door glass held the starting price to $43,749, while the Superior fleur-de-lis replaced the Chevrolet bowtie in the wheel centers.

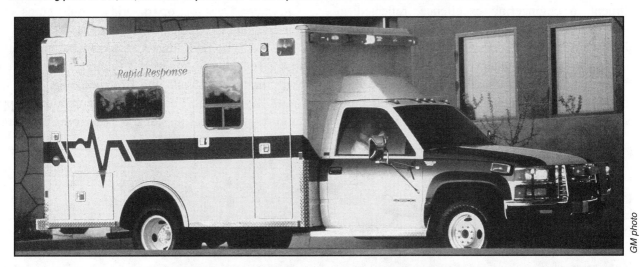

GM photo

A roof extension on the pickup cab indicates that this 1999 Chevrolet Type I ambulance, built by Wheeled Coach Industries of Winter Park, Florida, from a 3500 HD straight-frame chassis with dual rear wheels and a 6.5-liter turbo-diesel V-8 engine, has walk-through.

For 2003, Eagle Coach debuted a new-generation Alternative funeral coach based on the Chevrolet Venture. It features a 10-inch rear body extension with a hearse-style rear door and a raised one-piece composite roof cap. Its 96-inch-long casket floor is separated from the full-travel front seats by a structural steel roll cage partition. A pull-out casket extension table like those found on Eagle's Cadillac and Lincoln hearses is optional.

Eagle Coach Company

Chapter 5

Chrysler

Being the most iconoclastic member of Detroit's traditional "Big Three," the Chrysler Corporation has arguably had the most unconventional and thought-provoking relationship with professional vehicle buyers. Aside from a few years in the mid-1930s where the roomy, relatively inexpensive seven-passenger sedans sold by Dodge and DeSoto were pitched at funeral directors, the company has never pursued the business with the same fervor or consistency as other automakers. Still, the company's commitment to engineering excellence, reflected in the four-wheel hydraulic brakes and high-compression six-cylinder engine featured in the first 1924 Chrysler, the mighty Hemi-head V-8 unveiled in 1951, and the torsion-bar suspension that arrived for 1957, has earned it a small but loyal following among funeral directors and livery operators who were willing to think outside the box, which is certainly never a bad thing when one is trying to stand out from the competition.

Chrysler's willingness to completely reinvent itself aesthetically from time to time—think the 1934 Airflow, or the "Cab-Forward" look debuted on the 1993 LH sedans, or the difference between a 1953 New Yorker that was tall enough for people to wear hats while sitting inside and a much lower-slung 1957 model sprouting tailfins—has also assured us that the relative handful of professional cars that did get built from Plymouths, Chryslers, DeSotos, or Imperials would be as visually varied as they were scarce.

The goodwill that Chrysler has engendered in emergency, livery, and mortuary circles began in earnest with the brothers John and Horace Dodge, who forged, quite literally, an outstanding reputation supplying engines and transmissions to Ransom Eli Olds and

Nathan Lazernick photo, NAHC, Detroit Public Library

Fifteen years before it merged with Maxwell and became an ancestor of the Chrysler Corporation, Chalmers built one of America's most capable medium-priced cars. In 1910, the $1,600 Chalmers "Thirty" became the first car costing less than $4,000 to win the famous Glidden Tour, and this $2,750 Chalmers "Forty" built on a 112-inch-wheelbase chassis promised to be an even quicker and more comfortable conveyance for patients of the Nassau Hospital in New York City.

Henry Ford before they built their first complete car in 1914. Some 45,000 Dodge Brothers cars, in fact, found buyers during the first full year of production in 1915, setting a new industry record that was also good enough to stake a No. 3 spot in the sales charts behind Ford and Willys-Overland.

While the standard touring car went into history as the first mass-produced automobile with a welded all-steel body, and General "Black Jack" Pershing further boosted Dodge's image by using 150 of them to chase Pancho Villa through Mexico. The 212.3-cubic inch L-head four (initially rated at 35 brake or 24 NACC horsepower) used all the way through 1927 proved itself to be an extremely good lugger that would easily resist overheating in a slow-moving funeral procession. Often compensating for the utilitarian flavor of the base vehicle with elaborate carvings, columns, and beveled glass windows, companies mounting hearse, ambulance, service car, or casket wagon bodies on the dependable Dodge Brothers chassis in the 'teens and 1920s included the Keystone Vehicle Company of Columbus and Owen Brothers of Lima, Ohio; the Hoover Body Company of York, Pennsylvania; Babcock Body of upstate Watertown, New York; the McCabe-Powers Carriage Company of St. Louis; Holcker Manufacturing of Kansas City; the William Pfeiffer Auto & Carriage Works of Falls City, Nebraska; and the entirely unrelated E.M. Miller and A.J. Miller companies respectively situated in Quincy, Illinois, and Bellefontaine, Ohio.

After Walter P. Chrysler purchased Dodge Brothers for $170 million in stock in 1928 and added it to a stable that would also include Plymouth, DeSoto, and the Graham Brothers' truck operations by year's end, the 1930s would see a few professional cars constructed from increasingly powerful and elaborate straight-eight Dodges and Chryslers. This included companies such as A.J. Miller, the Eureka Company of Rock Falls, Illinois, and the Knightstown Funeral Car Company of Knightstown, Indiana, which really went all out by using a 1931 Imperial to build a limousine-style hearse for Leatherman's Funeral Home of Tipton, Ohio. To make sure that funeral directors could assemble a matching fleet, Chrysler marketed a Mortician's Service Car mounting a Detroit-built Procter-Keefe panel body on a 1936-37 Dodge LC chassis stretched to a 127-inch wheelbase, and positioned the seven- and (later) eight-passenger sedans it offered through every sales channel—including Plymouth as a less-costly, more economical alternative to Cadillac or Packard limousines. Quite a few of these long-wheelbase models, especially in the postwar years

when more-sophisticated combination coaches were in short supply, were converted into sedan ambulances that could admit a cot or wheelchair by removing the right front seat and center pillar. Derham of Rosemont, Pennsylvania, the Isenhoff Auto Rebuilding Company of Grand Rapids, Michigan, F.H. McClintock of Lansing, Michigan, and John J.C. Little of Ingersoll, Ontario, led the list of shops most actively involved in such endeavors.

By the 1950s, the number of full-fledged funeral cars and ambulances constructed from Chrysler Corporation vehicles was still regrettably small, though Superior created some memorably stylish Chryslers, Dodges, and DeSotos in both six- and eight-cylinder variants in the 1948 model year. Such Memphis-based concerns as Economy Coach and Weller Brothers achieved impressive results with relatively little effort by affixing squared-off roofs and side-swinging rear doors to the factory-built long-wheelbase Dodge, DeSoto, and Chrysler sedans.

The 1957-59 Memphian line, taking full advantage of Virgil Exner's compound-curved windshields, dramatically lowered beltlines, and sweeping tailfins, likely represented the stylistic apex with regards to Chrysler, Dodge and DeSoto professional cars, while the Mississippi-based Pinner Coach Company turned out some attractive high-top ambulances employing the toned-down themes developed by Elwood Engel for the 1963-up models. One thing people almost never saw, with the notable exception of the 132 limousines hand built in Turin, Italy by Carrozzeria Ghia between 1957 and 1965, were Imperial-based professional cars, though Economy Coach did construct a 1953 Imperial ambulance with a high-headroom roof and fender-mounted fire extinguisher for the New Brunswick, New Jersey, Department of Public Safety. The House of Diggs in Detroit commissioned a 1957 model hearse from National Coaches of Knightstown, Indiana, and Comet Coach of Blytheville, Arkansas, built a one-off 1959 high-top ambulance, nicknamed the "Blue Guardian," for the Guy Mullen Company of St. Louis.

Looking back, it could be claimed that Chrysler's greatest contributions to the funeral, ambulance, and livery fields were made by cars that filled in special needs, which were rarely met by more conventional coaches based on General Motors or Ford chassis. DeSoto convertibles, for some reason, were always used to advertise the drop-on Reilly flower car units made from lightweight fiber glass in Belmar, New Jersey, during the 1950s. Chrysler's spacious full-sized station wagons, especially when they were built in extra-stylish hardtop form from 1960 to 1964, were similarly useful for raised-roof, standard-wheelbase ambulances.

A majority of the colossal, eight-door airport limousines created by Armbruster/Stageway of Fort Smith, Arkansas, during the 1960s and 70s were Chrysler-based as well. The extended-tail Dodge Tradesman introduced in 1970 offered the emerging paramedic profession the longest floor available in any U.S. van. And, after Ford and GM discontinued their full-size, rear-wheel drive station wagons in 1991 and 1996, the front-drive Chrysler minivan became the vehicle of choice for first calls and other everyday duties around the funeral home. The landau panels on these vans, added by aftermarket converters like the Braun Corporation of Winamac, Indiana, Imperial Coach of Pittsburgh, and Royal Coachworks in St. Louis, could be easily slipped off the pivoting quarter windows to permit a discreet pickup at a private residence or retirement community.

NAHC, Detroit Public Library

Five years after founding the Maxwell Motor Company in 1905, Benjamin Briscoe brought together a number of well-known early carmakers in his $16 million United States Motors combine. Another firm that could claim Chrysler lineage through Briscoe's empire before its 1912 collapse was the Alden-Sampson Truck Company of Pittsfield, Massachusetts, which built the 18-horsepower, horizontally opposed two-cylinder, shaft-drive platform for this stately casket wagon. Sold by John V. Carr to A. VanLeberghe around 1910-11, this vehicle was said to be very first auto hearse in Detroit. Since the passenger was past complaining about the ride, solid rubber tires were certainly a good way to ensure that "first calls" would be handled reliably.

This 1917 Dodge, originally exported to New Zealand as a touring car, was fitted with an Auckland undertaker's horse-drawn hearse body and used continually until 1949. There was little woodwork left behind the doors when Whangerei, New Zealand, funeral director J.H. "Jim" Montgomery purchased the vehicle and began a three-year restoration in 1969.

American Funeral Director

With its high-compression six-cylinder engine and four-wheel hydraulic brakes, the first 1924 Chrysler stood out from the competition in the crowded medium-price field. It was no wonder then that the Kunkel Brothers of Galion, Ohio, who built this wood-bodied casket wagon on a 1924 Chrysler chassis, eventually became DeSoto and Plymouth dealers.

Thomas A. McPherson collection

Thomas A. McPherson collection

Knowing dependability was crucial when it came to first calls, the Erving Dress Funeral Home employed this Kunkel-bodied 1924 Dodge Brothers service car in Cleveland, Ohio.

145

Thomas A. McPherson collection

By the time it completed this nicely proportioned hearse/ambulance combination on a 1933 Dodge chassis, the Knightstown Body Company had been building vehicles in Knightstown, Indiana, for 33 years. Because the firm was controlled by Robert Silver, his son Ralph and daughter Jessie, these cars were marketed as Silver-Knightstowns to alleviate confusion with the rival Knightstown Funeral Car Company founded by the Silvers' former partners after an apparent falling out in 1922.

NAHC, Detroit Public Library

Attractively styled with a sloped grille and Ram hood ornament, the 1933 Dodges were good sellers. Commercial cars and trucks, built in greater numbers during the same 1933 period than in all of 1932, maintained this look without change through the 1934 model year. Few vehicles would have proved better suited to the "first call" than this coach body by Proctor-Keefe of Detroit.

Fitting a 40-inch center extension with a hidden door release, Silver-Knightstown built this streamlined 1934 DeSoto Airflow side-loading hearse for New Castle, Indiana, funeral director Frank Stanley. In August 1940, the Chrysler Corporation tracked this vehicle down and quickly refurbished it in Detroit for use at Walter P. Chrysler's funeral in New York City.

Featuring three beveled windows beneath arch-motif ornamentation, the "Art Model" hearses introduced by the A.J. Miller Company of Bellefontaine, Ohio, in 1934 revived the traditional carved funeral coach with a new streamlined twist. Dale Schmidt's 1935 Chrysler version had been purchased new by his grandfather, Morris Clinton Schmidt.

Gillig Brothers of San Francisco used a 1935 Chrysler Airstream Eight sedan to build this long, sleek ambulance for the San Jose Ambulance Company. Purchased secondhand from a mortuary in Vallejo, this vehicle also became the City of Petaluma's first municipally owned ambulance before hobbyist Edward Fratini acquired it in the early 1950s.

Sporting a pleasant-looking convex grille divided by four horizontal bars, the 1936 Dodges were promoted as the "Beauty Winner Line." In addition to a dignified wreath of cycus leaves and attractive Art Deco coach lamps, this 1936 Dodge Model D 296 Mortician's Service Car bodied by Proctor-Keefe of Detroit featured a substantial rear overhang and a wheelbase extended to 127 inches to ensure plenty of space for first-call cots, flower baskets or gravesite chairs.

Offering some of America's least-expensive seven-passenger sedans, Chrysler was most proactive when it came to courting value-conscious funeral directors. Announced in March 1938, this 136-inch-wheelbase DeSoto "Double-Duty" sedan could be quickly converted from a livery vehicle into an ambulance by removing the right enter post (shown resting against the running board) and the right front seat to make space for a hospital cot. Not counting the sedan ambulance equipment, this body style sold for a reasonable $1,195.

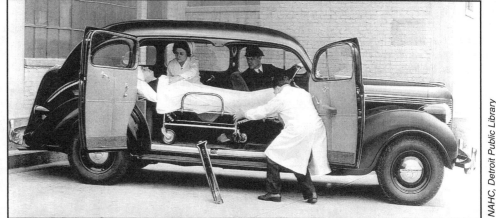

A factory-built 1941 Chrysler Royal Six eight-passenger sedan on the 139.5-inch wheelbase served as the basis for this invalid car conversion, created by Derham of Rosemont, Pennsylvania.

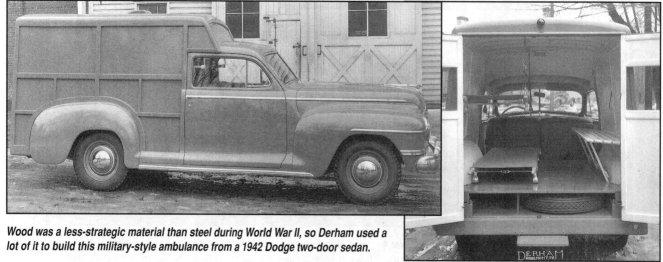

Wood was a less-strategic material than steel during World War II, so Derham used a lot of it to build this military-style ambulance from a 1942 Dodge two-door sedan.

Dropping its budget-priced Pontiac coaches, Superior used the October 1948, NFDA Convention in Detroit to debut a line of Dodge, DeSoto, and Chrysler professional cars that were themselves discontinued when Chrysler launched its "second series" postwar cars in January 1949. The effort was made, nevertheless, because Chrysler continued to offer a factory long-wheelbase chassis that didn't require lengthening. This landau style hearse, owned by John Ehmer of Pittsburgh, was one of only six built by Superior on the six-cylinder Chrysler chassis.

CCCA Museum, courtesy Dale Wells

Derham built this four-stretcher ambulance using a Dodge B-1 Series half-ton panel truck with the full-fendered styling introduced in 1948. Though the vehicle's destination is unconfirmed, Mungeli is a city in the Madhya Pradesh state of India, implying it was donated by a missionary organization.

Superior converted this 1948 Chrysler into a searchlight rig for the Lenoka Harbor Vounteer Fire Department in Ocean County, New Jersey.

In the late 1940s and 1950s, Memphis, became a major manufacturing center for low-cost professional cars because it was situated in a "right to work" state where few factories were unionized. Brothers George and Harold Weller had been building hearse and ambulance conversions in Memphis since at least 1936, and their postwar portfolio included this 1949 Chrysler Royal landau hearse created from a factory long-wheelbase sedan.

Roger D. White MD collection

Weller Brothers of Memphis used the "cut-and-stretch" method to turn a 1949 Plymouth Special DeLuxe sedan into this inexpensive, but attractive, funeral coach/ambulance combination. Competing 1949 Fords and Chevrolets might have been more dramatically styled, but Plymouth's emphasis on practicality encouraged an impressive 47.5-percent sales gain over 1948.

Roger D. White MD collection

Already selling sedan delivery-derived Chevrolets and Pontiacs, the Economy Coach Company of Memphis added eight passenger sedan-based Chryslers to its lineup for 1951. Fitted with the Saratoga's new Fire Power Hemi V-8 or the Windsor's Spitfire six, the five models offered were: the no. 2100 straight ambulance, 2200 three-window combination, 2300 landau combination, 2400 end-loading landau hearse and 2500 service car. These are 1953 models, which were upgraded with a one-piece curved windshield.

Roger D. White MD collection

When Weller Brothers of Memphis was in charge of the modifications, a 1951 Dodge Coronet eight-passenger sedan proved a most-attractive basis for this combination coach. 1952 would still be the last year that Dodge sold a long-wheelbase model, and the division's deep involvement in Korean War work limited styling changes to such details as a painted lower grille and non-connected rear fender moldings and taillight bezels.

"Doc" Armstrong photo, Rich Litton collection

Obviously a source of pride to the Lions Club members who raised funds for its construction, the Lakewood First Aid and Emergency Squad's 1953 Dodge medium-duty truck ambulance was photographed in Atlantic City in September 1954. The spacious patient module, repainted white after being transferred to a new chassis in 1963, was constructed by the Adam Black Company of Jersey City, New Jersey, which also made moving vans and other varieties of commercial truck bodies.

Turned into a "Sedambulance" by the F.H. McClintock Company of Lansing, Michigan, Len Langlois' 1952 DeSoto Firedome eight-passenger sedan was one of only 80 built with Hemi V-8 power. Output of six-cylinder Custom and Deluxe long-wheelbase models, in contrast, amounted to 1,712 cars that year.

Advertised on a 1953 DeSoto, the Reilly Conversion Unit could turn a convertible into a flower car for just $1,095. Made of lightweight fiberglass with stainless-steel trim, the bed assembly was hinged at the middle for easy access to the trunk and spare tire.

American Funeral Director

Steve Loftin collection

Still situated at 2087 York Avenue, Economy Coach changed its name to the Memphis Coach Company in 1955 and began marketing its professional cars as the "Memphian" line. The side trim on this most-unusual 1956 Plymouth ambulance used in New Jersey tells us that the base vehicle was a Savoy sedan or Custom Suburban station wagon, while the V-emblem in the center of the grille proclaims the fitting of a Hy-Fire V-8 engine.

Given lower beltlines, larger glass areas, and soaring tailfins, Memphian's best work was arguably based on 1957 model MoPars like this DeSoto Firesweep high-top ambulance owned by West Haven, Connecticut, EMT Dawson Blackmore Sr.

In addition to funeral homes that owned a matching hearse, Memphian suggested that its 1957 DeSoto seven-passenger sedans would also interest airport limousine services, sight-seeing companies, and school sports teams. Fireflite and Firedome-based cars had a 148-inch wheelbase and 240-inch overall length, while the less-expensive Firesweep used a 144-inch wheelbase for a 237.8-inch overall length.

Employing its top-of-the-line "two-step" roof, the National Body Manufacturing Company of Knightstown, Indiana, built this long-wheelbase 1957 Chrysler high-top ambulance for the New Castle & Henry County Police Department in Indiana.

Richard J. Conjalka collection

Built by the National Manufacturing Company of Knightstown, Indiana, this long-wheelbase 1957 Chrysler high-top was used as a transport ambulance by the America Emergency Squad in Mount Holly, New Jersey, until 1961.

Rich Litton collection

Richard J. Conjalka collection

National's willingness to build on any chassis is epitomized by this raised-roof 1959 Plymouth and 1958 Buick built for Butcher's Mortuary in Knightstown, Indiana. This funeral home, now known as Todd-Butcher's Chapel, is still situated in this Main Street building.

This Riverview Rescue 1959 Chrysler had a raised roof and side-swinging rear door, making the most of a relatively inexpensive station wagon conversion. This vehicle, believed to be a Memphian, stayed in service until it was destroyed by fire in the early 1970s.

Terry Lange photo

Tim A. Fantin photos

Whimsically dubbed "Kount Kennedy's Mobile Blood Bank," complete with rather lethal-looking batfin exhaust extensions, this extremely rare 1959 Memphian Dodge ambulance warranted attention at a recent Blueberry Festival Car Show in Plymouth, Indiana. Interestingly, the high-top body had one door on the driver's side and two on the passenger side.

Richard J. Conjalka collection

Headquartered in Eaton Rapids, Michigan, the Richard Brothers Division of Allied Products Corporation fitted a 6-inch raised roof and a 2/3-1/3 split folding second seat to create a "Briarean" funeral coach, ambulance, or combination from a 1960 Chrysler four-door hardtop station wagon.

Richard J. Conjalka collection

In situations where a Cadillac limousine was simply too ostentatious, this 1960 Chrysler formal from National Coaches was ideal. Considerable skill was needed to keep the factory tailfin contours maintained through the extended center section.

Steve Lichtman

Stretched 3 feet by McClintock of Lansing, Michigan, this 1962 Chrysler sedan ambulance was custom built for DuBois, Pennsylvania, funeral director and avowed MoPar partisan Paul J. Short. The stretcher was loaded through interlocking suicide doors on the passenger side, while the attendant sat in a jump seat between the factory stock rear bench and the driver's bucket seat. This unique car was restored after it sat unused for 25 years. It is now owned by Mike Riefer of Owensville, Missouri.

Walt McCall collection

With a squared-off rear roof adorned with Ford Thunderbird landau bars, this 1962 Plymouth was turned into a hearsette by the W.S. Ballantyne Company of Windsor, Ontario. Though the firm also built some raised-roof Chrysler station wagon ambulances between 1963 and 1967, this project went no further than the prototype when it was calculated that the conversion would have had to cost around $8,000.

The Belmar, New Jersey, First Aid Squad was the proud recipient of this extended-wheelbase 1964 Chrysler high-top ambulance built by Pinner Coach, which then had offices in Memphis with its factory in Victoria, Mississippi.

Another seller of ambulance and funeral coach conversions based on Dodge station wagons during the 1960s was the Universal Coach Corporation of Detroit. Universal went on to build a truly intriguing Cadillac Eldorado suicide-door limousine towards the end of the decade. A padded landau top and a palm leaf rear window motif transformed this 1965 Polara into Universal's No. 501PT Standard Hearse.

The New Chicago Volunteer Fire Department in Hobart, Indiana, bought this 1965 A-100 van from Broadway Dodge in nearby Merrillville and converted it into an ambulance. After retirement from ambulance work in the early 1970s, it served the department for another two decades as a rescue equipment van.

Tim A. Fantin photo

Roger D. White MD collection

Chrysler celebrated a record 1966 with 255,487 cars delivered during the calendar year, but this imposing New Yorker high-top built by Pinner was still an extremely rare sight. Just the ticket for responding to emergencies, the 1966 New Yorker's standard engine was a brand-new 440-cubic inch "big block" V-8 making 350 horsepower.

Richard J. Conjalka collection

Prior to delivery, National Coaches posed this 1967 Chrysler Town & Country service car outside its Knightstown, Indiana plant. The landau panels covering the quarter windows were secured with thumbscrews, allowing them to be easily removed if a discreet first call was required or the funeral director wanted to use the car outside of business hours.

157

Walt McCall collection

Furnished with a raised roof and extended wheelbase by National Coaches, this attractive and extremely unusual 1968 Chrysler combination served the Gerner & Wolf Funeral Home of Port Clinton, Ohio. Small supplemental panes were used to inexpensively extend the Town & Country base vehicle's quarter windows, while the Plexiglas "Ambulance" signs were quickly removed for funeral duty.

Tim A. Fantin

Stageway Coaches created this stately six-door funeral limousine, once owned by T.C. McDaniels of Cincinnati, Ohio, from a 1972 Chrysler New Yorker sedan. The Fort Smith, Arkansas, firm also continued to offer sedan and wagon-based Chrysler airport limousines with four rows of seats, which were available with four doors on each side of the body or a single door on the driver's side.

Roomier, better-equipped van-type ambulances were encouraged in a highly influential 1970 report by the National Academy of Sciences' Ambulance Design Criteria Committee, especially after qualified buyers began receiving federal aid under the Department of Transportation's Highway Safety Act. Tim A. Fantin's 1973 National Dodge Minute Man Ambulance, built from a "display" van with passenger-side only windows, served the small town of Paradise, Michigan, for 30 years.

Tim A. Fantin photo

Wayne Works of Richmond, Indiana, responded to the NADCC's dimensional specifications with its 1974 Dodge Care-O-Van. Under the Department of Transportation's new KKK regulations, these "cutaway" chassis vans became known as "Type III" ambulances, while raised-roof vans were called "Type II" ambulances and box body modulars were designated as "Type I" ambulances.

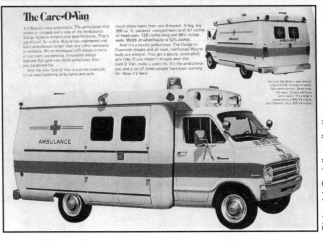

Richard J. Conjalka collection

Richard J. Conjalka collection

1974 Chryslers were 5 inches shorter than the 1973 models, but the Town and Country was still America's most-spacious full-sized station wagon with 104.9 cubic feet of cargo capacity. Sporting slim, almost spear-like landau irons, this service car conversion by A.G. Solar of Dallas worked well with Chrysler's new sheet metal.

Tim A. Fantin photo

With its half-vinyl roof reflecting style trends in the auto industry at large, this 1977 A.G. Solar Chrysler served a funeral home in White Plains, New York, before being sold to Merrillville, Indiana, resident Tim A. Fantin.

Jerry W. Kayser

Adding a custom grille with stacked rectangular headlights and a padded vinyl roof with landau bows, brushed B-pillar trim, and a double bar beltline, Professional Cars Incorporated of Tacoma, Washington created this novel first-call coach from a 1977 Dodge Tradesman for Kayser's Chapel of Memories in Moses Lake, Washington.

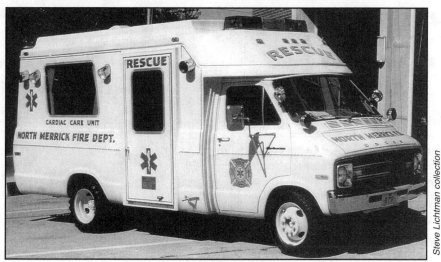

Steve Lichtman collection

Built by Tec Coach of Goshen, Indiana, using a motor home body shell and a Dodge van cutaway chassis with dual rear wheels, this cardiac care unit saw action on Long Island with the North Merrick Fire Department. The Safety Lime Green paintwork championed by period regulations quickly became known as "Slime Lime" among those pining for a return to red fire apparatus.

Lacking the funds for a full response to GM's downsized 1977 big cars, Chrysler put a squared-off body its mid-sized Fury/Monaco platform to create the 1979-81 Chrysler New Yorker/Newport, Dodge St. Regis, and 1980-81 Plymouth Gran Fury. A pillarless hardtop roofline made for an attractive, airy look, though a *Car & Driver* tester discovered that you could fit a pencil in the gap between the windows and the seals above 80 mph. This six-door New Yorker was built by Breece Custom Limousines of Dallas.

Richard J. Conjalka collection

Richard J. Conjalka collection

Based in Belleville, Michigan, Andrew Hotton Associates built show cars for Ford, as well as LTD and Mercury limousines in 1965-66, and subtly stretched Lincolns in the early 1970s. Having sold the AHA name to Canadian coachbuilder Mel Stein, Hotton organized Andy Hotton, Inc. and started offering these "bustle-back" Imperial executive sedans through Chrysler dealers in 1981.

Having saved Chrysler, the front-drive K-car became the basis for nearly all of the company's 1980s products, including an Executive Limousine unveiled in spring, 1983 E Class catalogs. After prototyping two cars in 1983, American Sunroof Corporation converted 1,687 LeBarons near Chrysler's St. Louis assembly plant from 1984 to 1986. A 131-inch-wheelbase limousine seating seven passengers was offered all three model years, while just 196 examples of the five-passenger Executive Sedan were built the first year.

NAHC, Detroit Public Library

Being space-efficient, inexpensive, and maneuverable, the front-wheel-drive Dodge Caravan and Plymouth Voyager minivans showed potential for first calls and other everyday funeral home duties when they debuted as 1984 models. Caskets called for quarter panel extensions or other modifications until longer-length "Grand" models with V-6 engines became available in mid-1987. One of the most ambitious early attempts was The First Car from Minneapolis, which featured a 30-inch wheelbase stretch and a 108-inch-long rear compartment.

Richard J. Conjalka collection

The Gems of Turin

Ghia's 1957-1965 Crown Imperials

Since they sold for several thousand dollars more than a Cadillac Fleetwood Seventy-Five, and six months might elapse between order and delivery, it is extremely unlikely that any of the 132 Crown Imperial limousines built by Carrozzeria Ghia of Turin, Italy, between 1957 through 1965 ended up in funeral or commercial livery service. Instead, these supremely elegant cars would make their mark on Chrysler history by reviving, at least for a little while, the great traditions of custom coachwork that had also yielded unforgettably beautiful and lavishly appointed bodies for the first Imperials more than 30 years earlier.

The main reason why Chrysler went to an outside firm for limousines that it had previously built in-house was that the overall demand for these vehicles had been steadily declining for a number of years, and the only customers buying them by the mid-1950s were the wealthy scions of society and politics. In earlier days when every Chrysler division, including Plymouth, catalogued long-wheelbase models and the DeSoto and Chrysler versions even offered a choice of six- or eight-cylinder engines, most of these cars were slated for livery, hotel, or taxi service where luggage space and seating capacity were emphasized more than luxury or prestige. Naturally, the number of available variants was gradually reduced as the sales volumes shrank, with the final eight-passenger Dodge Coronet sedans, sitting on a 137.5-inch wheelbase, sold in 1952 while the 139.5-inch wheelbase DeSoto, Chrysler Windsor and Chrysler New Yorker models got the ax in 1954.

Though the 1955 and 1956 Crown Imperial limousines and partition-less eight-passenger sedans left behind touted a 149.5-inch wheelbase and a dramatic new "100 Million Dollar Look" dominated by a twin-port egg crate grille and free-standing

Old Cars Weekly

Debuted toward the end of the 1957 model year with 1958-style grilles and fender trim, the first Ghia-built Crown Imperial limousines combined elegance and flamboyance with a level of success rarely achieved elsewhere. The first year was the best in terms of production, with 36 examples complete, while another 31 were built in 1958.

taillights. After only 398 were built over the two model years, Chrysler concluded that it could not amortize the $3,300,000 projected cost of tooling up for all-new 1957-59 versions unless it charged more than prospective customers were willing to pay or took a several thousand dollar loss on every unit in exchange for the "halo" effect. Instead, it was determined after further study that the incredibly skilled craftsmen of Carrozzeria Ghia, who had already constructed a number of Chrysler's show cars and limited-production vehicles for since the beginning of the decade (including the 1956-58 Dual Ghia sports car and a clean-looking limousine created for the Vatican in 1952), could hand build the next generation of Imperial limousines on a contract basis at a total tooling cost of just $15,000.

Taking full advantage of the massive bumpers, wrap-around windshields, lowered beltlines, and forward leaning tailfins seen on other 1957 Imperials, the styling developed for the Ghia limousine was extremely dramatic. "Hy-bridge" doors opened into the roof to enhance entry/exit ease, while the rear roof section touted intimate quarter windows and a padded, black leather covering with a wraparound Tiara band. With the understanding that a complete, delivery-ready car would be returned to the United States, the base vehicle shipped to Ghia was a purpose-engineered Imperial Southampton two-door hardtop with a primer finish, a convertible frame contributing an extra X-member for additional rigidity, and a special selection of parts. Switching the base vehicle to a LeBaron four-door sedan in 1960 somewhat simplified the modification process, but it still took at least a month to complete each limousine and further delays sometimes resulted from Ghia's policy of building the cars in batches after enough individual orders had accumulated.

The Carrozzeria's alterations began with the body and chassis being extended 20.5 inches to create a 149.5-inch wheelbase and 244.7-inch overall length. Much hand finishing was required to reconcile sedan rear doors with two-door hardtop quarters, and 17 hours might be spent per car adjusting door and panel gaps to a tolerance of 4 millimeters. All of the large exterior panels, including the roof, were formed in the traditional Italian fashion using wooden mannequins and air hammers, after which 160 lbs. of lead was applied to each body and laboriously hand sanded to eliminate surface imperfections and fill the seams inside the door and trunk openings. Following a thorough acid cleaning, the painting process began

with a pale green zinc chromate "stucco" and a coat of black fog revealing any ripples on the exterior, which subsequently received several coats of hand-sanded lacuqer in black, maroon, deep green, or dark blue. Once the paint had dried, remaining surface imperfections were removed with a special paste made from cuttlefish entrails.

The five different rear compartment interior designs motiffs were similarly bespoke with their top-grade silk and broadcloth trim, mouton carpeting, and aged wood accents. The chauffeur's quarters were more utilitarian, with nylon carpeting and piped black leather uphostery, though the space between the instrument panel and partitian was adjusted to the driver's stature.

With only 36 examples completed in 1957 plus another 31 in 1958, seven in 1959, 16 in 1960, nine in 1961 (all with 1960 exteriors), none in 1962, 13 in 1963 (one of which was an eight-passenger sedan) and 10 each in 1964 and 1965, the Ghia Crown Imperials were certainly more exclusive than the equivalent Cadillac limousines. The last two years' worth of cars had squared-off styling, recalling the 1961 Lincoln Continental that Chrysler's new design chief Elwood Engel also created, and were especially classy looking.

As would be expected of a car selling for $15,000 at its launch and at least $18,500 when production ended, the customer list read like a "Who's Who" of the rich and famous, comprising such luminaries as RCA founder David Sarnoff, New York Governor Nelson Rockefeller, heiress Anna Dodge, and *The Good Earth* author Pearl S. Buck. Overseas clientele included the king of Saudi Arabia, the rulers of Kuwait and Qatar, and Generalissimo Rafael Trujillo of the Dominican Republic, while Great Britain's Queen Elizabeth II and Prince Philip used a bubble-top version, now on display at the Guild of Automotive Restorers in Bradford, Ontario, during their 1959 tour of Canada. John F. Kennedy's White House had two Ghia Imperials—a 1960 style 1961 that was the first car in line behind the slain president's horse-drawn caisson at his November 25, 1963, funeral and a 1964 model with an extra-private four-window roof that Lyndon B. Johnson loaned to Jacqueline Kennedy when she lived in Georgetown for the first months after the assassination.

Still, the logistical effort involved in building such a small run of cars, individually shipping them across the Atlantic from Genoa, and preparing them for delivery to demanding U.S. customers compelled

Chrysler executives to re-evaluate their commitment to the program on an almost annual basis. Even though most of the sales were handled through Chrysler's company-owned Manhattan dealership, each car required a thorough pre-delivery examination in Detroit since Ghia's craftsmen were unaccustomed to the complexities of the power assists and the dual-compartment air conditioning system. As a "content added" tax had to be paid on all labor and parts fabricated in Italy, U.S. Customs officials also had to

do two inspections of their own—the first when the base vehicles left the country, and the second when the finished cars returned from overseas. With an all-new, unit-bodied Imperial scheduled for introduction in 1967, tooling for the Ghia limousines finally ended up at Chrysler's Barreiros Diesel subsidiary in Spain, where 10 more cars were completed with 1966 grilles and trunk decks.

Cliff Gromer photos, courtesy Jan Witte

Jan Witte of Chester, New York, is the proud owner of two Ghia Imperial limousines, a 1964 with an extra-private four-window roofline delivered to the White House in September, 1963 and a six-window 1965 model originally owned by novelist Pearl S. Buck. With their formal lines and necklace-like fender trim, the exteriors of both cars recalled the 1961 Lincoln Continental that Elwood Engel created for Ford before he replaced Virgil Exner as Chrysler's design chief.

Chapter 6

Ford

With the exception of the early Model T days when it was No. 1, and a few extremely lean years in the 1930s and 40s where it was No. 3 after Chrysler, the Ford Motor Company has spent most of its first 100 years in business as the No. 2 automaker in America behind General Motors. A strong case could be made that this state of affairs has engendered a "we try harder" attitude and an audacity with new product that is most often evident when the "Blue Oval" has its back against the wall. The rise of Chevrolet in the 1920s at the Model T's expense, for example, inspired the development of a Model A delivering much-improved performance, styling, and creature comforts. The increased popularity of low-priced cars powered by six-cylinder engines, which Henry Ford had detested ever since his troublesome Model K of 1906, spurred his introduction of the industry's first inexpensive V-8 engine in the depths of the Depression. The 1953 appearance of the Chevrolet Corvette, and the concurrent ascent of imported sports cars, motivated the creation of a two-seat Thunderbird whose novel emphasis on "personal luxury" would create a lasting niche for the larger four-seat version launched in 1958. The failure of the 1958-60 Edsel, proving that market research paves no path to success if it makes one an imitator instead of a leader, would be more than compensated for by the positive reception given the 1960 Falcon and the Baby Boomer generation's even more-intense embrace of the first Mustangs sold in 1964.

Perhaps the main reason why Ford has enjoyed so many comebacks and second chances is because it is the company whose Model T, a rolling expression of Henry Ford's desire to improve the lot of the common man, put the country on wheels, and the country has never stopped being grateful. In the 1915 section of Tom McPherson's 1973 book *American Funeral Cars & Ambulances Since 1900* there is a thought-provoking photo of a casket sitting sideways on the back of an early

William Foley collection, courtesy Peter Winnewisser

Drafted into ambulance service during World War I, the Ford Model T could get closer to the front line trenches than just about any other automobile. This unit belonged to the 18th Section of the American Field Service, which had 1,100 mostly Ford-built vehicles tending to the wounded on the Western Front by 1917. The extremely long rear overhangs on the wood-planked, canvas-topped ambulance bodies might look comical in retrospect, but this layout delivered excellent maneuverability in tight quarters and a surprisingly comfortable ride for the patients. Up to 10 casualties could be carried by using the fenders and running boards.

164

brass radiator Model T Runabout fitted with a simple pickup box. While the vision is by no means dignified, this essentially stock Tin Lizzie was probably the best thing that the Ibbonbay mortuary in Cut Bank, Montana, could afford at the time, and it makes an important point about how much the added mobility was needed and appreciated in the small towns and wide-open prairies of rural America. Undertakers with a little more to spend, of course, could have their old horse-drawn hearse bodies transferred to a Model T chassis by a local carriage shop. They could also purchase a purpose-built Model T funeral coach or casket wagon from any number of firms, and there is no doubt that the thousands of Fords serving faithfully as ambulances on the World War I battle fronts also contributed to the general feeling of affection for the Flivver in the 'teens and early 1920s.

The Flathead V-8 arrived on the scene in 1932, and the coachbuilder that would be best remembered for professional cars on this chassis would be the Shop of Siebert and Associates in Toledo, Ohio. This firm, founded as a wagon making business by Fred L. Siebert all the way back in 1853, built no Lincolns to anyone's knowledge, but it did produce an eminently practical succession of low-priced hearses, ambulances, service cars, combinations, and limousines in the 1933-64 period using cut-and-stretched Ford and Mercury platforms. The company previously earned its stripes in the auto field by building screen-side delivery bodies that were most often mounted on Toledo-built Whippet and Willys vehicles.

The hard times of the early 1930s, which compelled many body builders to employ less-expensive chassis and many of their customers to hang on to their old hearses just a little longer, were almost tailor-made for modern, low-priced coaches like the Siebert Aristocrat. These cars made clever use of standard Ford side doors, cowls, windshields, hoods, and running boards while furnishing such expected amenities as a large, side-swinging loading door and an extra-long wheelbase initially stretched to 148 inches.

With its 1935 model "Advanced Aristocrats" selling for just $1,300 as a service car, $1,370 as a funeral coach, and $1,470 as an ambulance including bumpers, spare tire and all applicable taxes, Siebert could rightfully claim in its trade journal advertising that "this streamlined car offers economical operation, dignified appearance, and luxurious appointments at a price that makes it unnecessary to use obsolete, shabby equipment." Its product line, soon expanded with a six-door pallbearers coach and side-loading "Tu-Way"

built from a two-door sedan given a chassis stretch and an extra pair of side doors, could be ordered from the local Ford dealer to foster community goodwill or from an exclusive distributor named the National Hearse and Ambulance Company that shared Siebert's address in Toledo. As noted hearse-torian Walt McCall would write when recalling the company's history in a 1983 issue of The Professional Car, "Siebert was to the low-priced end of the U.S. funeral coach and ambulance market what Cunningham was at the other end of the price spectrum—best in class and the most conspicuously successful in its chosen market segment."

While Siebert, eventually owned by Inkster, Michigan, tool and die maker Carron and Company, built its last professional cars at a Waterville, Ohio, plant in 1964, there were a number of other firms offering Ford, Mercury, and even Edsel-based funeral cars and ambulances following World War II. Since it came from the factory with a side-hinged, hearse-style rear door through the 1956 model year, the Courier sedan delivery was a favorite platform for professional car conversions by such builders as Economy Coach of Memphis, the National Body Manufacturing Company of Knightstown, Indiana, the Welles Corporation of Windsor, Ontario, and the small but skilled body shop of John J. C. Little of Ingersoll, Ontario. The astounding success of the four-door, steel-bodied station wagons added to the Ford and Mercury lines in 1952 prompted the Automotive Conversion Corporation of Birmingham, Michigan, to introduce its first "Amblewagon" in the fall of 1955. This presented the value-conscious funeral director with a vehicle that could be quickly reconfigured from a first-call car into a back-up ambulance, flower coach, or personal family transport without the use of tools, on top of which the exterior and interior modifications could be easily reversed for resale as a conventional station wagon.

The Ford Ranchero "pickup car" debuted as a 1957 model and found itself employed for a small but interesting run of Pickway All-Purpose Funeral Cars. These featured a lengthened wheelbase and a covered casket compartment with an aluminum flower deck and vertically divided, saloon-style rear doors. They were built in Johnstown, Pennsylvania, by the Miller-Picking Corp., which was founded by auto body man Harold E. Miller and local mortician Howard M. Picking.

The Ford Econoline van, originally launched in 1961 but considerably enhanced in interior space, performance and utility seven years later, emerged as the preferred departure point for the truck-based ambulances endorsed by the emerging paramedic movement in the early and mid-1970s. Its total share of the market was boosted into the 90-percent range by the 1975-91 generation models that touted full walk-through capability and easy servicing with the engine and front axle further forward than competing Dodge and GM vans. Full-sized, rear-wheel-drive Ford and Mercury station wagons, fitted with padded landau roofs and, in some cases, extended quarter panels or wheelbases, can still be found handling first-call and back-up hearse duties at many funeral homes today, even though the last new ones were built in 1991.

Lincoln, the most-prestigious brand in Ford's domestic stable, had a conspicuously low profile in professional vehicle circles through the late 1970s. Such well-regarded firms as the Eureka Company of Rock Falls, Illinois, Brownell & Burt of Taunton, Massachusetts, and the almost-identically named Knightstown Body and Knightstown Funeral Car Companies based in Knightstown, Indiana, nevertheless built some classic funeral cars and ambulances from the V-8 Lincolns of the 1920s and the even-mightier V-12 models launched in 1932. Derham of Rosemont, Pennsylvania, which never shied away from the special demands of its Main Line Philadelphia clientele, even created a memorably streamlined Zephyr ambulance for the Chester, Pennsylvania, Hospital in 1938.

Taking advantage of the supremely elegant, almost timeless shape of the suicide-door Continentals, the four-door stretch limousine, as we know it today, saw its genesis at the Chicago coachbuilder Lehmann-Peterson in 1963,

but it would be another 15 years before the AHA concern in Canada unveiled the first viable, series-produced extended-wheelbase Lincoln hearses as an antidote to the downsized Cadillacs debuted in 1977. Even though the Continental, officially re-branded the Town Car starting in 1981, went to a trimmer body of its own in the 1980 model year, its traditional, easily stretched separate chassis and rear-wheel-drive V-8 power train enticed a number of funeral coach builders after Cadillac shrank its professional car platform for a second time and switched it to front-wheel drive in 1985. Preceded by smaller, lesser-known concerns like the Century Coach Company of Dallas and Duncanville, Texas, Marquis Custom Coach of Canoga Park, California, and Paul Demers & Sons of Beloeil, Quebec, relatively important players like S&S/Superior and Eagle Coach added Town Cars to their lines in 1986, while Collins Industries of Hutchinson, Kansas, previewed its first "Miller Meteor" Lincoln Paramount hearse at the October 1987 NFDA Convention in Salt Lake City. It was joined on display by a companion six-door limousine reviving the Premiere model name used by the Lincoln in the 1950s.

Further growth in Lincoln's share of the funeral coach market, currently touching 25 percent, followed the appearance of all-new or extensively facelifted Town Cars for the 1990, 1995, 1998, and 2003 model years. The factory-built, 6-inch-longer-wheelbase "L" Series Town Car sedans debuted in 2000 proved an even-bigger hit with limousine services, comprising an incredible 85 percent of all Town Cars ordered with the 535 Livery Package by the 2002 model year.

Shortly after the United States formally entered World War I in May, 1917, the U.S. Army Ambulance Corps was established with Camp Crane in Allentown, Pennsylvania, designated as its mobilization and training center. Substantially augmenting the 2,113 Ford ambulances already serving in existing volunteer units at the time, the U.S. government would order 10,042 Model T ambulances by November 1, 1918. The first ambulance bodies built by Ford in the U.S. were too short to be used since the American Field Service's specifications were erroneously converted from meters to yards.

Peter Winnewisser collection

Belying the low base price of the donor chassis, this elaborate eight-column carved hearse body was fitted to a 1917 Ford Model T by the Williams Carriage & Hearse Company of St. Louis. It is currently on exhibit at the Flying W Guest Ranch's Museum and Art Gallery in Sayre, Oklahoma.

A.L. Whinery

The old-fashioned "Mosque Deck" roof and curved rear doors on this 1921 Ford Model T child's hearse created by Brownell & Burt of Taunton, Massachusetts, suggests that the body was transferred from a horse-drawn chassis.

Steve Lichtman photo

Thomas A. McPherson collection

No one could deny that Henry Leland's first Lincolns, completed in September, 1920, were impressively engineered, but the make's future was not ensured until Edsel Ford convinced his father Henry to purchase the company in 1922. An extra-long 150-inch-wheelbase Commercial Chassis debuted in September, 1925, and a total of 37 were sold to professional car builders in the ensuing year. The Eureka Company of Rock Falls, Illinois, put one of the first to good use, creating this Model 194 DeLuxe Burial Coach for E.A. Horrigan & Son Morticians of Davenport, Iowa. It was photographed without a wheel on the side-mount carrier.

Large curves in the upper rear corners of the quarter windows identify this heavy-duty 1929 Ford Model AA funeral coach as a creation of the Lagerquist Auto Company of Des Moines, Iowa. Catering to the budget-conscious, this company also built professional cars on the six-cylinder Chevrolet chassis.

Arched side windows with an etched sunburst pattern accentuated the elegance of this Eureka Lincoln Model 29-R DeLuxe end-loading funeral coach constructed for Howard A. Loss & Company of Flint, Michigan in 1930. This basic body, also featuring hand-crafted clear ash framework and a seven-degree sloped windshield, could be fitted to any chassis the customer requested or supplied for $1,550, though the selection of Lincoln's 150-inch wheelbase chassis/cowl unit in this case likely earned a discount or a waiver of the standard $125 chassis alteration charge.

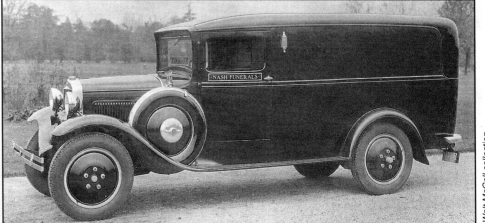

The Proctor Keefe Body Company of Detroit was the most likely builder of this service car from a 1930 Ford AA chassis, whose cowl now flowed smoothly between the hood and the doors for a more unified appearance. Considering the name of the firm it served, a Nash might have made a more appropriate base vehicle!

A double drop frame with a 6-inch-longer wheelbase, skirted fenders, angled hood louvers, and a heart-shaped grille topped with a leaping greyhound hood ornament worked wonders on the 1933-34 Fords, transforming a previously utilitarian platform into a rakish mini-Lincoln. Eureka's body draftsmen shared a similarly keen aesthetic sense, furnishing this extended-wheelbase 1933 Ford Princess service car with elegant bodyside scrollwork and a fashionable "beavertail" rear end. Underneath the hood the year-old Ford V-8's teething problems were essentially solved, and horsepower had increased to 75.

Museum of Funeral Customs

Thomas A. McPherson collection

Walt McCall collection

Thomas A. McPherson collection

Alvaro Casal Tatlock

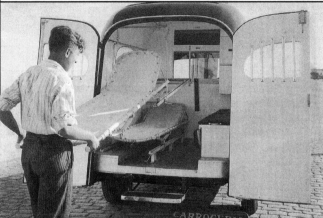

Aside from their acceptance in the U.S., Ford's sturdy half-ton V-8 trucks were in demand virtually anywhere in the world where roads were rough. This 1935 ambulance was constructed for the Uruguayan Air Force by Enrique Feuerstein, a German immigrant who settled in Montevideo in the 1920s and built a number of unusual bodies through the 1950s.

Originally purchased by his father's funeral firm for $1,470 and kept in service until 1953, this 1936 Siebert Ford hearse/ambulance combination was re-acquired by Oscar Seagle of Pulaski, Virginia, at a 1990 auction.

Winner of the Best-in-Show at both the 1997 and 1999 PCS International Meets, this 1938 Siebert Ford Aristocrat owned by Harry W. Foor of Frostville, Maryland, handled everything from first calls to burials for a funeral home in the 100-person hamlet of Brandonville, West Virginia, until the 1950s. This stretched sedan delivery used very Spartan Standard series trim, with only one windshield wiper and one taillight.

Built by Derham in just three months, this streamlined 1938 Lincoln Zephyr ambulance was donated to the Chester, Pennsylvania, hospital by two sisters, Mrs. Arthur E. Copeland and Mrs. Gideon M. Stull. Mrs. Stull was married to the owner of the local Gash-Stull Lincoln/Ford agency, who furnished the chassis and co-designed the body with hospital superintendent Lee P. Wray. The light brown leather interior could seat four in addition to the driver and patient, and the right front seat could swivel around to face a chrome-and-stainless steel stretcher fitted with balloon tires.

Gerald T. Nesvold of Pitman, Pennsylvania, owns this extremely rare first year 1939 Siebert Mercury Tuway ambulance, which was built by stretching the wheelbase of a Tudor sedan to 155 inches and fitting the body with extra side doors. The stretcher loads through the trunk opening, which must have intimidated injured workers when this rig was used at an anthracite coal company in Shamokin, Pennsylvania, during the late 1950s.

American Funeral Director

A landau-style "Triple Purpose" service car/ambulance/funeral car priced at $1,545 F.O.B. Toledo was added to the Siebert line in 1940, and conversions were now offered on Ford's sedan delivery trucks as well as Ford and Mercury passenger cars.

Rich Litton collection

When new-car production was suspended in February 1942, the U.S. Government's Office of Price Administration imposed strict rationing on existing stocks and allowed only a handful of high-priority civilians to take delivery starting in June 1943. Since the America Emergency Squad in Mt. Holly, New Jersey, covered a large service area, it could secure the permission needed to purchase this 1942 Siebert Ford ambulance. Even though attractive fender skirts were fitted, bright trim was banned except for existing stocks so the grille surrounds and headlight rings were painted "blackout" items.

The Avondale, Pennsylvania, fire department was another lucky purchaser of a Siebert-bodied 1942 Ford ambulance. Having ordered a large number of 1942 Fords and Mercurys in advance, Siebert claimed it was the only coachbuilder able to maintain production for priority customers during World War II.

Steve Lichtman collection

As Edsel Ford was the guiding force behind Lincoln's greatest achievements, it was most fitting that his April 29, 1943, funeral in Grosse Pointe, Michigan, involved a 1937-40 K-Series hearse from an unknown coachbuilder and several of the Ford family's Brunn-bodied Zephyr Town Cars.

Walt McCall collection

The Shop of Siebert was one of the first coachbuilders to resume sales as World War II wound down. As its postwar model "Super Ford" and "Luxury Mercury" passenger car ambulances were offered only in sedan-style "Tuway" layouts with a lift-up rear door, Siebert stressed that its Ford truck ambulances touted 43-inch-tall side and rear doors offering easy access to a 110-inch-long, 51-inch-tall patient compartment.

American Funeral Director

Roger D. White MD collection

This handsome 1946 Ford Landau hearse was built for the White-Wilcox Funeral Home by Weller Brothers of Memphis, Tennessee, which became a major center of low-cost hearse and ambulance manufacturing during the 1940s and 1950s.

By November 1945, Siebert was able to announce in *American Funeral Director* that it had re-initiated production of its "long-awaited" Luxury Mercury Models, promising that they were "the fulfillment of all that was hoped for in postwar vehicles." In addition to a 154-inch wheelbase, noteworthy features included a fully adjustable three-passenger front seat "upholstered in finest broadcloth," a partition fitted with medicine cabinets, and a linoleum-covered 109-inch-long rear floor accessed through a swing-up rear door that afforded effective protection from the elements.

American Funeral Director

Graeme Lemin of Oak Park, Victoria, Australia, still uses this all-original 1946 Mercury hearse for funerals. Like most funeral cars in Australia, it features an end-loading two-door body with long, slim side windows and a rooftop flower rack.

Graeme Lemin

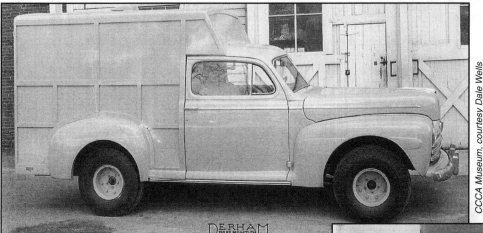

CCCA Museum, courtesy Dale Wells

Fitted with oversized Goodrich low-pressure tires for added traction in the sand, this military-style 1946 Ford ambulance was built by Derham of Rosemont, Pennsylvania, for the Arabian-American Oil Company.

Belonging to the Branchville Volunteer Fire Department Rescue Squad of Prince George's County, Maryland, this 1946 Siebert Ford sedan ambulance was followed by the company's 1947 Meteor Cadillac as it participated in a 1954 parade.

Harry Foor of Frostburg, Maryland, owns this 1948 Siebert sedan ambulance. It shows the subtle trim changes made to Fords in mid-1947, including a hood medallion identifying six-cylinder or V-8 power, and round parking lamps relocated below the headlights. Gene Lichtman purchased this vehicle from the Greenfield Township Fire Department near Wilkes-Barre, Pennsylvania, in the 1980s, and it was painted red and white to appear in the movie *Avalon* before Lichtman's 1947 Flxible Buick ambulance was used instead.

Siebert did not build any vehicles from the all-new, slab-sided 1949 Ford passenger cars, but its Triple Purpose Car conversion of an F-Series panel truck offered an extra set of side doors and a 116-inch-long, 55-inch-high interior that could handle tall flower arrangements, two large packing cases, or a steel grave vault. The customer could choose between a six-cylinder or V-8 engine.

Weller Brothers of Memphis was the first coachbuilder to market a combination ambulance and hearse built from the sleek new 1949 Ford cars. The wheelbase and rear end were extended slightly on this landau-style coach, which promised significant purchase and operating cost savings over larger equipment.

American Funeral Director

Typically subjected to very limited use during their service lives, plant ambulances are a tempting proposition for the professional vehicle enthusiast. To cite one example, this 1949 Siebert Ford F-Series had its original tires and less than 6,400 original miles when it was purchased as a public relations piece by John R. Perkins of Gold Cross Ambulance (with operations in Rochester, Duluth, Mankato and Owatonna, Minnesota) in the mid-1980s.

Powered by the base 95-horsepower flathead six, this vehicle had been purchased new by a U.S. Steel plant on the west side of Duluth. It was never even licensed for street use since it was intended for transferring ill or injured workers to the on-site infirmary. An outside ambulance would have been dispatched if the patient required transfer to a downtown hospital. Any trip beyond the plant gates in this vehicle would have been an arduous one for the driver and passenger alike, with no rear compartment heating or power assistance for the steering or brakes. Exterior warning devices were limited to add-on directional signals, two small flashers at the upper corners of the rear doors, and a front-facing roof siren/beacon controlled by a floorboard switch.

Having gone into on-site storage when the facility closed in the 1970s, the ambulance was brought to Perkins's attention by a retiring plant site manager who worried that it might be junked or sold to someone who would not appreciate its history. While the exterior needed repainting and rechroming—the vehicle had been garaged near a building that was used to treat steel with acid—the wood-framed doors and well-preserved interior required no refurbishment during the restoration.

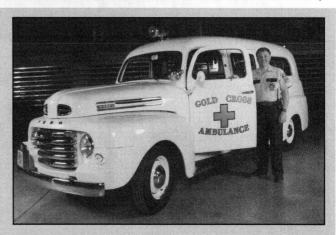

Even the rubber floor mats and the cot mattress are entirely original. Aside from a collapse-a-cot for a second patient and a scoop-style "stokes basket" to facilitate the removal of victims from difficult locations, the vehicle had no oxygen, splints, backboards, or other equipment now taken for granted in the most basic of ambulances. With no rear compartment attendant's seat either, Perkins said that the "attendants were called 'drivers' as they only loaded the patient and then rode to the infirmary in the front seats, leaving the patient to live or die on their own in the back."

175

Having spent its entire service life at U.S. Steel's Duluth, Minnesota, plant, this 1949 Siebert Ford six-cylinder truck ambulance had covered less than 6,400 miles when it was purchased by John R. Perkins in the mid-1980s. Aside from a scoop-style "stokes basket" and a collapse-a-cot for a second patient, the rear compartment carried little equipment as the vehicle was intended for short trips to the plant's on-site infirmary.

John R. Perkins

Employing a heavy-duty 1949 Ford truck chassis, the Boyertown Body Works of Pennsylvania custom built this massive crash wagon for the America Emergency Squad of Mount Holly, New Jersey. Last in service around 1960, this vehicle presaged the equipment-packed combination ambulances/rescue trucks embraced by modern day fire departments.

Rich Litton collection

Roger D. White MD collection

The luxury hearse market pretty much belonged to Cadillac and Packard after World War II, but this did not deter Weller Brothers of Memphis, Tennessee, from constructing this standard-wheelbase, extended-tail 1949 Lincoln Cosmopolitan Landau. This was the first year since 1932 that Lincolns had V-8 engines.

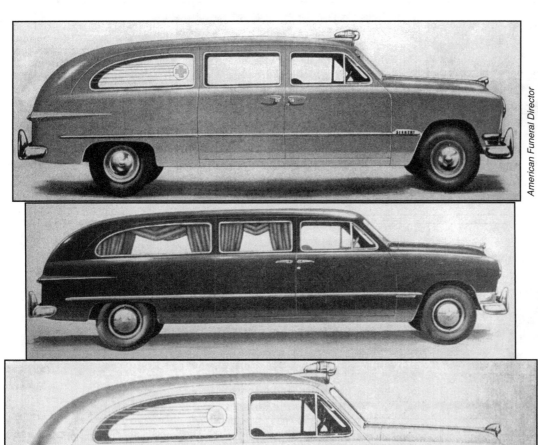

The first Siebert Aristocrats built from "postwar" Ford passenger cars appeared as 1950 models. The five-door landau hearse, ambulance, and combination models were offered with 147-inch or 156-inch wheelbases, while a three-door "Emergency Ambulance" built on an unaltered 114-inch wheelbase could be fitted with a factory-width rear Tudor seat for use as a standard sedan. Both series featured full-sized rear doors and Ford's 100-horsepower flathead V-8 engine.

In mid-1951, The Shop of Siebert moved from Toledo to suburban Waterville. Billed as "a car of engaging beauty" and "abundant roominess," its Ford-based hearse or combination was now called the Leeland, while the ambulance model was renamed the Leeds.

The Professional Car

Though it was better known for building Chevrolet and Pontiac professional cars, the National Body Manufacturing Company of Knightstown, Indiana, catalogued this Ford-based landau hearse and service car in 1952. Fords were entirely new and much improved that year, adding one-piece curved windshields, an overhead-valve six-cylinder engine making 101 horsepower, suspended brake and clutch pedals, concealed fuel fillers, and all-metal-bodied station wagon models in two- and four-door variants.

Stretching a Courier sedan delivery 22 inches, the Economy Coach Company of Memphis touted this Style 1000 Ford Junior Ambulance in its 1953 catalog without updating the grille design in the drawing. Standard kit included a Federal flashing siren flanked by faired-in tunnel lights, decorative quarter windows with roller shades and pivoting vents, and a 110-horsepower flathead V-8 that would be replaced by a modern OHV engine for 1954. The interior appointments also emphasized practicality at a "popular" price with art leather trim, "fine quality inlaid linoleum" floor covering and the option of a reversible right front seat to supplement the standard fold-down attendant's seat. A rear compartment fan and utility cabinet were also fitted as standard.

Tim A. Fantin photos

Powered by the new, 239-cubic inch "Y-block" V-8 that had finally replaced the faithful Flathead, this standard-wheelbase 1954 National Ambulette conversion of a Courier sedan delivery was fitted with a rear-facing right front seat, faired-in tunnel lights and louvers in the C-pillars to enhance ventilation in the patient area. This Highland Green beauty, sourced from Colorado and subjected to a ground-up $30,000 restoration by C. Thomas Hutton of Chestertown, New York, reputedly traveled only 5,080 miles in the service of a U.S. Steel plant in Pennsylvania and an Iowa funeral home.

The Professional Car

The new Thunderbird's influence was readily apparent on the rest of Ford's 1955 lineup, even the Mainline trim Couriers used by National-Knightstown to build this limousine-style funeral coach and fully enclosed standard-wheelbase flower car. The latter body style never really caught on with funeral directors, as a traditional open deck permitted taller floral arrangements.

Not all 1950s Ford professional cars were "strippers"—a point made clear by this spectacular Weller Brothers ambulance constructed from a 1956 Country Sedan station wagon with two-tone paint, fender skirts, and a 292-cubic inch Thunderbird "Y-block" four-barrel V-8 making 202 horsepower. After stretching the body between the rear doors and rear wheels, the Memphis-based coachbuilder fitted twirling Buckeye Roto-Rays to the front fenders and equipped the roof with a Federal Q2 siren, two Federal 360-degree Beacon-Rays, four tunnel lights and spotlights above the driver's seat and rear door.

Canadian Fords were not fitted with the overhead-valve "Y-Block" V-8 until 1955, one year after their American cousins. Once it was available, the Steadman Brothers Funeral Home of Brigden, Ontario, ordered this 1956 sedan delivery for $3,100, drove it home from Windsor plant, and sent it to John J. C. Little of Ingersoll, Ontario, who charged another $2,200 after fitting a landau roof treatment, extra interior insulation, additional chrome trim from the Parklane two-door station wagon and a wine-colored mohair casket compartment with a matching ceiling. This coach is still used as a flower car, child hearse, and cremains conveyance during the summer months.

Stressing that purchasing and servicing could be handled through any one of 6,400 local Ford dealers, the Automotive Conversion Corporation of Birmingham, Michigan, announced its first Ford "Amblewagon" to the funeral trade in November, 1955. Sand-blasted Plexiglas window inserts, a side-swinging rear door sourced from the Courier sedan delivery, a removable casket table, and a zippered headliner to facilitate quick removal of the rooftop beacon were just a few of the features on this versatile Country Sedan conversion.

Another Canadian concern that started a professional car conversion with a 1956 Ford Courier sedan delivery was the Welles Corporation of Windsor, Ontario, which was primarily a school bus builder. Modifications on this fairly inexpensive ambulance did not go far beyond a 360-degree rooftop beacon, front-facing tunnel lights and teardrop-shaped flashers for the upper corners of the side-hinged rear door.

Richard J. Conjalka collection

The 1959 Fords were among the most attractive of the decade with their broad, flat hoods, eyebrow-like headlamp housings and "Iris Eye Safety" taillights. Adding altered D-pillars and a side-swinging fiberglass door that could admit a 75-inch ambulance cot or an 86-inch long casket shipping box through its 31.5-inch-tall opening, the Automotive Conversion Corporation's basic A-1 rear end modification package cost Ford dealers only $550 plus another $13.63 for excise tax. The A-2 hearse, A-3 ambulance and A-4 combination conversions respectively cost the dealer $875, $960 and $1,175, on top of which an incredible array of stretchers, lights, sirens, draperies, flower trays, fire extinguishers and oxygen units could be ordered as options.

Steve Lichtman photo

Lance Alfieri of Plainview, New York, discovered this factory air-conditioned 1959 Edsel Amblewagon, originally used in Hays, Kansas, during an early 1980s family vacation in Arizona Its restoration earned the Best-of-Show at PCS Atlanta 1990. Interesting conversion details include a massive Federal C-6 flasher siren, a low-profile Ferno Washington stretcher, and front fender "Amblewagon" scripts that were obtained during a visit to ACC's old factory.

Richard J. Conjalka collection

In addition to dispensing with the windshield dogleg, 1960 Fords were longer and wider than their predecessors, and their lower profiles were used to full advantage on this limousine-style combination and "Minute Man" ambulance offered by National Coaches of Knightstown, Indiana. The largest units constructed had two-step roofs and a four-litter capacity.

In 1961, Siebert changed addresses again, officially relocating to Route 64 in Whitehouse, Ohio. The full-sized Fords used to build the company's Aristocrats re-emphasized practicality that year, with 4 less inches in their exteriors and a simple stamped aluminum grille.

The Professional Car

This 1962 Siebert Aristocrat, once used by the District 2 Rescue Squad of the Rotterdam, New York, Fire Department, highlights the many modifications made to Ford's Country Sedan station wagon (a Mercury Commuter could also be used) at Siebert's Whitehouse, Ohio, plant. The wheelbase was extended to 155 inches, with the extra sheet metal sourced from a third pair of doors, after which fiberglass was used to fabricate a side-hinged rear door and a raised roof cap offering 45 inches of interior headroom.

Ron Bogardus photo, Steve Loftin collection

Used only sparingly by the Springfield Township, Ohio, Fire Department, one of the nicest surviving Sieberts is this 1963 model 1045 Aristocrat owned by Bob & Jackie Collier of Fremont, Ohio. Power comes from a 352-cubic inch "Interceptor" V-8 with a Holley two-barrel carburetor, while a Federal "Q" siren visually blends the stock front roof section with the raised fiberglass cap above the patient compartment.

This battered and weather-worn 1964 Siebert, still used in Glasgow, Montana, by Roger's Ambulance Service around 1972 or 1973, represented Siebert's last year building Ford professional cars. The cone-shaped B&M siren above the front seat produced a distinctive stuttering tone.

Terry Lange photo

Richard J. Conjalka collection

Figuring that its padded vinyl roof and landau bars would fit right in with the hearse, a Canadian funeral director turned this 1964 Ford Thunderbird into a flower car. The hat rack-like post was used to prop up wreaths or tall floral arrangements. Like the rest of Ford's 1964 line, the Thunderbird was completely restyled with rectangular taillights and "mirror image" bodyside sculpturing.

Steve Loftin photo

Featuring all-new, squared-off styling with stacked headlights, this 1965 Ford station wagon worked for the Ninde Funeral Home in Jenks, Oklahoma. Superior window decals suggest that the car was converted by Southwest Superior Sales in Dallas.

Richard J. Conjalka collection

Andy Hotton started his auto industry career as a customizer in 1946, and by the 1960s his Belleville, Michigan, firm was constructing many of the Ford Motor Company's show cars. In 1965, Andy Hotton Associates introduced a limousine version of the new Galaxie 500 "LTD," and the price-conscious image they projected compelled many government fleets to choose them over the Cadillac Fleetwood Seventy Five. With a body stretched between the rear doors and the rear wheels, as well as the front and rear doors, these cars became known as "double-cut" limousines in industry parlance.

Richard J. Conjalka collection

This 1966 Ford LTD limousine shows how Andy Hotton Associates' handiwork appeared when all the windows were retracted, creating a discreet long-wheelbase four-door hardtop.

Ford strengthened its reputation as "The Wagonmaster" by debuting the industry's first two-way tailgate in 1966, making it standard on its full- and mid-sized models and optional on the Falcon. This so-called "Magic Doorgate," which could drop down conventionally for loading heavy objects or open sideways to enhance rear seat passenger access, considerably improved the convenience of ACC's F-2 hearse and F-3 ambulance conversions. General Motors, Chrysler and AMC had all introduced similar tailgate designs by 1969.

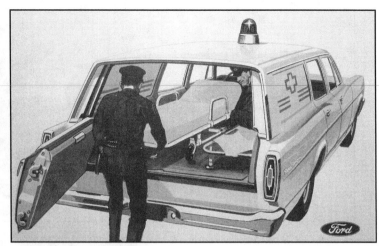

NAHC, Detroit Public Library

Terry Lange photo, Steve Loftin collection

Aside from a raised roof, side-swinging rear door conversion from National Coaches of Knightstown, Indiana, this 1966 Ford ambulance, operated by the Newton, Iowa, Fire Department, was very basically equipped. Twin pillar spotlights, a Federal C-series siren, a power rooftop ventilator, and a 360-degree Beacon Ray were augmented by rocket-style corner lights.

Strangely, a mid-sized Fairlane served as the basis for this rendering of a 1967 National Ford Minute Man ambulance. It's still useful for illustrating what the Knightstown, Indiana, coachbuilder's professional cars looked like when the customer didn't opt for commercial glass.

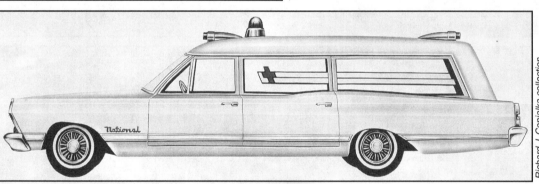

Richard J. Conjalka collection

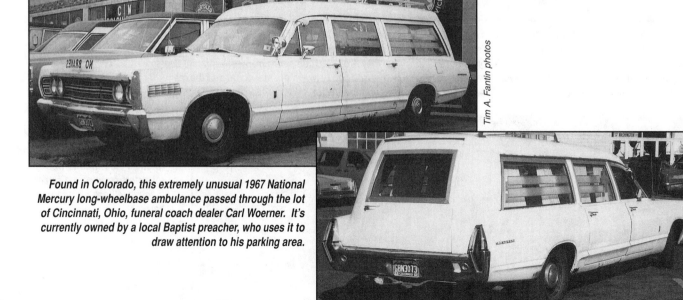

Tim A. Fantin photos

Found in Colorado, this extremely unusual 1967 National Mercury long-wheelbase ambulance passed through the lot of Cincinnati, Ohio, funeral coach dealer Carl Woerner. It's currently owned by a local Baptist preacher, who uses it to draw attention to his parking area.

Lehmann-Peterson: A Limousine Pioneer

While coach-built, six- or eight-door extended-wheelbase cars had been seen in resort, band bus, and airport service since the 1920s, the "stretch" limousine as we know it today didn't arrive on the scene until Lehmann-Peterson of Chicago unveiled its first Lincolns in May, 1963. The pioneering venture got its start when Robert Peterson, a builder of Indianapolis racecars for a number of years, was asked by fellow racing enthusiast George Lehmann if he would be interested in constructing a prototype limousine. "I had just rebuilt a Scarab automobile that had broken into three pieces and he was quite impressed by what I had done on that car," Peterson recalled during an interview published in *Limousine & Chauffeur* magazine's January, 1986 issue, adding "I had always been fond of the idea of building a limousine, but never had a reason to do it. The final deal we came to was that I would stretch the cars and he would provide the money."

The "suicide door" Continental was selected for the project simply because Lehmann was fond of Lincolns, though it turned out that the slab-sided body and admirably restrained ornamentation introduced on 1961 models stretched extremely well. The first two prototypes built from 1963 sedans had 36-inch wheelbase extensions, while the production cars, taking advantage of the 1964 Lincoln's 3-inch-longer 126-inch wheelbase, had 34-inch center stretches yielding a 160-inch wheelbase and 250.3-inch overall length. In marked contrast to the folding, forward-facing jump seats used in Cadillac Series Seventy-Five limousines and the Ghia-built Chrysler Crown Imperials, the interior's chief distinguishing feature was a pair of rear-facing seats flanking a walnut stereo and beverage cabinet mounted on the driveshaft tunnel. A padded leatherette (later vinyl) top with a formal backlight, thick mouton carpeting, and built-in umbrella stowage under the front seat further enhanced the feel of luxury.

Good looks and lavish appointments aside, the secret of Lehmann-Peterson's success was that the partners secured the Ford Motor Company's official blessing for their project from the very beginning. After completing their first prototype, Lehmann and Peterson brought it to Dearborn, where Peterson recalled "they got all of the engineers together and had no less than 60 people looking at the car. They were very cautious about building an automobile that was about 500 lbs. heavier than the standard automobile at the time, because they wanted something structurally safe." Asked to leave the prototype behind for some preliminary testing, Peterson learned some years later that "the Sales Department had taken the vehicle out and loaded it with as many guys as they could get into it. They drove it over dips and bumps and got it launched up into the air, but they were unable to break it."

Once a 1964 model limousine prepared in November, 1963, passed a more rigorous and systematic 40,000-mile durability test at the Dearborn proving grounds, Ford agreed to cover Lehmann-Peterson's conversion with the standard Lincoln two-year or 24,000-mile warranty and take orders for the cars through Lincoln dealers on an exclusive basis. "Incidentally," Peterson added, "those limousines tended to have a lower warranty cost than a standard Lincoln. That used to mystify both Ford and ourselves, until we realized that we really poured over a limousine when it was finished to find every possible defect and fix it."

The starting price for this 1968 model Lehmann-Peterson Lincoln limousine was $15,104 but optional equipment usually pushed the bottom line towards $20,000. A 2-inch raised roof was a new option that year at $950, joining such previously-offered amenities as air conditioning at $850, a $500 passenger intercom, a $295 9-inch television set, and a $200 beverage service.

Richard J. Conjalka collection

Though the $15,153.50 base price of a 1964 or 1965 Lehmann-Peterson Lincoln represented a $5,000 premium over a Cadillac limousine and a big boost from the $13,400 price originally announced in 1963, the model 53A found a ready market among customers seeking greater exclusivity than was possible with a Fleetwood Seventy-Five or a slightly cheaper alternative to the Mercedes-Benz 600 Pullman. As output increased from 15 units in 1964 to 85 in 1965 and 130 in 1966—other sources, while consistently-agreeing 1966 was the peak year volume-wise, offer figures ranging from 104 to 159 vehicles—the Lincoln plant in Wixom, Michigan, began to drop-ship cars in Chicago, where Lehmann-Peterson opened a 16,000-square-foot plant on Armitage Street that could complete four limousines a week. A-list purchasers included Robert F. Kennedy, Jerry Lewis, Sophia Loren, and Aristotle Onassis. The opening reel of the 1965 James Bond movie *Thunderball* featured the first of several onscreen appearances for the car. Heads of state felt right at home in the spacious rear compartment, with the Dutch royal family purchasing a pair of Lehmann-Petersons. One of the 1964 models used for Ford's durability testing was turned into an open-top parade vehicle in just nine days for Pope Paul VI's October, 1965, visit to New York City. Even the White House got an armor-plated Lehmann-Peterson Lincoln, developed at a record-breaking cost of $500,000, but leased by Ford for a token fee of $1 a year. It was placed into service as Richard Nixon prepared to take office in 1969. Its 2-inch raised roof fit extra quarter windows and a bulletproof glass skylight that could hinge open so the president could wave to the crowds during parades.

During the time they were on sale from 1964 to 1970, Lehmann-Peterson's Lincolns also raised the bar for amenities expected in limousines, introducing built-in TVs, fold-out secretarial desks, photochromically tinted rear compartment windows, and a high-tech paging system where the client carried a transmitter that was used to signal the chauffeur that the car was needed. To promote Lincoln luxury to the public, Ford initiated a subsidy program that put about 50 of the approximately 100 cars built each year into livery service, and Lincoln-Mercury's General Sales Manager Frank E. Zimmerman was especially pleased to see three Lehman-Peterson Lincolns simultaneously appear at one Park Avenue intersection during a 1967 business trip to New York City. "While the Lincoln Continental executive limousine is recognized as the ultimate in prestige and luxury motoring around the world," he said afterwards, "most of all we wanted to earn the 'Park Avenue Seal of Approval'—and it has."

In spite of the vivid, industry-founding first impressions created by its cars, Lehmann-Peterson shut down in 1970 because, Peterson explained in 1986, "with all the new auto safety rules being introduced at the time, Henry Ford (II) thought it would be better if they didn't participate anymore. We didn't feel that we were able to do an adequate amount of advertising without them." George Lehmann died in 1972 while Robert Peterson, who stayed in the business by affiliating himself with fellow Chicago limousine pioneer Earle Maloney in 1973, passed on in 1995.

Wearing 1969 exterior trim by the time it entered service in November, 1968, this 6-ton, armor-plated 1967 Lehmann-Peterson Presidential limousine had a 2-inch raised roof with opening glass panels that could be fitted with a vinyl cover to prevent heat build-up when the car was parked. Also featured was a two-way P.A. system that could transmit outside sound to the interior, front fender-mounted flag holders illuminated by three miniature spotlights, a fold-down bumper step, and a hydraulically retracted trunk rail for the Secret Service agents.

Courtesy Ford Motor Company

All-new Ford Econoline vans, with their engines moved forward to enhance driver comfort and expand the cargo floor, debuted in the spring of 1968. They proved effective in addressing emerging desires for more equipment and interior space in ambulances, and within a decade, these easily converted vehicles had pushed car-based ambulances to the brink of extinction. This 1970 model, said to be the first van ambulance built by Horton Emergency Vehicles of Grove City, Ohio, served the Prairie Township Fire Department outside Columbus.

Steve Lichtman collection

In addition to constructing box-bodied paramedic units on light-truck chassis, the aptly named Modular Ambulance Corporation of Dallas sought out mortuary customers with this 1971 Mercury Marquis Demi-Coach intended for "airport pick ups, cross country deliveries, and baby funerals." The car could also be used by the pallbearers or the funeral director's family when the second row seat was folded up, and the purchaser had the choice of furnishing a wagon purchased from a favored hometown dealer or arrange for MAC to procure a base vehicle at its fleet discount rate.

Richard J. Conjalka collection

After debuting an all-new Continental with front-hinged rear doors and a separate perimeter chassis in 1970, Lincoln celebrated its 50th anniversary in 1971. Given that the new frame was easier to stretch than the unit bodies used from 1958-69, it was a good time for Andy Hotton Associates to launch a Continental limousine lineup that included a six-passenger model with a 1-foot wheelbase extension, and a range of eight-or-nine passenger cars with 2-foot wheelbase extensions, 1-foot-longer rear doors, and a choice of jump- or bench-seat auxiliary seating.

Richard J. Conjalka collection

Since a Ford LTD station wagon cost only $350 less ($5,061 versus $5,411) in 1975, it made sense for funeral directors to choose the more-prestigious Mercury Marquis as a base vehicle for their first-call cars. Note that the casket floor of this Elegante conversion built in Kitchener, Ontario, was offset to make space for a church truck well within the right side #2 door.

Richard J. Conjalka collection

Matching six-door limousines were also offered to funeral directors who used their Mercury Marquis station wagon conversions as hearses. Seating nine passengers, this 36-inch stretch was built by Breece Custom Limousines of Dallas, Texas, in 1978.

Fitted with an ACC conversion, a Federal Twin Sonic light bar, and a factory police package with the 460 Interceptor V-8, this 1977 Ford LTD station wagon served the Ainsworth-Deep River Fire Department in Hobart, Indiana, as a back-up ambulance. It showed just 10,000 miles on the odometer when it was retired in 1996.

Tim A. Fantin photo

Tim A. Fantin photo

As GM and Chrysler had, respectively, downsized and discontinued their full-sized station wagons in 1977, Ford and Mercury enjoyed a one-year Extra Large Wagon market exclusive as funeral directors and other traditional buyers snapped up the last of the "whoppers." This 1978 Mercury Arlington by Automotive Conversion Corporation, showing just 52,000 original miles when Tim A. Fantin purchased it in 1998, was operated by the Brough-Getts Funeral Home in Miamisburg, Ohio.

The Professional Car

With the 1977 Cadillacs delivering, in the opinion of many livery customers, less car for more money, Mel Stein sensed an opportunity and acquired the rights to manufacture Andy Hotton Associates Lincoln limousines in Canada. His sales manager, Tom McPherson, convinced him there might also be a market for a long-wheelbase Lincoln funeral coach. The first prototype, completed in 1978, which utilized the rectangular quarter windows of the Lincoln Town Coupe, would become known as the AHA Viceroy.

The rear door of AHA's 1978 Lincoln Viceroy prototype was adorned with a Mark V-style tire hump, which was also a popular option on the company's limousines. The casket compartment beyond, which was equipped with a slide-out table, measured 125 inches, with 93 inches between the front and rear bier pins and 31 inches of clearance between the door top and the rollers.

AHA's basic Lincoln Landau hearse, shown here as a 1979 model, was ultimately called the Viscount. In addition to the Viceroy with its Town Coupe windows, the initial April, 1978 catalog also showed silhouettes of a Verona with oval opera windows and a Westminister combining larger quarter windows with a wide D-pillar.

Walt McCall collection

Richard J. Conjalka collection

Full-sized Fords and Mercurys adopted severely angular styling when they downsized in 1979, but the look proved durable enough to last through the 1991 model year. Adding a padded vinyl roof with S&S-style landau bows, A.G. Solar of Dallas, Texas certainly did a nice job turning this 1979 Marquis into a service car.

Richard J. Conjalka collection

McClain Sales & Leasing of Anderson, Indiana, which usually converted Cadillac Coupe DeVilles, built this novel Ford flower car from a 1980 LTD station wagon. It was one of a handful commissioned by Hispania Trading/Royal Coachworks of St. Louis for export to Venezuela, where company president Joe Molina speculates "they're probably still in service today." A few Mercurys were also altered in this fashion.

Walt McCall collection

The success of its Lincoln hearses prompted AHA to seek larger quarters in the Toronto suburb of Downsview in early 1979, but limousine production returned to Mississauga after Tom McPherson and Vancouver, B.C. coach dealer Howard Carter purchased the professional car division in the fall of 1980 and renamed it the Eureka Coach Company Ltd. The Lincoln Viceroy Landau was still on sale after a smaller Continental Town Car bowed for 1980, but 1981 would be its last year as Eureka's Buicks and a new Cadillac Concours series assumed center stage.

American Funeral Director

Characterized by giant display windows for the #2 side doors, some of the decade's most imposing-looking Lincoln hearses were constructed by Marquis Custom Coach of Canoga Park, California. Three-way loading via a 122-inch table with 12 casket rollers was a notable option, and this example wears the angled taillights, flush bumpers, and heavy crosshatch grille added to the Town Car in 1985.

With experience dating back to the band busses it constructed in the late 1920s, Armbruster/Stageway of Fort Smith, Arkansas, remained a favorite source for six-door limousines as matching Lincoln hearses became more popular in the mid-1980s. The car shown here has solenoid-released center doors to eliminate the outside handle, allowing it to handle business and recreational roles as effectively as funerals.

Accubuilt

Extending the quarter panels instead of the wheelbase, the Eagle Coach Company of Cincinnati debuted this Lincoln Town Coach at the beginning of the 1986 model year. The 4-inch raised roof was covered with convertible canvas instead of the usual vinyl.

Richard J. Conjalka collection

Rick Davis

In the mid-1980s, Paul Demers & Sons of Beloeil, Quebec, began to sell large numbers of its funeral cars in the United States. This 1985 model, which spent its career at a succession of Hamilton, Ontario, funeral homes, has been owned by Rick Davis of Winona, Ontario, since 1995.

Ford's position as the dominant chassis supplier for van-based ambulances was sealed by the 1975-91 generation Econoline, which touted full walk-through capability and easier servicing with the engine and front axle further forward than competing Dodge and GM vehicles. This impressive unit, built around 1985 for the Hammonton, New Jersey, Volunteer Rescue Squad as a first-response truck for auto accidents, also featured a Quigley four-wheel-drive conversion, more than 80 cubic feet of illuminated exterior storage, and powerful spotlights mounted on extending poles at each corner of the body.

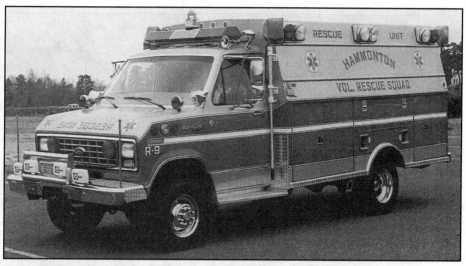

Steve Lichtman collection

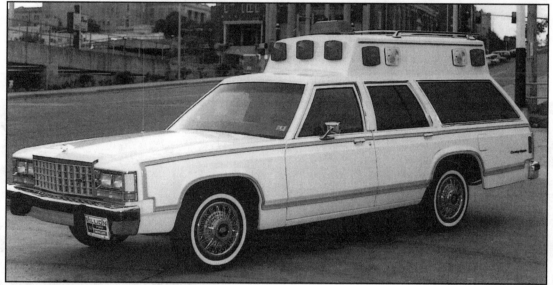

Steve Loftin photo

Brand new, passenger car-based ambulances were essentially extinct by 1980, but this 1986 Ford Crown Victoria station wagon converted into a standard-wheelbase high top for a California transfer service by CRS Coach of McAlester, Oklahoma, proves there's always an exception.

Tim A. Fantin photo

Six-window landau hearses like the Paramount and Eterna were some of the most-distinctive models offered by the original, Piqua, Ohio-based Miller-Meteor company during the 1960s and 1970s, so it was no surprise that a similar-looking LeClassic would appear in the revived Miller-Meteor line introduced as 1986 models by Collins Professional Cars of Hutchinson, Kansas. To create a matching procession, this 1988 vintage funeral coach could be teamed with a Collins Premiere four-door Lincoln limousine sharing its side window design and squared-off rear doors.

Accubuilt

The 1988-89 Lincoln Town Car had a finer-featured grille that integrated subtle horizontal crossbars, and it proved a tasteful starting point for this Superior Renaissance funeral coach. Commercial glass wasn't fitted like it was on Superior's Cadillacs, Chevrolets, and Buick Sovereigns, but roll-down power front door vent windows were a major selling point to smokers, and the stainless-steel moldings spanning the roof and windshield header neatly crowned the steel-reinforced fiberglass cap.

Richard J. Conjalka collection

Utilizing Lincoln taillights so the rear end would not need a redesign (which also maintained a more-prestigious look where it counted most), Eagle introduced a traditionally sized Mercury hearse at the October, 1987 NFDA convention in Salt Lake City. In addition to the standard full-length Elk Grain vinyl top, the customer could specify a 3/4 vinyl or 2/3 convertible-style carriage roof.

Richard J. Conjalka collection

Professional car enthusiasts perpetually pine for a revival of the traditional extended-wheelbase first-call/service car, which no doubt inspired the wreath motif and painted quarter panels on this early rendering of Eagle's all-new 1990 Lincoln Town Coach.

Retaining the aerodynamic sheet metal added for 1990, the 1991 Lincoln Town Car received a more easily assembled 4.6-liter "modular" V-8 with chain-driven overhead cams, distributor-less ignition, and an alternator bolted directly to the engine to reduce vibration. 1992 models like this Eureka Brougham Landau built in Norwalk, Ohio, were further improved with a passenger-side airbag and electronically controlled automatic overdrive transmission.

Richard Shelly

As Richard Shelly, who established Imperial Coach in Pittsburgh, was also a Ford dealer, it was no surprise that his 1993 model line included this Explorer L-Mini hearse in addition to the more common Chrysler minivan and GM station wagon conversions. Four-wheel drive added $2,000 to the $30,900 sticker, while an identically priced EX Conversion retained the factory rear quarter windows and covered them with removable landau panels.

The Town Car added a revised grille with rounded-off upper corners for 1993—the same year that S&S courted Lincoln loyalists by launching a Majestic Landau with a 31-inch chassis stretch. Interior appointments included S&S emblems for the front seat headrests, a deluxe cloth headliner and an optional air extraction system that exhausted the rear compartment every two minutes. Linked to the Town Car's self-leveling rear suspension, an electric switch inside the rear door lowered the casket floor to 23 inches for easy loading and unloading.

S&S celebrated its 120th anniversary by introducing the industry's first commercial-glass Lincoln funeral cars at the beginning of the 1996 model year. The first car completed, previewed to the trade in April, 1995, was a Park Lane combining tall commercial glass with a rakishly-low roofline sharing its 67.3-inch height with the standard glass S&S Lincoln Majestic. This was soon joined on sale by an S&S Lincoln Park Hill with a 72-inch roof, and a line of matching high-headroom commercial glass limousines with 44- or 60-inch chassis extensions. For added distinction, either hearse could be ordered with a Limousine Styling Option that added picture windows to the quarter panel for a better view of the casket and floral tributes.

THE STANDARD OF EXCELLENCE... THE TRADITION OF LEADERSHIP.

LIMOUSINES

S&S Lincoln Limousines are the perfect companion cars for S&S Lincoln funeral coaches while at the same time eloquently reaffirming your professional image. With commercial or standard glass, they combine style, luxury, innovation and comfort with high levels of quality and numerous standard features. These are professional limousines as distinctive as your own services, limousines that will immediately impress all who view them.

The available S&S Custom CEO and 24-Hour packages easily transform your limousine into a profit generating corporate or entertainment vehicle. The reversible center seat easily changes from forward facing to the conference position. Seat belts are permanently attached to the seat.

S&S limousines feature an adjustable, forward facing center seat as standard. Leather, as shown, is optional.

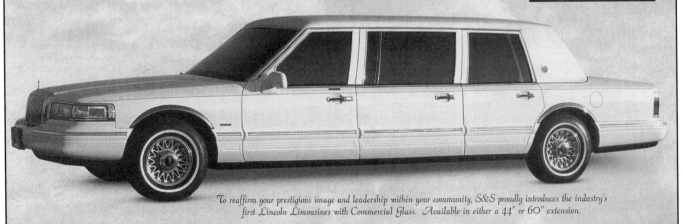

To reaffirm your prestigious image and leadership within your community, S&S proudly introduces the industry's first Lincoln Limousines with Commercial Glass. Available in either a 44" or 60" extension.

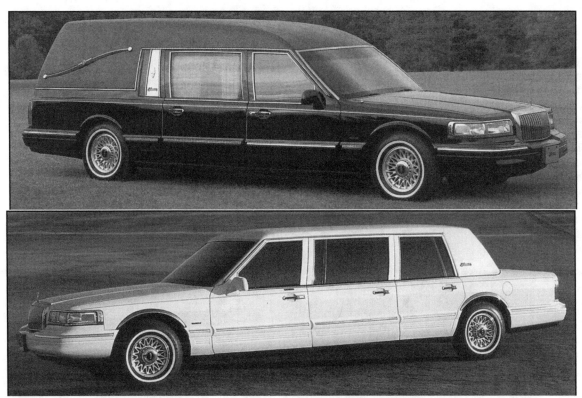

1996 marked the 10th year since Superior had introduced its first Lincoln hearse, and the Lima, Ohio, builder marked the occasion by debuting its own commercial glass Town Car called the Monarch. The construction of this coach, 4.7 inches taller than the standard-glass Superior Diplomat at 72 inches, involved nearly 400 specially designed components ranging from an oversized windshield to reduced-angle roof pillars. Companion six-door limousines were also available.

Richard J. Conjalka collection

Though a majority of the 400 flower car conversions completed by McClain Sales and Leasing between 1959 and 1997 were built from Cadillac Coupe DeVilles, the last vehicle to emerge from its Anderson, Indiana, shops was this all-white Lincoln Town Car.

Tom Caserta

Tom Caserta, a Piqua, Ohio, native who had been national sales manager at the original Miller-Meteor company before it closed in 1980, built his first Meteor Mort from a Ford Crown Victoria in 1996. The conversion featured a one-piece composite roof cap reinforced with 16-gauge steel tubing, widened rear fenders fitting less-intrusive vertical taillights from a Ford F-150 pickup to permit a 44.5-inch-wide rear door, and a 90.5-inch casket table. Most subsequent cars were based on the Mercury Grand Marquis, wich offered more prestige for virtually the same cost.

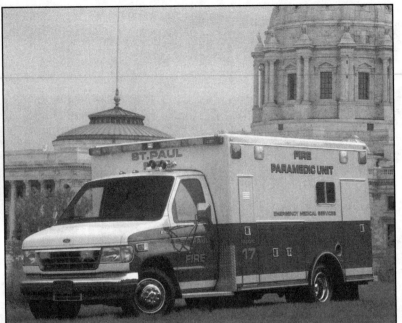

By the time Road Rescue of St. Paul, Minnesota, completed this 1996 Type III Supermedic and posed it in front of the Minnesota State Capitol, 85 to 90 percent of its ambulances were built from Ford Econoline chassis-cab units with the PowerStroke turbo-diesel engine. This was because diesel fuel burns cooler than gasoline and was less likely to start a fire when the ambulance was used as a stationary power plant on a combustible surface like grass or leaves.

Road Rescue Ambulances

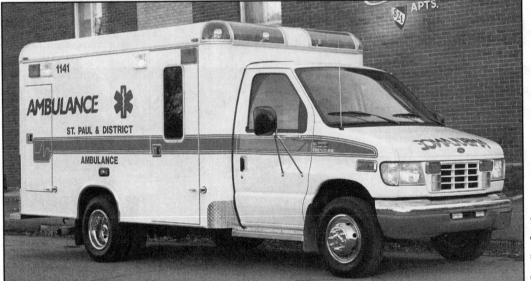

Crestline Coach of Saskatoon, Saskatchewan, intended to enhance the fuel economy expected of a Ford Econoline ambulance by introducing this wind-tunnel-tested NU*ERA model with emergency lights faired into the upper corners of its "AirCurv" bodies. Other interesting features included clamshell-style equipment doors in the rear corners of the body, and an electro-pneumatic CrestRide system for the cot that dampened ride vibrations.

Crestline Coach

To prepare funeral directors for the 1998 Town Car's dramatic styling changes, S&S/Superior was commissioned to build this generically badged prototype funeral coach for Lincoln's exhibit at the NFDA Convention in Las Vegas in October, 1997. In addition to an almost Bentley-esque body with a prominently fluted radiator grille, bright chrome door handles and rounded-off taillights, the 1998 Town Car featured triple door seals, a limp-home "failsafe" cooling system, and 16-inch wheels that allowed bigger brakes. Production S&S/Superior Lincolns would have rearward-leaning C-pillars.

To replace the Chevrolet Chancellor it could no longer build after the Caprice was discontinued in 1996, S&S/Superior debuted an all-new entry-level funeral coach built from the Ford Crown Victoria heavy-duty fleet platform at the 1997 NFDA Convention. Named the Superior Regent when in went on sale, this model featured a 16-inch chassis stretch, a jig-built all-steel superstructure, a sliding glass partition, and a 95.3-inch-long casket floor with a stainless-steel threshold.

In 1997, W. Rance Bennett, a vintage funeral coach dealer and restorer from Lowell, Michigan, began to offer old-fashioned carved panel hearses custom-built from modern Ford Econoline vans. The body sides and rear loading doors had decorative drapery panels accented by ornate columns and wire wheels, while the casket compartment featured cathedral-style cherrywood paneling, ornate brass lanterns, and a remote-controlled electric casket table that also opened the rear doors automatically. The division panel was etched with a scene of an ornate carved-panel hearse drawn by four horses.

W. Rance Bennett

Image Coaches

Having previously built a more conventional-looking Lincoln landau hearse, Image Coaches of Warsaw, Indiana, embraced the more contemporary character of the 1998 Town Car by creating this distinctive hatchback-style family hearse. It had six-passenger seating, all-steel construction, an externally accessed right-side storage compartment for the church truck, and a full-length casket floor with built-in floral spray storage at the rear of the coach.

Eagle Coach Company

The slanting taillights used on 1998-2002 Lincolns posed an aesthetic challenge to any builder trying to combine them with a squared-off hearse body, and it was the main reason why competing Cadillacs often had wider-opening rear doors. This 2000 Eagle Kingsley was nevertheless a quality conveyance, with corrosion-resistant galvanized-steel frame extensions, floors and interior panel backings, stainless-steel exhaust components and door lock rods, BASF base coat/clear coat paintwork, and advanced composite exterior panels.

Accubuilt

After S&S/Superior acquired the Miller-Meteor and Eureka brands in 1999 and moved production to Lima, Ohio, the Superior Regent Ford Crown Victoria was also sold as the Miller-Meteor Rockford (top) and Eureka Ashford (bottom). Both models, aimed at larger firms that wanted a professional-looking first call vehicle, and smaller homes that wanted a new hearse, but couldn't justify the expense of a Cadillac or Lincoln, offered a 16-inch wheelbase extension and a 95.3-inch long casket floor, accessed through an all-steel rear door 44 inches long, 34.5 inches wide, and 31.2 inches off the ground.

Accubuilt

The European flavor of 1998-up Lincolns lent itself nicely to limousine-style funeral coaches, as confirmed by this 2002 Miller-Meteor Paramount fitted with an unusual light-colored vinyl roof. Its 115.3-inch-long casket compartment, accessed through a 44.3-inch wide rear door with a 115-degree maximum opening angle, was equipped with 10 rollers, eight skid plates, and a clever suspension switch that lowered the floor threshold to within 25 inches off the ground.

Federal Coach

Funeral and livery customers were elated with the changes made to the 2003 Lincoln Town Car, which re-embraced traditional themes with a more-assertive grille topped by a stand-up hood ornament, squared-off front fenders, and a slightly higher and larger trunk. Federal Coach of Fort Smith, Arkansas responded to these changes with all-new hearse molds with a significantly larger casket compartment and a dramatically increased rear door aperture of 130 degrees.

Chapter 7

Oldsmobile

If one counts from the official founding of the Olds Motor Vehicle Company in Lansing, Michigan, on August 21, 1897 (Ransom Eli Olds had, in fact, tested an experimental three-wheeled steamer an entire decade earlier), 2004 will mark the last of 107 model years for Oldsmobile, bringing to an end its remarkable reign as America's oldest manufacturer of automobiles. As the curtain rings down, it is appropriate to think, in light of its long, heretofore unbroken history and well-deserved reputation as a technical innovator, that Oldsmobile should have enjoyed a bigger, more-consistent role in the affairs of funeral coach and ambulance builders. But the division's contributions in this arena warrant admiration even if they were largely concentrated in the mid-1930s and a 30-year period spanning the mid-1950s through the late 1980s.

During the Depression, General Motors' unparalleled resources allowed Oldsmobile to grow and prosper at a time when many other medium-priced makes were exiting the auto business (including, ironically, REO, which Ransom Eli Olds had founded after leaving Oldsmobile in 1904), and in 1934 the division's straight-eight engines played a pivotal role in developing a less-expensive LaSalle that could be sold in greater numbers. As far as funeral cars and ambulances were concerned, the high esteem in which Oldsmobile was held in this era was epitomized by the fact that it was one of the first cars that America's most prestigious coachbuilders turned to when they wanted to debut lower-priced models that would still uphold their hard-earned reputations. James Cunningham, Son & Company of Rochester, New York, indisputably one of the country's greatest horse-drawn carriage and motor hearse makers, with roots dating back to 1838, fielded Oldsmobiles after delivering the last professional cars constructed on its own V-8 chassis in 1934. The no-less-venerable Henney Motor Company of Freeport, Illinois, (established 1868) also based its 1934 "Progress" line on the division's Series L straight-eight

Bernie Weis collection

James Cunningham, Son & Co. turned to "straight-eight" Oldsmobiles and Packards after it ceased constructing funeral cars and ambulances on its own chassis in 1934. This allowed the 96-year-old Rochester, New York, firm to price this elaborately carved model 315A eight-column town car hearse in the $3,500 range, making it at least $3,000 less expensive than an equivalent coach on Cunningham's old Model W chassis.

after deciding that the cost of building its own chassis from scratch no longer outweighed the benefits. The following year, Sayers & Scovill of Cincinnati (a relative youngster dating from 1876) became the third great funeral coach builder to adopt Oldsmobile componentry, employing its front-end sheet metal and eight-cylinder engines for the Arcadian series, though a Sayers radiator badge and S&S hubcaps carefully de-emphasized the link to Lansing.

To the future detriment of the marque's enthusiasts, however, all three firms did not build Oldsmobiles for very long. Cunningham departed the funeral coach building field in 1936, while the same year saw S&S switch to Buick platforms for two seasons before settling on the even more-prestigious LaSalle and Cadillac Commercial Chassis. Henney, having secured an exclusive arrangement to build Packard funeral cars and ambulances, similarly discontinued its Oldsmobile Progress after 1937, though the A.J. Miller Company of Bellefontaine, Ohio, stepped in to satisfy any remaining demand by offering Oldsmobiles in ambulance, service car, combination coach and carved drapery, Gothic panel, and six-window limousine hearse styles through the war-abridged 1942 model year.

While one might have thought that Oldsmobile's 1940 introduction of Hydra-Matic Drive and its 1949 debut of the Rocket overhead-valve V-8 would have immediately boosted its profile in hearse and ambulance circles, coachbuilders expressed no interest until the Flxible Company of Loudonville, Ohio, trying to fill a backlog of bus and national defense orders, suspended production of its Buick professional cars between 1952 and 1959. As the next rung up the General Motors price ladder from the Pontiacs that were already America's most-popular low-cost professional car platforms, Oldsmobile quickly became a favorite "prestige" offering of such firms as Vernon Z. Perry's National Body Manufacturing Company of Knightstown, Indiana, the Dixie Coach Company established in Lebanon, Tennessee, and the bevy of budget-market builders centered around Memphis.

It was certainly appropriate that the Memphis area concern that would ultimately become most closely associated with the Rocket in the 1950s was called Comet, even though the firm's co-founders Waldo J. Cotner and Robert Bevington would sell the name to Ford for its upcoming Mercury compact by decade's end. Having moved into a new plant in Blytheville, Arkansas, during 1959, Cotner-Bevington (as the operation became known) pretty much culled the Chevrolets and Pontiacs from its

model line to concentrate on Oldsmobiles by 1961. Its attractive range of extended-wheelbase Cotingtons was augmented at the lower end by a standard-wheelbase Seville series in 1963, while 1964 saw the company absorbed by the Wayne Works that already manufactured Miller-Meteor Cadillacs in Piqua, Ohio. Until the rise of truck-based ambulances in the early 1970s undermined production volumes, the product ranges of the two subsidiaries complimented each other beautifully and, in contrast to the fiberglass caps used to build high-headroom ambulances at other coachbuilders, all-steel roof construction was an important selling point to the "safety-first" crowd. Oldsmobile's massively overbuilt V-8 engines, increased in size from 394 cubic inches at the beginning of the 1960s to 425 cid in 1965 and 455 cid in 1968, were another crucial Cotner-Bevington asset, keeping many hard-working ambulances and hearses in service for decades after Blytheville's lights were dimmed in 1975.

After General Motors trimmed the external bulk and curb weight of its full-sized cars for 1977, the Buick Electra and LeSabre promised funeral buyers more prestige at very little added cost compared to Oldsmobile's equivalent 98 and 88, but there were still a number of firms that constructed professional cars from the latter. Before the Wayne Works' bean counters shut it down as well in 1979, Miller-Miller used the standard-wheelbase 98 sedan to build its standard-wheelbase Athena funeral coach. A considerable number of boxy, 1977-90 generation Custom Cruiser station wagons were converted into hearses and first-call cars fairly easily and inexpensively by such companies as B&B Custom Coachworks of Waxahachie, Texas, A.G. Solar of Dallas, and Eagle Coaches of Amelia, Ohio, with the most-ambitious creations adding raised roofs, wide-angle rear door hinges, and extended quarter panels or wheelbases.

Teamed with matching four- and six-door Mayfair limousines, the ultimate, Oldsmobile-related achievements in this period were likely the traditional commercial glass hearses offered by the Toronto-based Eureka Coach Company Ltd. starting in mid-1982. These were offered in 98 series Regent and 88-based Carlton variants that could be finished with four-window landau or six-window limousine rooflines. Even though these cars continued in production with front-drive power trains and purpose-engineered, low-profile rear suspension systems after 1985, Oldsmobile was beginning its long, sad decline from the million unit years it had enjoyed from 1983-86 to 714,394 sales in 1987, 600,037 in 1989, and just 426,306 in 1991.

Even if a funeral director wanted a hearse with a Rocket badge, the rear-wheel-drive, aerodynamic generation Custom Cruiser best suited to such work was only sold in 1991 and 1992 and it was apparently never offered as a stripped-down, heavy-duty "coachbuilder"

wagon. Instead, the division's final contributions to funeral service would come in the form of humble Silhouette minivans, fitted with casket tables, first-call cot cups, and slide-off landau panels by such companies as Royal Coachworks of St. Louis.

Bernie Weis collection

1934 was a fine year for Cunningham to switch to Oldsmobile's 90-horsepower L-Series straight-eight chassis, given its addition of hydraulic brakes, "Knee Action" independent front suspension, a rear stabilizer bar, and double-acting shock absorbers at all four wheels. The resulting improvements in ride quality were further enhanced by extending the wheelbases 29 inches on the limousine-style 347A hearse and 354A ambulance models to 148 inches overall.

William N. Schwartz photo, Rich Litton collection

Launching its "Progress" line in 1934, the Henney Motor Company of Freeport, Illinois, was another builder that embraced the Oldsmobile Series L straight-eight chassis when the costs of building its own frame outweighed the benefits. This 1935 model ambulance belonging to the Ocean Grove, New Jersey, Fire Department First Aid Squad benefited from bigger brakes and a horsepower boost from 90 to an even 100. Henney's body frame, resting on a beefed-up chassis with 8.5 inches of road clearance and an oversized self-aligning mid-ship bearing, was glued and screwed together from air-and-kiln-dried White Ash coated with lead, oil, and waterproof paint to prevent squeaking and repel moisture.

Before switching to Buick mechanicals for its 1936 models, Sayers & Scovill of Cincinnati adopted Oldsmobile sheet metal and straight-eight engines—installed in S&S' own 159-inch-wheelbase chassis—for its 1935 Arcadian funeral car and Ablington ambulance. Deferring to industry tradition, S&S hubcaps and Sayers badges for the radiator and spare tire covers were used to de-emphasize the Oldsmobile connection. The only example ever seen at a Professional Car Society event was this car owned by Dan Becker of Struthers, Ohio.

HENNEY PROGRESS MODEL 760

The eight-cylinder Oldsmobile platform used for this 1936 Henney Progress Model 760 Nu-3-Way Side Servicing Limousine Hearse offered only a few changes over the previous year. Electro-hardened aluminum pistons that reduced the break-in period, and fender-mounted parking lights and new hood trim (obscured by the side-mount spare) with nine vertical vents arranged in threes were new. An Elecdraulic casket table with manual override was a new feature, though a table lock controlled by the sliding front seats (which ran on ball bearing casters in a steel track) had been used by Henney since 1932.

As Henney had secured an exclusive arrangement to build Packard funeral cars and ambulances, 1937 was the last year for the Oldsmobile Progress. An egg-crate pattern grille with matching hood louvers distinguished the Oldsmobile L-37 eights from their six-cylinder siblings, and horsepower went up to 110 through an increase in displacement from 240 to 257 cubic inches. Henney's 1937 improvements included Leveldraulic side-to-side leveling on its Nu-3-Way hearses, offset-adjustable bier bins for its casket tables and all-steel roof inserts bolted into place against an angled rubber seal.

While it specialized in Cadillacs and LaSalles, A.J. Miller of Bellefontaine, Ohio, catalogued Oldsmobile hearses and first-call cars from 1937 to 1942. Combining an eight-cylinder Series 90 Custom Cruiser chassis ($775 including hood, fenders, and dashboard instruments) with a Gothic panel body style debuted in 1939, this 1940 Miller Oldsmobile three-way served the D. J. Robb Funeral Home in Sarnia, Ontario, until it was succeeded by a new Miller-Meteor Cadillac landau in 1956.

After a decade on the sidelines, Oldsmobile received renewed interest from funeral coach and ambulance makers after Flxible put its Buick professional cars on hiatus between 1952 and 1959. The budget market builders based in Memphis particularly took to them as prestige models, with the Comet Coach Company producing this attractive ambulance with two-tone paint, faired-in tunnel lights, and a Federal C-5 siren. Tubeless tires and a Power Ride front suspension with direct action shock absorbers and a front stabilizer were important improvements on the 1955 Oldsmobiles.

Advanced engineering,
superlative quality,
and unsurpassed value
will have ambulance operators
talking about the new 1955 COMET
with chassis by Oldsmobile

*See you at the
Tri-state convention*

*The Prestige of a new
COMET in your fleet
will pay dividends
for years to come*

comet

*Oldsmobile Chassis
(Also available on Pontiac chassis)

COMET COACH COMPANY
3723 Lamar Ave.   Phone 62-4653
MEMPHIS, TENNESSEE

Built on an extended Super 88 chassis by the Memphis Coach Company, this 1956 Memphian Oldsmobile sported wraparound rear corner windows and new front end where the grille and bumper were combined into a single unit. The renowned Rocket V-8 engine retained its 324-cubic inch block, but earned a new T-350 designation after a bump in compression increased the torque and horsepower.

Walt McCall collection

NATIONAL BODY MFG. CO., KNIGHTSTOWN, INDIANA   O-56-1

Richard J. Conjalka collection

Always willing to build a coach on any chassis desired by the customer, Vernon Perry's National Body Manufacturing Company of Knightstown, Indiana, published renderings of Oldsmobiles as early as 1954. With their mighty Rocket V-8s, this 1956 model limousine hearse and ambulance was certainly a tempting step up from National's more common Chevrolets and Pontiacs.

NATIONAL BODY MFG. CO., KNIGHTSTOWN, INDIANA   O-56-2

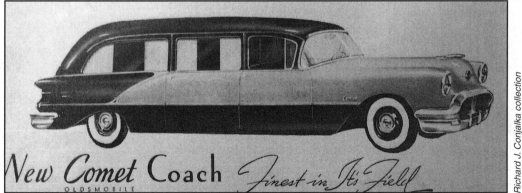

New Comet Coach *Finest in Its Field*
OLDSMOBILE

Richard J. Conjalka collection

This 1956 Comet Olds as a model 5260 combination relied on removable aluminum casket racks and a pair of folding attendants seats to alternate between funeral coach and ambulance duty. With the welded all-steel body's overall length totaling 235.29 inches, a sliding glass partition could be combined with a 105-inch-long rear compartment offering 43.5 inches of headroom and 99 inches of space at cot level.

Little is known about the Dixie Coach Company of Lebanon, Tennessee, beyond the fact that it was founded in 1956 by Wilburn Adams, George Middlebrook, and Meteor dealer Perry Lanius, who evidently toured the Weller Brothers plant in Memphis for manufacturing ideas. Dixie was acquired from its founders by the Bland Casket Company of Lebanon and moved to 405 South Maple Street in April, 1956, where it produced Oldsmobile and Pontiac professional cars through the 1962 time frame. The company subsequently became a Cotner-Bevington and Miller-Meteor distributor.

Jeremy D. Ledford collection

Richard J. Conjalka collection

Even when it came to this Memphis-built Comet combination, 1957 Oldsmobiles were nearly 2 inches lower than their predecessors thanks to 14-inch wheels and an 8-inch-wider frame with rugged X-bracing. A repositioned front cross member allowed the engine (making 277 horsepower and 400 lbs.-ft. of torque from 371 cubic inches) and the cowl to move further forward for a smaller transmission tunnel and more interior space.

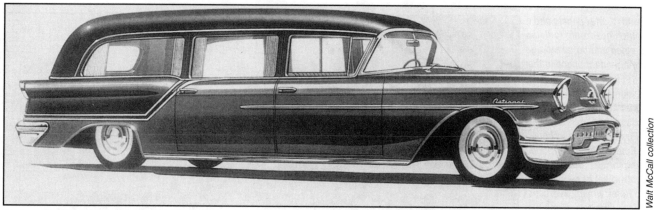

Walt McCall collection

National's 1957 Oldsmobiles started at $6,600 compared to $6,313 for its Pontiacs and $5,730 for its Chevrolets, making them the company's most expensive professional cars aside from Buicks and Chryslers. For the first time since 1950, funeral directors could avail themselves to matching Oldsmobile station wagons (now offering pillarless hardtop styling) for first-call duties.

Steve Loftin collection

Stunned by Chrysler's 1957 models, General Motors spent $730 million restyling its 1958 car lines, but the Oldsmobiles fared badly with chrome-slathered flanks and dual headlights sitting rather uncomfortably atop an anodized aluminum grille. Handed a lemon, Comet Coach of Memphis made lemonade with new hardtop-inspired window frames and wraparound rear quarter windows that eliminated blind spots.

Richard J. Conjalka collection

1959 was an extremely eventful year for the Comet Coach Company, which transferred factory operations from Memphis to larger quarters in Blytheville, Arkansas, and sold the rights to the Comet name to the Ford Motor Company for its 1960 Mercury compact. The Oldsmobile 98 chassis used to build its Panoramic landau hearses was all-new for the third year in a row, with 4.6-inch-longer "Linear Look" bodies boasting 36 percent more glass area, more effective electric windshield wipers, and rear leaf springs in place of 1958's trouble-prone New-Matic Ride air suspension.

Blind quarter panels and a 48-inch-headroom roof cap created additional storage and attendant space in this 1959 Comet Oldsmobile, making it a more effective community servant in the hands of the Lake View, New York, Fire Department. Though the Emergency Relief Squad sprung for twin Beacon Rays and a mixed set of secondhand Buick wheel covers, the prodigious amounts of salt that were needed to thaw the roads along the Lake Erie shoreline south from Buffalo each winter made it unlikely that this impressive rig kept its good looks for very long.

Leo Duliba photo, Steve Loftin collection

Ted Bruehl period photo, Roger D. White MD collection

Hardtop station wagons had been dropped from Oldsmobile's model line for 1959, which certainly simplified matters when Weller Brothers of Memphis built this standard-wheelbase high-top ambulance from a 1960 Super 88. It is still a mystery why the factory luggage rack was retained.

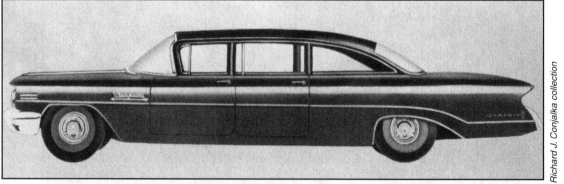

Richard J. Conjalka collection

Stageway Coaches of Cincinnati sold this 1960 Olds Sedan Limousine on a 153-inch wheelbase, which offered space for eight passengers distributed between a fully adjustable front seat, a pair of folding second-row jump seats, and a 60-inch-wide rear bench. The base vehicle was a Dynamic 88 two-door sedan with a 240-horsepower 371-cubic inch V-8 engine, and Jetaway Hydra-Matic transmission, which was beefed-up with heavy-duty springs and shock absorbers, encasement-style frame extensions, and 8.00 x 15 nylon tires on heavy-duty wheels.

The Professional Car

After Comet Coach of Blytheville, Arkansas, sold its name to Ford in 1959, the firm was renamed Cotner-Bevington and its extended-wheelbase Oldsmobiles were dubbed Cotingtons. Whether the funeral director chose a limousine or landau-style hearse, C-B's coachwork worked surprisingly well with the scoop-like grilles, torpedo-themed side sculpturing and inverted "skeg" fins used on 1961 Oldsmobiles.

Richard J. Conjalka collection

Cotner-Bevington sold a four-door Oldsmobile formal limousine to match its Cotingtons as early as 1961, but those in need of something larger could turn to National Coaches of Knightstown, Indiana, with its Dynamic 88 six-door and 98-derived eight-door. Oldsmobile's 1961 chassis marked a major philosophical change from the rigid frames used on previous models, featuring a relatively flexible perimeter frame bolted to a rigid body shell with fewer body mounts. This approach, combined with nylon-sleeved shock absorbers and a return to coil springs at all four wheels, promised a better ride and reduced noise, vibration, and harshness.

Resting on an Oldsmobile 98 chassis extended by 2 feet to yield a 150-inch wheelbase, this 1962 Cotner-Bevington Cotington Landau sold for $8,524 as a single-purpose hearse, $8,354 as an ambulance and $8,657 as an easily reconfigured combination. A matching Oldsmobile eight-passenger limousine with the same wheelbase shared such 1962 enhancements as factory-sealed lubrication fittings and improved air conditioning systems. Further aided by cleaner-looking styling, Oldsmobile sales increased and the division leapfrogged Rambler to become the industry's #4 make behind Chevrolet, Ford, and Pontiac.

Richard J. Conjalka collection

Priced at $8,688 in 1962, Cotner-Bevington's top-of-the-line 44-inch-headroom limousine ambulance represented a $467 premium over the standard-height model. This example, painted in an unusual mustard color, was eventually sold to Texas enthusiast Steve Diamond. Note how Oldsmobile's taillights were tilted on their sides to make space for the rear door.

Steve Lichtman photo

Capping the Cotner-Bevington price list with its $10,501 sticker, the high-top ambulance received a headroom increase to 46 inches in 1963. This example fitted with a massive Federal "Q" siren was promptly pressed into service by the Tuxedo-Cheverly Fire Department in Prince George's County, Maryland.

Steve Lichtman collection

The angular contours of the 1963 Oldsmobile 98 worked well with Cotner-Bevington's eight-passenger limousine body, though the standard hubcaps afforded a rather austere appearance. Producing 330 horsepower and 440 lbs.-ft. of torque, Oldsmobile's massively overbuilt 394-cid V-8 remained a trusty servant in funeral and ambulance service.

Richard J. Conjalka collection

Tim A. Fantin photo

The 1964 Chicago Auto Show witnessed Oldsmobile's introduction of the mid-sized Vista Cruiser station wagon, touting tinted glass roof panels and a 5-inch-longer wheelbase than other F-85s (120 inches). It proved so successful that full-sized Oldsmobile station wagons were dropped for 1965 and Buick borrowed the body for its Skylark Sport Wagon. As the patient had 100 cubic feet of space and something to look at besides the ceiling, the Vista Cruiser proved a fine platform for this Automotive Conversion Corporation Amblewagon. Still showing less than 30,000 miles, this car is now owned by Jim Vowell of Romeo, Michigan.

While the wheelbases still spanned 150 inches on Cotingtons and 126 inches on Sevilles, 1965 Cotner-Bevington Oldsmobiles enjoyed an entirely new look featuring kicked-up rear fenders, more-pronounced rocker panel transitions, reduced-angle roof pillars and GM's new commercial cowl assembly and extra-height windshield. Instead of being S-shaped, the decorative bars on C-B landau hearses now resembled elongated diamonds.

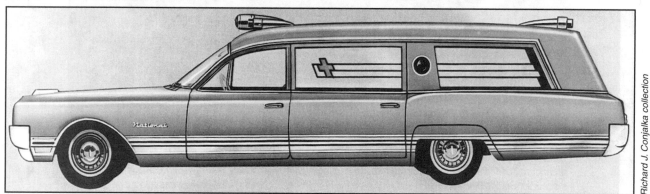

Richard J. Conjalka collection

Thanks to tooling purchased from Flxible, National Coaches of Knightstown, Indiana, could also offer ambulances that took advantage of Oldsmobile's new 1965 styling. The 98 chassis also underwent important changes that year, with the faithful 394 superseded by a substantially lighter and more efficient 425 Super Rocket V-8.

213

Decorative wreaths, traditionally associated with service cars instead of hearses, adorned the thumbscrew-secured window covers of this dark green 1966 Cotner-Bevington Oldsmobile Seville combination used by the Becker Funeral Home in Jewell, Iowa, until 1989.

Tim A. Fantin photo

Kirk & Nice of Germantown, Pennsylvania, claimed to be America's oldest funeral home with roots dating back to 1761. It operated this 1966 Cotner-Bevington Oldsmobile commercial glass limousine as part of a matched fleet that included hearses and first-call cars. It is now owned by Mike and Joyce Satterthwaite of Huntingdon Valley, Pennsylvania.

While the side sculpturing was simplified, the 1967 Oldsmobile 98 recalled the '59 model in its use of prominent headlight pods that were taller than the middle grille. With safety taking center stage in the national discourse, Cotner-Bevington stressed that even its 48-inch-headroom high-top ambulance had a one-piece all-steel roof for additional roll-over protection. Other enhancements in this spirit included a collapsible steering column, self-adjusting dual-circuit brakes (with optional front discs), four-way emergency flashers, rubber-tipped overhead stretcher hooks and frame extensions made from one-piece girders.

1968 Cotner-Bevington Oldsmobiles co-opted the split grille and concealed windshield wipers that debuted on Pontiacs the year before, and a longer 4.25-inch stroke for the 98's V-8 engine yielded a 455-cubic inch displacement, 375 horsepower, and 510 lbs.-ft. of torque at 3000 rpm. This 150-inch-wheelbase Cotington landau was changed from a black to a white exterior in 1981 and used actively by the Browning-Yates Funeral Home in St. Maries, Idaho, until 1992.

Tim A. Fantin photo

Richard J. Conjalka collection

Though a front-wheel-drive Oldsmobile hearse would not appear until the mid-1980s, 1968 Toronado underpinnings were employed by American Quality Coach of Blytheville, Arkansas, to create a flat floor, tandem-axle "Jetaway 707" limousine that seated 15 passengers between a 185-inch wheelbase chassis and an all-steel raised roof with tinted skylights. The Sands Casino in Las Vegas was one of the hotels that used these tremendous vehicles as airport and tourist shuttles.

Richard J. Conjalka collection

Cotner-Bevington built its last commercial glass Oldsmobile limousine in 1967, so Knightstown, Indiana's National Coaches was tapped to turn a 98 Town Sedan into this low-slung stretch during the 1968 model year. The seams on the extended rear door moldings were a bit obvious, but opera windows would become ubiquitous in the coming decade.

For 1969, Cotner-Bevington's most basic 150-inch-wheelbase ambulance remained the 42-inch-headroom Cotington 42, illustrated here with a flat-top Beacon Ray and torpedo-shaped corner lights that warned traffic to the front and sides. The year's most important changes were variable-ratio power steering and revised rear suspension geometry.

215

Ziebart rust-proofing was an important durability enhancement on 1970 Cotner-Bevingtons, and Oldsmobile concurrently increased the service life of the 455 V-8 powering these vehicles by adding intake and exhaust valve rotators that gave the stem a part turn every time the valve opened. This 1970 Seville combination was purchased new by the Schmidt Funeral Home in Brookshire, Texas, and used until 1995. Tim A. Fantin sold it to Terry Kennedy of Kokomo, Indiana, in 1998.

Tim A. Fantin photo

GM's full-sized "B" and "C" platform cars were longer and lower for 1971, with bigger windshields, more-pronounced body curvatures, and lower compression ratios, allowing the engines to run on low-lead or no-lead fuel. Performance was compromised, but the Oldsmobile 98-based Cotner-Bevington ambulances were undeniably attractive with subdued tailfins and V-shaped headlight clusters echoing the grille design.

Standard-wheelbase passenger car ambulances were falling out of favor when an all-new Cotner-Bevington Oldsmobile Seville bowed in 1971, but this model still commanded a following from purchasers who wanted a relatively low-cost coach that could give their patients a smoother ride than a truck or van-based vehicle. The 99-inch-long rear compartment was wide enough for two cots when the single jump seat was folded into the floor, and the 37-inch-high rear door permitted cardiac cases to be loaded in the elevated position.

Called Custom Cruisers, full-sized station wagons returned to Oldsmobile's model line in 1971. Taking advantage of the loading ease delivered by the cars' novel sliding tailgates, Adam & Hense of St. Paul, Minnesota, wasted no time in converting these vehicles into first-call cars and mini-hearses by adding casket rollers, bier pins, vinyl roofs, and sandblasted palm leaf motifs to the rear window.

Richard J. Conjalka collection

Replacing the thin, diamond-shaped bars used since 1965, more conventional-looking landau bows appeared on 1971 Cotner-Bevington funeral cars. They were fitted to removable panels in the case of this 75th anniversary 1972 Oldsmobile combination operated by the May Funeral Home in LaGrange, Indiana, until 1995.

Tim A. Fantin photo

An easily reconfigured interior was the key to Cotner-Bevington's 1972 "Dual-value Combination Cars." To prepare for an ambulance call, all the funeral director had to do was reverse the casket rollers and unfold a pair of attendant seats from the floor. The exterior transformation was completed by removing the landau panels from the quarter windows (which often had ambulance decals) and bolting a rotating beacon to the roof.

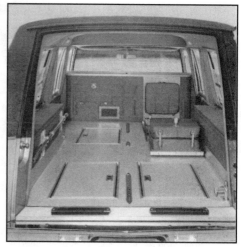

Tim A. Fantin photo, John Rabold collection

When it was owned by Michael Armentrout of Belle Center, Ohio, this 1973 Cotner-Bevington Seville standard-wheelbase landau hearse was used for company co-founder Waldo Cotner's funeral in April, 2001. The 98's new split taillight housings conveyed a suitably Gothic flavor when combined with a funeral coach body.

Mary Little

With a recession wreaking havoc on the U.S. auto market, the Wayne Corporation advertised its 1974 Cotner-Bevington Oldsmobiles and Miller-Meteor Cadillacs with the slogan "To Meet The Challenge Of Change." Despite the so-called "energy crisis," it was the last year standard-wheelbase Oldsmobile Sevilles were available and the combination ambulance models had already been discontinued.

In addition to being the first year for rectangular headlights and catalytic converters, 1975 was the last year for Cotner-Bevington-bodied Oldsmobiles and one of the most unusual final cars was this 54-inch ambulance put on sale by Milwaukee, Wisconsin, coach dealer Robert Hedges. Its numerous one-off touches included "Ful-Vu" corner beacons normally limited to Miller-Meteor Cadillacs, a rooftop fracture board compartment, and a windowless M-M Cadillac Criterion-style body without the usual walk-through partition.

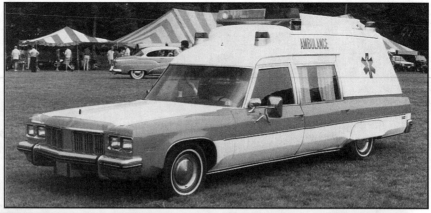

Steve Lichtman photo

Richard J. Conjalka collection

Like the rest of America, funeral directors had to downsize if they wanted an Oldsmobile 98 after 1976. Aiming at the old Cotner-Bevington Seville's budget-minded customers, Miller-Meteor introduced the standard-wheelbase Athena as a 1978 model. A creditably large casket compartment was created by fitting extended bumper filler panels, while other basic expectations were addressed by a one- or two-level raised roof, a side-swinging rear door, and a driver's compartment partition with sliding glass panels. A Cadillac Sedan DeVille could also be converted in this fashion.

One firm filling the demand for commercial-sized Oldsmobile hearses after Cotner-Bevington's departure was Bob Beitel's B&B Custom Coachworks of Waxahachie, Texas, which built this halo-style landau from a 1979 Custom Cruiser station wagon.

Tim A. Fantin photo

For the first time since Cotner-Bevington shut its doors seven years earlier, commercial-glass Oldsmobile hearses with reduced-angle roof pillars became available when the Toronto-based Eureka Coach Company introduced the Regent in the middle of the 1982 model year. To yield a suitably large interior, a 98 sedan was stretched 26 inches to create a 145-inch wheelbase and an overall length of 247.1 inches. Eureka's exclusive ExTend table was offered as an option to further facilitate casket handling, and the top-of-the-line Regent Tiara featured a half-padded vinyl roof with a painted front section.

Thomas A. McPherson collection

Encouraging purchasers of its Regent funeral coach to assemble a matched procession, Eureka also used the Oldsmobile 98 to build a Mayfair IV limousine with a 152.9-inch wheelbase and 256.1-inch overall length. A six-door, 261.3-inch-long Mayfair VI on a 158.9-inch wheelbase was also offered.

Based on the Oldsmobile Delta 88, this 1983 Eureka Carlton Landau offered funeral directors the opportunity to own a modestly priced, extended-wheelbase, commercial-glass coach without buying used.

Armbruster/Stageway of Fort Smith, Arkansas, was the builder of this rust-free, 55,000-mile 1983 Oldsmobile 98 six-door limousine that Cincinnati, Ohio, funeral car dealer Carl Woerner purchased in 2002.

Situated near Miller-Meteor's old Piqua base in Bradford, Ohio, Master Coach courted Oldsmobile buyers on a smaller budget with a standard-wheelbase 98 funeral coach stretched 7.4 inches in the quarter panels to allow a 93.5-inch-long, 33.5-inch-wide casket floor behind the partition. Only six examples were completed before the rear-wheel-drive 98 was discontinued at the end of 1984.

Tim A. Fantin photo

A 10-inch quarter panel extension and a custom-designed 110-degree rear door hinge from Cincinnati's Eagle Coach converted this 1985 Oldsmobile Custom Cruiser into an inexpensive landau hearse. The roof over the front seat was also raised slightly to create a traditional looking windshield header. This well-kept 66,000-mile car, finished in black with a blue velour interior, served a West Virginia funeral home until 2001.

Thomas A. McPherson collection

Eureka continued to offer Oldsmobile Mayfair VI six-door limousines after the front-drive "New Generation" professional cars debuted as 1986 models at the 1985 NFDA convention in Minneapolis. Suitable comfort and space for nine forward-facing passengers was promised by the 151.2-inch wheelbase, split 55/45 six-way power driver's seat, and commercial-duty suspension system fitting automatic level control and oversized tires. The Mayfair Formal added solenoid-released center doors and privacy sail panels to the third-row windows.

John Rabold collection

As the same sheet metal was used on Custom Cruiser station wagons all the way from 1980 to 1990, the Klaehn, Fahl & Melton Funeral Home of Fort Wayne, Indiana, found this 1988 A.G. Solar conversion contemporary enough to use for first calls through 2000. Oldsmobile dropped its 350-cubic inch diesel after the 1985 model year, so the sole engine choice at this stage was a four-barrel, 307-cubic inch gasoline V-8.

Tim A. Fantin photo

One of the last—and most-elaborate—conversions built by A.G. Solar of Dallas, this 1989 Oldsmobile Custom Cruiser was equipped for service at a Florida funeral home by fitting a raised roof and a formal rear window with fixed tailgate glass. Its white exterior, tastefully combined with blue upholstery and wire wheel covers, still reflects prevailing paintwork preferences among Southern and Southwestern morticians. Eric Chapman of Three Rivers, Michigan, is the current owner.

Richard Shelly

Replacing body shells that first appeared on 1977 models, General Motors redesigned its full-sized wagons for 1991, but the Oldsmobile Custom Cruiser was dropped after 1992. As a result, this GLS hearse conversion from Imperial Coach of Pittsburgh was more commonly ordered as a Buick Roadmaster or Chevrolet Caprice.

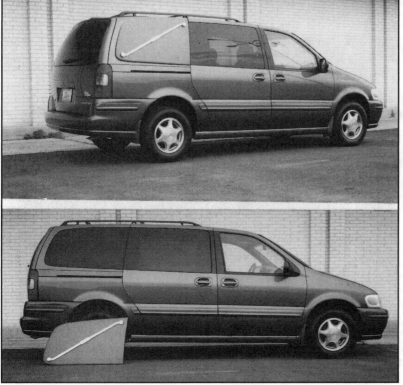

Joe Molina, Royal Coachworks

Dropping the "Dustbuster" noses and plastic body panels used before, the second-generation General Motors minivans launched as 1997 models were far more viable "first-call" vehicles, especially since long-wheelbase versions were available and the body (so it could be sold in Europe as an Opel) was 3 inches narrower than a Chrysler minivan for superior city maneuverability. The foam-padded aluminum landau panels on this Oldsmobile Silhouette by Royal Coachworks of St. Louis incorporated top and bottom grooves so they can be slipped over the pivoting quarter windows and clamped into place. The casket floor and its fold-out carpeted bumper protector are also easily removed, allowing the original seats to be quickly reinstalled for family use.

Chapter 8

Packard

There have been Miller-Packards and Knightstown-Packards, Eureka-Packards and Cunningham-Packards, but the Packards with the greatest impact on American funeral coach and ambulance history were indisputably the ones that wore the magic lamp medallion of the Henney Motor Company of Freeport, Illinois. After 1937, this was the only builder you could go to if you wanted a professional vehicle based on Packard's factory-engineered, long-wheelbase Commercial Chassis, and the cars that would be created under this exclusive arrangement epitomized a marriage of equals with their uncompromising quality and undisputed dignity. While both firms would be forced to leave the field together in 1954 as Cadillac assumed almost total control of the high-end hearse and ambulance market, for nearly 20 years the Henney-Packard pairing was the ultimate partnership between carmaker and coachbuilder, that competitors most admired, that customers most aspired to, and that vintage car collectors with an interest in professional vehicles would most revere in retrospect.

As third-generation funeral director James Broussard, president of Broussard's Mortuary in Beaumont, Texas, would recall in a 1990 letter to the PCS journal, *The Professional Car,* after acquiring a 1938 Henney-Packard hearse that was exactly like the one he had learned to drive on, "My dad was a Packard man from the get-go. His theory was that if you saw a black Cadillac you had to look at the nameplate in the window to know whose it was, but if you saw a blue Packard a mile away you knew it was Broussard's."

The story of the Henney-Packard alliance and its awe-inspiring achievements actually begins with John W. Henney Sr.'s 1868 establishment of a buggy building business in Cedarville, Illinois, which was ultimately moved 5 miles south to the larger town of Freeport in 1872. The surrounding region was already home to great numbers of extremely skilled Scandinavian immigrant

W. Rance Bennett collection, courtesy The Professional Car

Taken in an unknown location, this interesting photo of a circa 1910 Packard casket wagon from the collection of Lowell, Michigan, vintage hearse restorer W. Rance Bennett raises a lot more questions than it answers. The huge crowd surrounding the vehicle, not to mention the presence of a photographer beside the rear doors, indicates that the deceased was a person of importance. The double-panel wreath-type ornamentation on the body offers no firm clues as to a builder, and the curved casings ahead of the rear wheels suggest a chain-drive transmission, even though the Packard Model Thirty used a bevel gear differential.

craftsmen who found gainful employment in the area's many furniture and carriage factories, not to mention other noted Illinois hearse makers like the Eureka Company of Rock Falls, and the Rock Falls Manufacturing Company of Rock Falls and Sterling.

With success assured by its high standards and talented labor pool, Henney soon became one of the largest employers in Freeport, with its standing in the community symbolized by the block-square, five-story plant it erected at the intersection of South Chicago Avenue and Spring Street in 1888 (it still stands today, housing Honeywell's MicroSwitch Division). In the middle of 1916, by which time interest in its horse-drawn wagons had waned, Henney introduced its first motor-driven hearses and ambulances and managed to complete about 60 by year's end. While a number of the company's early coaches were mounted on a sturdy Velie long-wheelbase chassis manufactured in nearby Moline, Illinois, the vast majority of vehicles completed prior to 1933 employed a purpose-designed chassis of Henney's own manufacture, incorporating such similarly trustworthy components as Continental engines and Lockheed hydraulic four-wheel braking systems.

At the Professional Car Society's 2003 International Meet in Pittsburgh, Bill Alexander would assert with admiration that that the Continental straight eight-powered, limousine-style 1927 Henney combination coach he purchased in 1964 was "made for funeral processions. The fastest I ever drove it was a 48 mph out-of-gear down Paris Mountain in Virginia, but you could shift it into high at 10 mph and run it in a parade without changing gear or overheating. The radiator is solid bronze 4 1/2 inches thick." Under the leadership of a second-generation John W. Henney, the company also earned top honors in the 1928 evaluation of ambulance builders by the U.S. Bureau of Standards and, in spirited rivalry with Eureka, became an early pioner in the development of three-way-loading funeral cars.

While the Depression would compel virtually every funeral coach and ambulance builder to abandon the tradition of assembling their own chassis by the mid-1930s, Henney was not alone in having a hard time settling on the most suitable platform available from a mainstream automaker. Velie cars could no longer be employed as company founder Willard Lamb Velie and his son Willard Jr. had both died, but Henney bodies did find their way onto Chevrolet and Pontiac chassis. From 1931 through 1933, Freeport also teamed up with the National Casket Company of Boston to produce funeral coach and ambulance bodies (including some with town car-style

driver's compartments) for mounting on the beautifully streamlined Reo Royale chassis styled by Count Alexis de Sakhnoffsky. Straight-eight Oldsmobiles and Pierce-Arrows were also used by Henney, respectively, to build its Progress and Arrowline series professional cars from 1934 to 1937.

The missing piece of the puzzle finally fell into place when Packard, in concert with its 1935 introduction of a medium-priced One-Twenty Series, got serious about the funeral coach and ambulance market by debuting a 158-inch Commercial Chassis variant, officially designated 120A, that no longer had to be altered or extended by the purchasing coachbuilder. This platform, along with Senior Packard 1200A Eight and 1203A Super Eight Commercial Chassis, also introduced in 1935, found immediate acceptance with important funeral coach and ambulance builders such as Eureka, the A.J. Miller Company of Bellefontaine, Ohio, the Superior Body Company of Lima, Ohio, and the 97-year-old firm of James Cunningham, Son & Co. in Rochester, New York. But Henney was indisputably the biggest and most-enthusiastic customer.

Henney's affection for Packard automobiles was fully consummated on January 16, 1936, when the company secured an exclusive agreement (effective with the 1938 models) to be the sole consumer of Packard Commercial Chassis. Many years later, in 1953, A.J. Miller would assert in one of its brochures that it had refused an autumn, 1937 demand from Packard that "Miller must discontinue all use of all chassis other than Packard," but the bulk of evidence assembled by Henney-Packard authority and Professional Car Society co-founder George Hamlin suggest that the demand for exclusivity came from Henney instead. "It was the other way around," former Henney council William A. Alfs related to Hamlin when he was questioned about Miller's claims, elaborating "We had Packard under exclusive contract not to sell commercial chassis to any other body maker." Further confirmation came from industry competitor Willard Hess, the one-time company office boy who purchased Sayers & Scovill in partnership with Charles Eisenhardt in 1942, who added "Packard never gave us any ultimatum like that. Henney landed that agreement. We all thought that it was a real 10-strike for John Henney."

Thanks in large part to this exclusive alliance—which did not, interestingly, apply to Canadian coachbuilders like Brantford—Henney was likely America's largest professional car concern in the late 1930s, commanding an estimated one-third to 40 percent share of the total market. In the absence of firm prewar output figures, Hamlin estimated that the company produced approximately 1,300 vehicles in 1937, 800 units in the more economically distressed 1938 model year, 1,000 coaches in 1939, and another 1,200 cars apiece in 1940 and 1941. Henry Ford even took his final ride in a 1942 Henney-Packard when no Lincoln-chassied hearse could be located in the Detroit area for his April, 1947 funeral.

The company's position of leadership was further-bolstered by such professional car industry "firsts" as the Elecdraulic casket table debuted in 1936, the all-steel tops (initially a giant insert bolted against an angled rubber seal) and Leveldraulic side-to-side leveling system introduced in 1937, and the hydraulically-operated flower car deck, built-in "singing chapel" and air-conditioned ambulance that appeared in 1938. Still, in a stunning reversal of fortune, the much-envied partnership with Packard turned out to have a fatal double edge in the dramatically different postwar automotive marketplace. To start with, the Twentieth Series Packard Eight and One-Sixty platforms used by Henney to build its funeral cars and ambulances through 1942 were not continued after the war. Then chronic shortages of steel and other crucial materials forced the company to postpone production of its postwar models (with the exception of two Clipper-based prototypes and a contract to produce Twenty-First Series Clipper limousines and seven-passenger sedans) until the bathtub-themed Twenty-Second Series Packards bowed in mid-1947. The coaches Henney created from this platform were certainly attractive with their clean slab sides and height-accentuating extra row of grille bars, and 1,941 examples were built during the 1948 model year compared to 2,067 Commercial Chassis Cadillacs bodied by Eureka, Miller, Meteor, S&S, and Superior. But their momentum could not be sustained when there were five firms selling Cadillacs that touted annually refreshed styling and an up-to-date overhead-valve V-8 engine. By 1949 the professional car production score was Packard 380, Cadillac 1,861, and the spread was even wider in the 1950 model year.

As if there were already not enough changes and challenges to contend with, John W. Henney Jr. had sold his interest in the company founded by his father, retired to his home at Henney Farms, and died on November 27, 1946. Henney's new owner was the National Union Electric Corporation's Chairman C. Russell Feldmann, a colorful wheeler-dealer who had started out in business as an auto dealership office boy, made his fortune during the 1920s by buying, reorganizing, and reselling Winton

Engine, Victor Peninsular, and (oddly enough) Henney, and billed himself as "the man who first put radio into an automobile" after founding the Transitone Automobile Radio Corporation in 1928. One of the most important things to take place on his watch was the debut of entirely new, Twenty-Fourth Series Henney-Packards as 1952 models. Teaming wide C-pillars with wraparound rear quarter windows, a dramatically lowered exterior profile, and a significantly widened selection of interior colors and materials, veteran industrial designer Richard Arbib did a masterful job building on the basic body shape that John Reinhardt developed for Packard, and Henney's model year output climbed accordingly from 244 units in 1950 to 401 in 1951.

Cadillac, nevertheless, confirmed that Packard was nearly finished as a player in professional car circles, producing 2,052 Commercial Chassis in 1950 and 2,960 units in 1951, and the high hopes that Henney had for its Clipper-based, 127-inch-wheelbase Junior were dashed by its three-door body, relatively-short interior floor, and unsustainably low pricing. While the NFDA convention held in Washington, D.C., in the fall of 1953 featured an elaborate, eight-car "Henney Parade of Progress" exhibit anchored by an all-white 1954 ambulance and a matching horse-drawn hearse, Feldmann was being financially squeezed by a shareholder lawsuit related to his 1950 sale of the Newport Steel Corporation, his late 1953 purchase of the Eureka Williams electric firm, and his unsuccessful attempt to acquire Reo Motors in April, 1954.

Simply put, there was no money left to develop Henney bodies for the 1955 Packards with their wrap-around windshields, cathedral taillights, and torsion-bar suspensions, let alone any money that could be used to switch to the now-dominant Cadillac Commercial Chassis. After 120 Clipper Juniors and 205 longer-wheelbase Packard coaches were produced in 1954—another thirty chassis left at year's end were dismantled and returned to Packard—Feldmann announced the Freeport plant's closure on January 18, 1955, and subsequently had its essential tooling and personnel transferred to a Canastota, New York, plant where Oneida manufactured missile trailers and airport crash trucks and brokerage buses on the Marmon Herrington chassis. The grand old Henney name would see its final use on the Henney Kilowatt electric cars made with Renault Dauphine body shells at Eureka Williams' Bloomington, Illinois, plant between 1960 and 1964. Only 100 or so were built, with 58 of them sold to utility companies for promotional purposes.

American Funeral Director

Up-to-date limousine styling and a "startlingly low" price ensured that the A.J. Miller Model 102 on the 1926 Packard Six chassis would be a successful offering in funeral circles. The Bellefontaine, Ohio, firm also built a Nash-based Model 101.

George Hamlin collection

Adopting tire presses to fit its needs in 1927, A.J. Miller became the first funeral coach and ambulance body builder to stamp out its steel exterior panels using hydraulic presses. Prior to this, quarter panels and other curved sections were hammered or wrapped around corners in the body framework. This technology allowed the company's limousine-style Packard hearse, priced at $3,350 with a six-cylinder engine or $4,400 as a straight eight, to take on a less-boxy appearance in concert with a length-accentuating double beltline.

American Funeral Director

Countering the table-type "Side-Way Burial Coach" introduced by Eureka the year before, Indiana's Knightstown Body Company stressed that the "scientifically placed" ball-bearing rollers in the casket compartment of this 1927 Packard left "no track to jam at the critical moment." In addition to dispensing with the need for pallbearers to step into a muddy street while loading the casket, side servicing eliminated the gap between the hearse and the rest of the procession when they were parked outside the church or funeral home.

Even though the body frame comprised premium-quality seasoned white ash, it cost just $1,900 for the Eureka Company to take this 1928 Packard, lengthen the chassis, and fit one of its Model 40 DeLuxe Side-Way Burial Coach bodies. $1,650 bought the funeral director a Model 194 end-loading hearse with a back door, while ambulance coachwork sharing the same basic body shell sold for $1,950. Packard offered undeniable prestige to a mortician's motor fleet, but other makes like Buick, Nash, Studebaker, Reo, Lincoln, and Hudson also benefited from Eureka's skill during this period.

George Hamlin collection

Walt McCall collection

Superseded by a small block Standard Eight displacing 319.2 cubic inches, six-cylinder Packards went on an eight-year hiatus in 1929. A more modern appearance was afforded by chrome-plated trim and parabolic (as opposed to drum-shaped) headlights—both of which mated nicely with the two-tone paint and contrasting-color window surrounds on this A.J. Miller-bodied hearse used by the Petroshius Funeral Home of North Chicago, Illinois.

A 1930 Packard town car could impart prestige at a cemetery or hospital just as easily as it could at a polo field or country club. This Silver-Knightstown funeral coach (top) was built in Knightstown, Indiana. The A.J. Miller ambulance (bottom) is from Bellefontaine, Ohio. Twin fan belts and four-speed transmissions were notable technical improvements that year.

Thomas A. McPherson collection

George Hamlin collection

George Hamlin collection

With luxury car values in a free fall due to the Depression, a 1930 Seventh Series Packard made a promising foundation for this three-way loading funeral coach completed by Eureka in 1931. Arch-shaped flower trays, a walnut-finished casket table, and a slightly slanted windshield were among its many attractive features.

NAHC, Detroit Public Library

John Thomas Batts of Pasadena, California, completed this elaborate Art Deco hearse on a Seventh Series Packard chassis in 1932—most likely for a Central or South American country where flamboyant funeral vehicles were customary. The side panels flipped down to show off the glass-enclosed casket compartment, and the circular grille in the rear corner pillars could have been a speaker for recorded music. An aviation fixation is apparent in the rivet-covered trim, radically V-shaped windshield, and airplane hood mascot, while the rear door was adorned with a semicircular leaded glass rear window.

NAHC, Detroit Public Library

George Hamlin collection

Launched in July, 1932, the Eureka Chieftain series embraced emerging trends in streamlining with its fuller fenders, slanted windshield, and internal sun visors. This low-slung coachwork could be mounted on any chassis, but the Haley Funeral Home of Aurora, Illinois, opted for nothing less than a Ninth Series Packard Standard Eight in constructing this three-way limousine-style hearse.

The Tenth Series Packard Eights launched in January 1933 touted such significant refinements as a dual-downdraft Stromberg carburetor, three-point motor suspension, a lower-effort, single-plate clutch and an automatic choke. Even with the traditional tucked-under rear end on this limousine-style Miller hearse, the look was generally sleeker with an increased windshield slope, fully skirted fenders, and smaller 17-inch wire wheels.

George Hamlin collection

The V-shaped windshield on this magnificent 1933 A.J. Miller Packard town car hearse is complimented by a two-pane glass partition, suggesting it was hinged to allow side servicing in concert with forward-sliding front seats. The prominent beavertail, an option like Packard's steel disc wheels, could be fitted with a compartment for storing the church truck.

George Hamlin collection

In 1934, the Morris Funeral Service of Windsor, Ontario, commissioned a spectacular "Mobile Sanctuaire" on a 1931 Packard chassis from the Mitchell Hearse Company of Ingersoll, Ontario. Its all-aluminum light gray body was accented by black running gear and a solid walnut casket compartment with stained-glass windows, a Gothic-style beamed ceiling, and indirect lighting activated when the rear door was opened.

Walt McCall collection, courtesy Mary Little

Walt McCall collection

The Henney Motor Company of Freeport, Illinois, had earned many admirers with the funeral cars it had been building on its own assembled chassis since 1916, and the switch to outside-sourced chassis in the early 1930s hardly diminished its reputation—especially when the base vehicle was an Eleventh Series Packard Eight. Produced from August, 1933 to August, 1934, these were the first Packards specifically engineered for radios with a special dashboard, shielded wiring, and a heavy-duty generator.

George Hamlin collection

A.J. Miller modernized and re-popularized the carved hearse with its 1934 "Art" models. Bearing three beveled windows topped by a golden owner's initial in the center of a simple arch, this example, built on the new 1935 Packard 120A Commercial Chassis, highlights one of two basic variants offered by the Bellefontaine, Ohio, builder on a variety of chassis. "Art Carved" Millers had drapery-style carvings divided into three segments by vertical columns.

Photo by M. Bagby, courtesy Stuart R. Blond

In addition to retaining the rear-hinged front doors used on stock Packard 120s during 1935 only, this Miller-bodied ambulance built for Billups & Sons of Richmond, Virginia, was fitted with extra-wide #2 doors for enhanced patient compartment access.

George Hamlin collection

To ensure that its carved hearses had the largest and most elaborate panels in the industry, Eureka incorporated a pronounced rearward slope in the trailing edge of the driver's compartment doors. Furthermore, the draperies on this 160-inch-wheelbase 1935 Packard 1200 Series Eight were still carved from yellow poplar, as opposed to the stamped-steel or cast-aluminum panels being adopted by other coachbuilders.

The Grace Hospital in Detroit was the lucky recipient of this 1935 Eureka-Packard Princess ambulance on the 158-inch-wheelbase 120-A Commercial Chassis. Even though the Princess was Eureka's least expensive series, the patient compartment in the ambulance model offered a mirrored walnut medicine cabinet, an electric fan, and a pair of folding attendant's seats as standard equipment.

George Hamlin collection

Having been in business since 1838, it was no surprise that James Cunningham, Son & Co. of Rochester, New York, clung steadfastly to traditional carved funeral coaches and executed them with superb attention to detail. Distinguished by an elevated center arch, this hand-carved Cunningham model 355-A eight-column town car hearse was created on a 1935 Packard Super Eight Commercial Chassis for Drehmann-Harral of St. Louis, Missouri.

Bernie Weis collection

Prior to 1937, most professional cars built by Superior were Studebaker-based, so this 1935 Packard 120-A Commercial Chassis hearse built for the George J. Wetherholt & Sons Funeral Home of Gallipolis, Ohio, was extremely unusual. The wide #2 side door, allowing side servicing to be combined with a partition, was a distinguishing feature on Superiors in this period.

George Hamlin Collection

Apparently a straight end-loader, this 1935 Cunningham 361-A funeral coach constructed on the packard 120-A Commercial Chassis uses torch-style columns to divide its six carved drapery panels. The first owner of this lovely vehicle was Fred J. Lowe of Troy, New York.

Bernie Weis collection

The variety of styles catalogued by a true custom coachbuilder like Cunningham was emphasized by the subtle differences between the window-equipped model 365-A (left) and solid panel 367-A (right) flat-roof hearses it constructed on the Packard 120-A Commercial Chassis. The Rochester, New York, firm nevertheless discontinued funeral coach production in 1936.

Bernie Weis collection

George Hamlin of Clarksville, Maryland, has owned this Henney-bodied 1936 Packard 120-BA model 800 three-way hearse since 1967. It had originally been purchased in December, 1935, by J. Seth and Aubrey T. Richie of the Richie Brothers Funeral Home of Upper Marlboro, Maryland, where the paint was still polished regularly after its 1951 retirement.

George Hamlin collection

Fender skirts and a winter blind for the trademark Packard ox-yoke grille enhanced the purposeful looks of this 1936 Miller 120-BA funeral coach/ambulance combination, which also wears a bumper-mounted Federal Traffic Master Model Z siren.

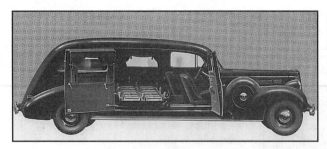

Beating Packard by a year, 1937 Henney professional cars had all-steel roofs, though the cost of dies ruled out a one-piece stamping in favor of a steel insert bolted into place against an angled rubber seal. The framework underneath remained air-and-kiln dried texture select hardwood as well. 1937 was also the first year that Henney Nu-3-Way hearses offered Leveldraulic, a lever-controlled electro-hydraulic device that kept the coach level from side-to-side during curbside loading and unloading.

Though the underlying framework was still seasoned Southern ash coated with oil and lead to deter rot, a one-piece stamped steel top was a notable addition to Eureka's 1937 Chieftains. It seemed the ideal time for the Derezinski Funeral Home to commission this three-way Packard hearse from a 4-year-old Series 1001 Eight. Disc wheels, metal side-mount covers, and squat proportions effectively de-emphasized the base vehicle's vintage.

George Hamlin collection

As Henney Packard professional cars were also built in Brantford, Ontario, it must have been a blow to company prestige when the Truscott Brothers Funeral Home in Brantford went to A.J. Miller for this 1937 model 120 art carved three-way funeral coach. The car is owned today by Neal Elliott of Mt. Brydges, Ontario.

George Hamlin collection

If "sporty" was a term that people normally applied to funeral vehicles, this coupe-style Silver-Knightstown flower car constructed from a 1937 Packard 120-CA by the Knightstown Body Company of Indiana would certainly qualify. Open well designs of this sort would ultimately become known as "Chicago" or "Western Style" flower cars. Vehicles with stainless-steel decks covering a casket compartment became known as "Eastern Style" flower cars.

Thomas A. McPherson collection

Impressive by any standard with its solid panel "Art Carved" body by A.J. Miller of Bellefontaine, Ohio, the Canton Classic Car Museum's 1937 Packard hearse truly stands out because it was built on a V-12 chassis with a gigantic 172-inch wheelbase. It was originally owned by a funeral home in Vermilion, Ohio, which also operated a matching 1937 Packard open well flower car that was also purchased by the Museum in the late 1970s. The company that created this vehicle from a standard wheelbase 1502 Super Eight sedan is unknown, though Silver-Knightstown is a likely candidate.

As purpose-designed flower cars started to replace tribute-filled phaetons and touring cars in the funeral procession, Henney trumped the competition with its 1938 Packard Model 886 "Combination Flower and Utility Car." In addition to a rear-hinged, adjustable stainless-steel deck that allowed bouquets and baskets to be arranged according to height, the body had an extra pair of doors for loading chairs or other equipment through the rear compartment sides and a drop-down tailgate for a casket or first-call cot.

From Stalin's Russia to Chiang Kai-shek's China, Packards could be found anyplace on the planet where prestige and stamina were desired in one vehicle. This spectacular glass-sided hearse, with an open driver's compartment and a rooftop flower rack, was used by Charles Kinsela, a long-established funeral firm in Sydney, Australia.

The builder of this British Packard funeral car is unconfirmed, but it could be Woodall Nicholson of Halifax or Thomas Startin of Birmingham. English four-door hearses were, and still are, typically outfitted as "Bearer's Coaches," where the pallbearers ride along with the casket. The "beavertail" rear, rooftop flower rack, and radiator-mounted cross were other interesting touches on this car.

Stuart R. Blond

A.J. Miller constructed this magnificent town car hearse in 1938 to show Packard what it was missing by giving all of its professional car business to Henney after 1937. It is reputed that John W. Henney expressed his displeasure by leaving 1939 Cadillac sketches in his office where his Packard liaison would not miss them. The survival of the intricate woodcarvings on this one-off coach, now owned by Marietta, Ohio, funeral director William Peoples, is all the more amazing since it ended up hauling chickens on a ranch in Mexico before returning to the U.S. for a West Coast restoration in the early 1980s.

Henney was the only major coachbuilder that did not catalog a carved panel hearse during the late 1930s, opting instead to offer a so-called "Formal Limousine" with cast-aluminum plaques bearing the owner's name on the side and rear doors. These were complemented by crinkle-finish backgrounds, decorative trim above the windows, and a matching Art Deco pattern for the interior woodwork. This first-year 1938 Nu-3-Way model, owned by Struthers, Ohio, funeral director Dan Becker, also features an electric casket table and Leveldraulic side-to-side suspension leveling.

Walt McCall collection

In November, 1961, Walt McCall paid just $350 to purchase this Brantford-built 1939 Henney Formal Limousine hearse off a farm implement dealer's lot. This coach was originally owned by the Jahnke-Greenwood Funeral Home in Chatham, Ontario, and later sold to the Addison Funeral Home in Otterville, Ontario.

Walt McCall collection

Still used for services upon special request at his Chapel of Memories in Moses Lake, Washington, Jerry W. Kayser's 1939 Henney-Packard Nu-3-Way Funeral Coach has double-sided name plates to enhance casket presentation. This original and unrestored car, showing less than 40,000 miles on the odometer, also went to British Columbia to appear in the movie *Snow Falling on Cedars*.

Jerry W. Kayser

Winner of the Best-of-Show award at the Professional Car Society's 1996 International Meet in St. Paul, Wayne Kempfert's 1939 Henney-Packard 120 ambulance originally served in Minnesota's Iron Range at the Erie Mining Company in Taconite Harbor. After sitting at an Aurora, Minnesota, gas station for nearly 30 years, this rig was rescued from further deterioration in the fall of 1992.

Stuart R. Blond

It is estimated that Henney produced 1,000 Packard professional cars on the 1701A Eight and 1703A Super Eight commercial chassis during the 1939 model year—enough for a solid one-third share of the entire market. As if its funeral coaches and ambulances were not impressive enough, the firm's Freeport, Illinois, factory also created this airport limousine for American Airlines. Interesting details include the bullet-shaped corner lights, the plethora of rooftop vents, and the protective trim on the rear fenders.

Stuart R. Blond

Two years before Packard introduced mechanical refrigeration on its 1940 models, Henney had delivered the world's first air-conditioned ambulance to the Kreidler Funeral Home in McAllen, Texas. The technology made perfect sense for these delivery vehicles used by the upscale San Francisco florist Podesta & Baldocchi. The cars were basically identical to Henney's 14095 first-call/service cars on the 1803-A One Sixty Commercial Chassis.

Walt McCall collection

Designated a 4098, 4198, or 4298 depending on the model year, Henney Packard's side-servicing Landaulet funeral coach resembled an oversized four-door convertible with its fabric-covered roof, sloping tail, and elongated, thinly framed side windows. For added impact, a town car version with a vertically hinged two-piece partition was also offered. Equipped with Leveldraulic and a "Singing Chapel on Wheels," this 1941 example built on the 1803-A One Sixty chassis belongs to Mike Burkhart of Dodge City, Kansas.

Dwight Heinmuller collection

With an "envelope" body designed by Howard "Dutch" Darrin that was a foot wider than it was high, the Packard Clipper proved to be a great commercial and aesthetic success when it went on sale in April, 1941. Only a few one-off funeral cars got to take advantage of the Clipper's attractive lines. One was this 1942 model with a traditional rooftop cross that was used by Raoul Alian of St. Raymond, Portneuf County, Quebec. The body builder was evidently John J.C. Little of Ingersoll, Ontario.

The Twentieth Series Packard Eight and One-Sixty platforms used by Henney to build its 1942 model funeral cars and ambulances were not available after World War II, so the company constructed one funeral coach and one ambulance prototype from various pre- and-postwar Custom Clipper parts. Accompanied by the headline "Worth Waiting For," an "unretouched" photo of the hearse shot directly from the front appeared in a January, 1946 American Funeral Director advertisement, but continuing shortages of steel and other essential components compelled Henney to postpone production of its postwar professional cars until the bathtub-themed Twenty-Second Series Packards bowed in mid-1947.

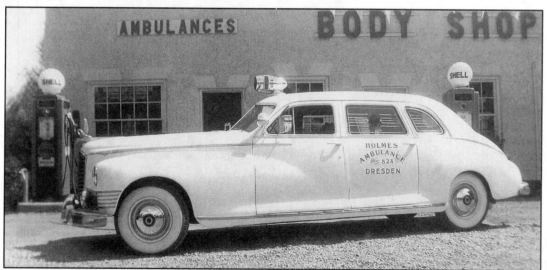

Until funeral coach and ambulance production resumed with the Twenty-Second Series Packards, Henney kept its Freeport, Illinois, plant busy by securing the contract to produce Twenty-First Series Clipper limousines and seven-passenger sedans on the 148-inch-wheelbase chassis. Some were converted into sedan ambulances with removable passenger-side center pillars and right front seats for admitting a stretcher, with John J.C. Little creating this example for Holmes Ambulance of Dresden, Ontario.

237

Weller Brothers of Memphis extended the wheelbase of a Packard Clipper sedan to create this attractive funeral coach/ambulance combination. Relying on rubber feet to keep the attendant's seat from moving around may seem precarious by modern standards, but Henney used the same approach in its combinations.

Appearing more than a year before the first postwar-styled professional Cadillacs in the summer of 1947, the Twenty-Second Series Henney-Packards were the most successful in Freeport's history with 1,941 built on the 156-inch-wheelbase Custom Eight commercial chassis during the 1948 model year. This model 14894 ambulance, last used in Santa Rosa, New Mexico, in the early 1970s, had "a couple of hundred critters living in it" when Mark P. Wilson of Ray Township, Michigan, found it in an Arkansas field in 1997. He had to buy a second 1948 ambulance from a Milwaukee junkyard for the parts needed to complete his award-winning restoration.

George Hamlin collection

With the possible exception of the panel truck-style service car, the rarest Twenty-Second Series Henney-Packard was the flower car with its rear-hinged, hydraulically adjusted stainless steel tray for arranging tributes in differently-sized banks. Having maintained a registry of 22nd/23rd Series flower car serial numbers, Rochester Hills, Michigan, PCS member Dale Cole made the surprising discovery that the bodies were apparently run off all at once and installed on a chassis when ordered.

Bernie Weis photo

This 1948 Henney-Packard shows how U.S. Army ambulances were built to a unique government specification. A rooftop ventilator was fitted, and the side doors were deleted to allow full-length folding benches that could carry up to 10 seated casualties or two reclined patients.

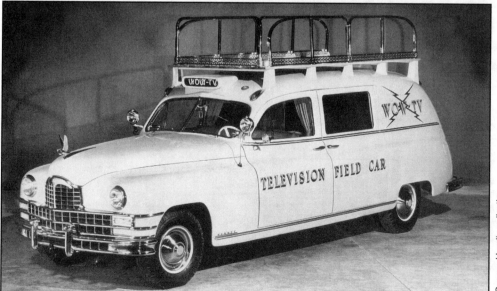

George Hamlin collection

A 1948 Henney-Packard model 14800-L landau funeral coach body served as the basis for this mobile television studio built for WOW-TV of Omaha, Nebraska.

The lack of vertical grille bars identifies Wayne and Olga Hogrefe's Briggs-built 1948 Packard seven-passenger sedan from Lorain, Ohio, as a Series 2222 Super Eight. It has the 141-inch wheelbase and the five-bearing, 327-cubic inch straight eight. Other variants included a six-cylinder, 141-inch-wheelbase Series 2280 targeted at the New York taxi market, and a 2226 Custom Eight combining an extra-long 148-inch wheelbase with the nine-bearing, 356-cubic inch straight eight.

Henney-Packard production fell precipitously in 1948 after Miller, Meteor, Eureka, Superior, and S&S debuted postwar Cadillac professional cars with tailfins and modern overhead-valve V-8s. The dignity, quality, and exclusivity of Henney's landau hearse was nevertheless undisputable. In 1949, this top-of-the-line three-way with Leveldraulic and Elecdraulic sold for $7,022.

American Funeral Director

George Hamlin collection

The Twenty-Third Series Packards, launched in May, 1949, to celebrate the company's Golden Anniversary, maintained the inverted bathtub theme, but added filled-in front bumper centers and shorter upper grille extensions that allowed full-length body-side moldings with traditional barbed ends. This 1950 Henney model 15096 flower car, owned by George Hamlin since October, 1990, was one of at least a dozen professional Packards acquired on the cheap by Hancock, Maryland, enthusiast Alvin Bain.

This view of the Twenty-Fouth Series 1951 Henney-Packard combination delivered to the Michael J. Colligan Funeral Home of Hamilton, Ohio, emphasizes the wrap-around rear quarter windows and their easily removed ambulance grilles. While the front bumper, grille, and windshield were shared with the Patrician 400, professional cars were now considered part of Packard's 300 line and, with the exception of the final 1954 models, used the five-main bearing version of the 327-cubic inch "Thunderbolt" straight eight engine.

Out of 320 Packards built by Henney on the Twenty-Fifth Series Commercial Chassis during 1952, it's a safe bet that only a handful were model 5296 flower cars. The airy, hardtop-style roofline introduced the previous year continued to turn heads in concert with the stainless steel deck and simulated tonneau cover, so appearance changes were limited to a sleeker-looking Cormorant and the replacement of the PACKARD block letters on the hood with a medallion in the upper grille surround.

Landau hearses like this 1952 Nu-3-Way model were the only Arbib-designed Henney-Packards that didn't have wraparound quarter windows. An Elecdraulic casket table combined with Leveldraulic side-to-side suspension balancing insured that the pallbearers could perform their duties with dignity.

To combat competition from Economy, Barnette, and other budget-price professional car builders, Henney launched an unaltered 127-inch-wheelbase commercial Clipper called the Junior in 1953. Cranbury, New Jersey, funeral director Mahlon Thompson's example is equipped as a combination service car and ambulance.

The 166 Henney-Packards built on the longer 2613 Commercial Chassis during the 1953 model year added stainless-steel trim from the Cavalier series that followed the front wheel opening. Other changes on the so-called 26th Series, represented by Maurice Baier's flower car from Paxton, Illinois, included a more imposing double-bar bumper, four-barrel carburetion, and power steering.

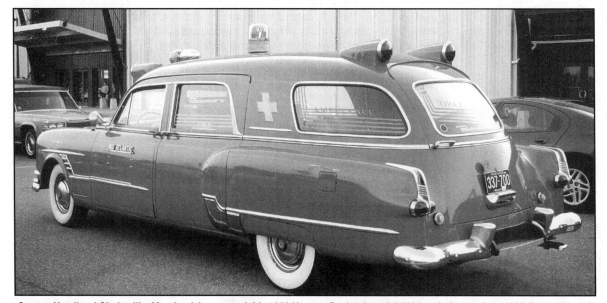

George Hamlin of Clarksville, Maryland, has owned this 1953 Henney-Packard model 5394 ambulance since 1969. It was the only 1953 example completed with rear tunnel lights. With its three-on-the-tree transmission retrofitted with overdrive, this car has logged an impressive number of miles attending Packard and Professional Car Society events.

Packard re-asserted its prestige by returning to the long-wheelbase market in the 1953 model year, teaming with Henney to produce 100 "Executive Sedans" and 50 "Corporation Limousines" on a 149-inch-wheelbase 26th Series chassis powered by the nine-bearing 327 engine. This dark blue example, owned by Mike Satterthwaite of Huntingdon Valley, Pennsylvania, was one of six originally purchased by the U.S. government as a Secret Service escort vehicle. It was, accordingly, a "stripper"—no radio, no power assist for the steering, brakes or windows, and a column-mounted three-speed manual gearbox in place of the more commonly seen Ultramatic. After spending time in a St. Louis museum, this car participated in the Reagan, Bush I, and Clinton inaugural parades.

George Hamlin collection

As Henney had already built a fleet of White House Lincoln Cosmopolitans and the 1952 Packard Pan American show car, company owner Charles Russell Feldmann investigated the custom car business as his hearse and ambulance output diminished. This 12-seat Super Station Wagon was realized as a prototype mixing 1953 and 1954 exterior trim. In addition to two second-row jump seats, a full-width third-row bench seat and a rear-facing double bench upholstered in two-tone blue leather, the car featured air conditioning, turquoise wool chenille carpeting and a fitted beverage cabinet. Packard nixed the idea on the grounds that the chassis would be overloaded. Sadly, this unique vehicle was torched and destroyed by vandals during the winter of 1962-63.

Hooded headlights, better-looking body-side moldings, and a switch to the nine-bearing straight-eight engine were welcome changes to the 1954 Henney-Packards. Still, Charles Feldmann's business empire was in trouble. The Freeport plant's permanent closure was announced on January 18, 1955, but the Henney Kilowatt name would be applied to an estimated 100 battery-powered Renault Dauphines built by Feldmann's Eureka-Williams Company from 1960-64.

Three decades after Henney built its last Packards, Bud Bayliff of the Bayliff Coach Corporation of Lima, Ohio, created a pair of Packard-inspired professional cars for the Long & Folk Funeral Homes of St. Mary's and Wapakoneta, Ohio. Both cars, respectively completed in 1987 and 1988, and believed to be the last funeral coach/ambulance combinations ever built, were based on front-wheel-drive 1985 Buick Rivieras. The first car completed was sold to Jim Tighe of Xenia, Ohio, in 1999, while the second car shown here was purchased by Patrick Martin of Palatine, Illinois, in November, 2002.

Chapter 9

Pontiac/GMC

It has been more than 15 years since the Toronto-built Eureka Chieftain ended its reign as the last commercial-sized Pontiac funeral coach, and almost 30 years since the last Pontiac ambulances and combinations were constructed by Superior, yet the make that made its way into our hearts with Silver Streaks and Wide-Track Wheels can still legitimately claim to be the most successful medium-priced professional car platform of all time. When you really get down to it, the chief reason why you rarely see an ambulance or hearse based on a Chevrolet, Ford, Mercury, Plymouth, or Dodge passenger car chassis is that the coach-built Pontiac offerings were so consistently varied, stylish, and capable.

Originally debuted at the 1926 National Automobile Show in New York City, the $825 Pontiac "light six" was designed to bridge the $330 price gap between Chevrolet and Oldsmobile and give struggling Oakland dealers a lower-cost car to sell (the name was certainly appropriate as the first 1907 Oaklands had been built by the Pontiac Buggy Company). It would end up making history as the only General Motors brand to set a first-year sales record and the only company "companion" car, in contrast to Cadillac's LaSalle, Buick's Marquette, and the similarly short-lived Viking offered by Oldsmobile, that proved successful enough to replace its parent entirely.

Only a couple of years would elapse before extended-wheelbase professional Pontiacs began to appear outside hospitals and funeral parlors in the United States and Canada. The Henney Motor Company of Freeport, Illinois, was evidently the first to body a six-cylinder version in 1929. The complex horizontal-valve V-8 model inherited from Oakland was employed for at least one 1932 ambulance by Superior Body of Lima, Ohio, and the Gardner line offered by the St. Louis Coffin Company at a $2,485 base price that included such niceties as seasoned oak body framing, Packard Blue mohair upholstery, and walnut flower trays. Pontiac would really hit its stride as a professional car platform after the division's first side-valve straight-eight engine

Walt McCall collection

Instead of using its own in-house assembled chassis powered by a Continental straight eight, the Henney Motor Company of Freeport, Illinois, employed a 6-28 New Series 1929 Pontiac for this limousine-style hearse used in Hamilton, Ontario, for many years. Pontiac's new heavier-duty Jaxon 10-spoke artillery wheels held up better in the long run than the spare tire well, which had rusted through by the time this car emerged from storage in 1962.

bowed in 1933, earning an enviable reputation over the next 21 years for smoothness, indestructibility, and surprising economy. Such attributes would, of course, make it an ideal power plant for cost-conscious funeral and livery service operators.

Surviving factory photos confirm that the Eureka Company of Rock Falls, Illinois, built an unknown number of straight-eight Pontiac funeral cars to order in 1934 and 1935, and the Flxible Company complemented its costlier, better-known Buick coaches with an impressive prewar output of Pontiacs, completing 12 examples in 1933, 50 in 1934, 78 in 1935 (including seven special three-door ambulances for the U.S. Navy) and 14 in 1936. Though they would end up being Flxible's penultimate Pontiacs, the 1935 models did introduce the raised hood and cowl lines that would become the Loudonville, Ohio, builder's chief distinguishing trademark through the 1948 model year.

Since 1925, the Superior Body Company of Lima, Ohio, renamed the Superior Coach Corporation in 1940, had grown into one of America's biggest coachbuilders by producing funeral cars and ambulances for the 3,000-outlet Studebaker dealer network, but the professional Pontiacs it launched in 1936 would play a crucial role in its establishment of an independent distributor organization initially consisting of 42 dealers. Touting such functional inducements as extra-wide #2 side door openings that could be fitted with a relatively inexpensive "Sidroll" casket loading system using angled rollers, the first models sold were based on an extended Pontiac Master Six chassis that, just like its larger straight-eight siblings, was "built to last 100,000 miles." The Master Sixes offered plenty of torque and flexibility at lower speeds (it was possible, for example, to leave the transmission in third gear down to 15 mph, a valuable attribute in a slow-moving funeral procession). These cars proved so successful that Superior expanded its 1937 Pontiac line with straight eight-powered coaches in two trim levels and, in spite of all that had been achieved through its alliance with South Bend, retired its Studebaker offerings entirely for the 1938 model year.

While the Superior- Pontiacs would, in 1948, go on a 5-year hiatus as the company focused its attention on the all-new postwar Cadillac Commercial Chassis, the 1949 debut of an inexpensive Streamliner sedan delivery (priced from just $1,749 as a Six or $1,817 as an Eight) insured that Pontiac would remain the industry's most popular platform for low-cost professional cars. By the early 1950s, there were many firms in North America cutting and stretching, or at least outfitting the interior, of these easily altered, entirely steel-bodied vehicles for funeral or ambulance service. The users ranged from such long-established builders as Eureka and Meteor to newer ventures, like the National Body Manufacturing Company of Knightstown, Indiana, the Acme Motor Company of Sterling, Illinois, the tiny, but versatile, workshop of John J.C. Little in Ingersoll, Ontario (often working with the interesting, Chevrolet-influenced Canadian Pontiacs), and the half-dozen different concerns centered around Memphis. This latter group included Guy Barnette & Company; Weller Brothers; Economy Coach, which renamed itself the Memphis Coach Company in 1955 and began to call its cars the "Memphian" line; the Comet Coach Company, which moved to Blytheville, Arkansas in 1959 and ultimately focused on Cotner-Bevington Oldsmobiles; and Pinner Coach, a relative latecomer to the group that established its first factory in Olive Branch, Mississippi in 1960.

Though the cost and effort involved with creating a Pontiac professional car increased considerably after U.S. market sales of the sedan delivery were discontinued in 1953, these firms maintained an impressive pace of sales as times were good and the Pontiacs were getting even better. As was the case with Chevrolet, the 1955 model year witnessed Pontiac's debut of a modern, overhead-valve V-8 dubbed the Strato-Streak, and the styling also got a lot flashier after 43-year-old Bunkie Knudsen came on board as the division's youngest-ever general manager. Even then, in spite of the excesses that the era was notorious for, Pontiac saw relatively few missteps compared to some other makes with the 1958 models, for example, being considerably more tasteful than a Buick or Olds from the same model year.

As was the case prior to World War II, the coachbuilder that gained the most from Pontiac's ascension was Superior Coaches, which celebrated the 30th anniversary of its 1923 founding by debuting a new generation of Pontiac professional cars at the NFDA's October, 1952 convention. Where the 1936-48 models had been built alongside the company's Cadillacs at the East Kibby Street facility in Lima, the 1953-up versions took advantage of less-expensive labor by being constructed at the "Southern Division" plant Superior dedicated in Kosciusko, Mississippi in 1951 to manufacture school busses and knocked-down transit buses for export to 62 different countries. Helped by the potent competitive advantage of being the only coachbuilder that Pontiac provided with a purpose-designed, standard-wheelbase chassis/cowl unit with a heavy-duty convertible frame, Superior ramped up Pontiac output fairly quickly from just 34 units in 1953, to 195 the following model year, 273 in 1955, and 356 during 1957.

Criterion-styled Superior-Pontiacs with hardtop-style pillars, wedge-shaped corner windows and arching roofs that could be fitted with "Super Headroom" fiberglass caps, appeared a year after the Cadillac versions in 1958, and the dynamic new profile worked especially well with the split grille, twin fin fenders and Wide Track stance (good for patient comfort as well as handling, when it came to ambulances and combination coaches) adopted by the considerably longer and lower 1959 Pontiacs. Paralleling Pontiac's leap to third place in total industry sales in 1961, Superior entered the fast growing "compact" coach market with a standard-wheelbase Consort that attracted 132 customers in its first year, thanks to a Pontiac-furnished, heavy-duty platform, and an attractive-looking, high-top roof that featured wide D-pillars and convertible-style chamfering for an entirely distinct appearance in comparison to the extended-wheelbase Criterions. With their pronounced Coke-bottle contours and all-new rooflines touting an extra-tall commercial glass windshield, the 1965 model Superior-Pontiacs were the most-popular of all with an even 500 produced at Kosciusko, out of which a record 210 units were standard-wheelbase Consorts.

All good things must come to an end, and Superior-Pontiac production endured a particularly severe contraction in the late 1960s and early 1970s, primarily because the majority of cars completed on this chassis were combination coaches that could never offer as much patient or equipment space as the emerging generation of truck-based emergency vehicles. After the Sheller-Globe auto parts conglomerate acquired Superior in 1969, the company's professional car production was consolidated at the Lima plant and total Pontiac output fell precipitously from 420 units in 1966 (of which 150 were Consorts), to 350 cars in 1970 (100 of them Consorts), and 240 examples of both models during the Consort's final year in 1973. Once this standard-wheelbase coach was gone, the Pontiac tally shrank again to 113 units in 1974 and just 60 units for the final run of Pontiacs in 1975.

With customer expectations and government specifications ruling out new car-based ambulances and combination coaches, an entire decade would elapse before the Eureka Coach Company Ltd. of Concord, Ontario, decided to expand its line of commercial-glass Cadillac, Buick, and Oldsmobile funeral coaches with a conceptually similar Pontiac Chieftain hearse. Attractive as it was, it did not get to stay on sale for very long, as the rear-wheel-drive Parisienne used to build it was discontinued at the end of the 1986 model year.

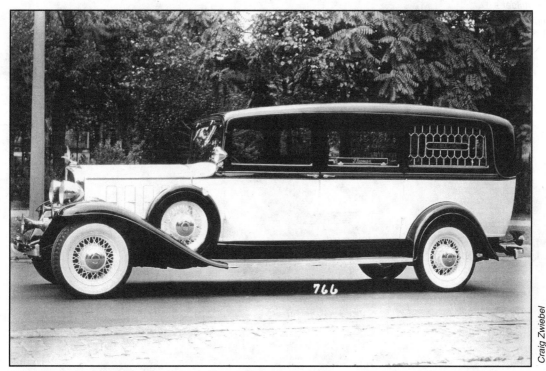

Most early 1930s Superior professional cars were built from Studebakers, but there were exceptions. This eye-catching two-tone ambulance was created for the Fleeman Funeral Home of St. Joseph, Missouri, from a 1932 Pontiac Series 302. Derived from the V-8 Oakland discontinued in 1931, this model proved costly to produce and was replaced by a simpler straight eight after a single season.

Pontiac styling hit a new high note when Franklin Q. Hershey initiated a two-week crash redesign of the 1933 models, heralding the division's smooth and tough new 233-cubic inch "Economy Eight" inline engine with an elongated hood and eyelash-like streaks for the skirted fenders. A 7-inch-longer hood with horizontal louvers and a shorter cowl further improved the car's lines for 1934. This Princess series funeral coach was constructed by the Eureka Company.

Thomas A. McPherson collection

In addition to one-piece stamped steel "Turret" tops, the 1935 Flxible-Pontiacs added raised hood and cowl assemblies that were 5 5/8 inches taller-than-stock in order to blend more smoothly with the bodywork. With raised headlight brackets added the following year, this would be the Loudonville, Ohio, builder's dominant design feature through the 1948 models.

Thomas A. McPherson collection

Moby's Eureka Autos

Pontiac funeral cars and ambulances, initially mounted on an extended Master Six chassis offering 80-horsepower from 208-cubic inches, were added to Superior's model line for 1936. Excepting a 1949-52 hiatus and the occasional Buick, LaSalle, Studebaker or Chrysler, Pontiacs would serve beneath Cadillac as the cheaper rung on Superior's two-step product ladder for the next 39 model years. While the slanted tail dictated prominent rear door hinges, the extra-wide 52.5-inch side doors proved an effective and distinctive way to combine a driver's compartment partition with Sidroll side servicing.

Six- and eight-cylinder Superior Pontiac professional cars were available for 1937, and both engines touted increases in displacement and horsepower. The top-of-the-line DeLuxe Eight Graceland hearse, Benevolent ambulance, and Woodlawn service car had restyled front ends like those on S&S Buicks, with Superior badges taking the place of the Pontiac Indian Heads on the bumpers, and thin horizontal slots topped by a new hood ornament supplanting the Silver Streaks.

Thomas A. McPherson collection

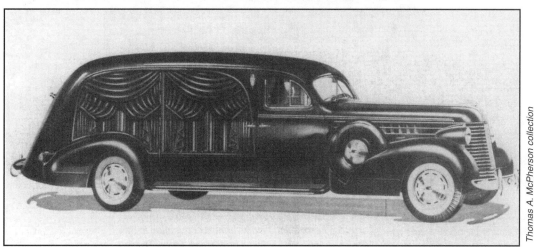

One year after Pontiac finished phasing out wood framing, Superior's 1938 models became the first professional cars in the industry with all-steel welded bodies. In addition to reducing cost, an issue also reflected in the switch to standard Pontiac grilles and hubcaps for 1938, this construction method did away with glued joints that tended to loosen and squeak over time.

Thomas A. McPherson collection

To hold its starting price to $1,795, this 1939 Superior Pontiac Rosehill service car had a three-door body and a six-cylinder engine. This incredibly well-preserved example was still riding on three of its original tires when it was purchased by Pittsburgh PCS member John Ehmer in 1995.

Growing up in Imperial, Pennsylvania, John Ehmer got to drive his 1940 Superior Pontiac straight-eight combination (used by the A.G. Armour Funeral Home until the mid-1960s) for the first time as a 12-year-old, though it was only from the apron to the service bay of the local garage at inspection time. Ehmer's chance to buy the well-preserved, 39,000-mile coach from Bock & Waters Pontiac came in 1985.

The Professional Car

Thomas A. McPherson collection

Ten years after Eureka introduced the basic style, Superior added a landau to its 1941 Pontiac line. It was initially regarded as a $300 appearance option, instead of a separate model. Since a painted roof was used instead of leather padding, the look worked best with two-tone color schemes.

Despite the war clouds looming as the National Funeral Directors Association held its annual convention in St. Louis in October 1941, Superior featured 15 major enhancements on its 1942 Pontiac professional cars. These included semi-concealed running boards, 5-inch-wider front seats with improved padding, a higher rear door opening, more rear compartment headroom, concealed interior trim fasteners, a full-width tool compartment behind the driver's seat, easier-working door locks, and stronger hinges with improved safety checks. The last new Pontiacs for 31 months were completed on February 10, 1942.

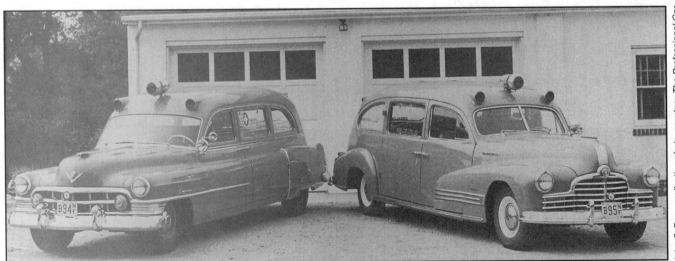

John C. Bauer collection photo, courtesy The Professional Car

Once civilian car production finally resumed, the Brick Township, New Jersey, First Aid Squad became one of the lucky early recipients of a 1946 Superior Pontiac ambulance that was eventually teamed with a 1950 Superior Cadillac. The "NF" suffix on the consecutively numbered license plates means "No Fee," a courtesy extended to non-profit organizations by the state Division of Motor Vehicles. Prices had inflated nearly two-fold since Pearl Harbor, with the 1946 Superior-Pontiacs retailing for $4,035-$4,290 versus $2,295-$2,495 for the equivalent 1942 eights.

Leon Allen collection photo, courtesy Nick Bliss

When he was 19 or 20 years old, Leon Allen of Bunker Hill, Indiana, posed with the maroon-over-off-white 1948 Superior Pontiac ambulance that the Jordan Funeral Home usually stationed behind Grandstand B at the Indianapolis Speedway during the annual 500 race. "At the track we were allowed to take our coats off," Allen recalled. "Otherwise you had better never be caught without (a) white shirt, tie and suit coat on."

Walt McCall collection

In Canada, Pontiac had displaced Plymouth as the No. 3 best-selling make in 1948, and the Fleetlander and Fleetlander DeLuxe names used through 1953 denoted Chevrolet bodies with the Pontiac 239.2-cubic inch L-head six. When an automatic transmission arrived in 1951, it was Powerglide instead of Hydra-Matic. In Ingersoll, Ontario, John J.C. Little was demonstrating his skill on an impressive array of one-off professional cars, with one of his most-distinctive postwar creations being this 1949 Pontiac (completed in 1950 and registered as a 1950 model) with external wooden drapes for the Armstrong Funeral Home in Oshawa, Ontario.

Steve Lichtman collection

With an 85.75-inch-long cargo floor that could fit a 7-foot stretcher, even a standard-wheelbase 1950 Pontiac sedan delivery could make a viable rescue vehicle. This Barnette ambulance used was in Prince George's County, Maryland, by Company 23 of the Forestville Volunteer Fire Department. Aside from a modest restyling where the front end added wraparound trim and five toothy horizontal bars to the grille, the 1950 Pontiac straight eight was bored out to 268.4 cubic inches to increase horsepower from 104 to 108.

251

Partners in a body shop at in Sterling, Illinois, F. J. "Fran" Cullins and Don Schultz might have been inspired by the Eureka Company across the river in Rock Falls when they established the Acme Motor Company in 1950. Their handiwork, easily identified by the nameplate on the rear corners of the hood, entailed a 36.5-inch stretch of an eight-cylinder Pontiac Model 2571 Sedan Delivery.

The Professional Car

Having already made its mark as a low-cost combination coach producer, the Meteor Motor Car Company of Piqua, Ohio, was one of the long-established firms taking on the up-and-coming Memphians with low-cost Pontiacs in 1951. In addition to this end-loading limousine hearse available on both the Series 25 Six and Series 27 eight-cylinder chassis, the company also catalogued a landau hearse, a service car, and a flower car.

American Funeral Director

American Funeral Director

As Meteor had introduced a Pontiac flower car the year before, the National Body Manufacturing Company of Knightstown, Indiana, was technically incorrect in billing its 1951 Pontiac Imperial as "the first flower car in the low-price field." But it was still an attractive vehicle with its extended wheelbase, whitewall tires, DeLuxe trim, concealed rear door releases, and simulated convertible top boot.

Mary Little

Sharing sheet metal and their 115-inch wheelbases with Chevrolets, 1951 model Canadian Pontiacs were more Spartan than their U.S. counterparts. This did not deter John J.C. Little from using one to create this classy three-way landau hearse at his small Shell station and body shop in Ingersoll, Ontario. Employing hand tools and a couple of trusted assistants, it would have taken him just three months to complete a coach like this, with the landau irons, torches and other decorative hardware cast to his specifications at the small Hahn Brass foundry in New Hamburg, Ontario.

Guy Barnette & Company claimed its 1951 Pontiac had a 3.5-inch-higher roof than any other funeral car in its field. Sporting an illuminated hood ornament, this rust-free three-door Landau combination from Arkansas was put on sale by Sheldon Weaver of Woodbury, Pennsylvania, in 1999.

American Funeral Director

DE LUXE LANDAU FUNERAL CAR

Handed a Korean War-related quota limiting its share of the U.S. light truck market, Pontiac produced only 984 sedan deliveries in 1952 compared to 1,832 units in 1951 and 2,158 in 1950. Quite a few still ended up as ambulances and funeral cars, with the National Body Manufacturing Company of Knightstown, Indiana, putting Pontiac's new double-tiered side trim to good use on this DeLuxe Landau hearse.

Dr. David Richards

Topping a stylish, but value-priced, product line that also included a standard-wheelbase Ambulette and an 18-inch extended-wheelbase Midway, this all-white 30-inch extended-wheelbase 1952 National Pontiac Imperial ambulance was constructed for the White Pine Copper Mining Company in Michigan's Upper Peninsula to service the small hospital it had built for the community. David L. Richards D.D.S. of Bloomfield Hills, Michigan, became the owner of this outstanding professional car in 1995.

Thomas A. McPherson collection

Celebrating its 30th anniversary in 1953, Superior debuted its first Pontiac professional cars since 1948. It employed a purpose-designed Pontiac heavy-duty eight-cylinder chassis/cowl unit extended to a 150-inch wheelbase and 230 11/16-inch overall length. This landau hearse shared many styling elements with the Superior-Cadillacs, including vertical vents on the rear fender and a body-colored sail panel surrounded by C-shaped trim.

254

STYLE 1700

In addition to a one-piece windshield and a 2-inch-longer wheelbase, 1953 Pontiacs promised better handling with the help of an all-new "Curve Control" front suspension. Saginaw-supplied power steering also became a $177.40 option, and it was worth every penny in professional car applications like this straight-eight Style 1700 Master Limousine Combination from Economy Coach of Memphis, Tennessee. With the wheelbase stretched 32 inches over stock to 154 inches, the rear floor measured 102 inches between the back door and the driver's compartment partitian.

STYLE 800

Claiming it invented the "triple service" concept early in 1950, Economy Coach pitched its Style 800 Junior Combination as a "secondary unit" effecting "great savings on operation of more expensive equipment." By deleting the partition and one of the folding attendants' seats found on larger models, the 24-inch-wheelbase stretch to 146 inches overall created a 104-inch-long floor and a 96 inch cargo space at window level, which was enough to fit a rough box for a casket.

THE ALL NEW 1953 BARNETTE LANDAU (Pontiac Chassis)

PRECISION BUILT

In presenting this chic, practical line . . . the ALL NEW Barnette Landau . . . we give you such outstanding features as: One piece top with far superior lines • new, longer wheelbase for greater roadability and comfort • new, one piece windshield with horizon vision • greater number of accessories as standard equipment • more gleaming chrome • outstanding trim selections • advance designing • built for service to you.

Barnette-bodied Pontiacs were promoted as the largest on the market with their 156-inch wheelbases and 239-inch overall lengths (Meteor and Economy coaches, by comparison, were 233 inches long while Superior-Pontiacs measured 230 and 11/16 inches), but a partition-mounted spare tire meant the 109-inch casket floor was only 3 inches longer than Superior's. The 1953 models still offered plenty of improvements, however, including a wider rear door and greater seat adjustment.

American Funeral Director

255

In December 1953, Meteor Motor Car announced that it was delegating construction of its Pontiac professional cars to Economy Coach of Memphis, Tennessee. While a new carburetor gave the 21-year-old straight eight a final horsepower boost to 122 with synchromesh, or 127 with Dual Range Hydramatic, 1954 Pontiacs would be best remembered as the first cars in the industry with totally under-hood air-conditioning systems.

METEOR COMBINATION (PONTIAC CHASSIS FOR 19

American Funeral Director

The Professional Car

While Pontiac celebrated the building of its 5 millionth car on June 18th, 1954, it was the only GM division to see a sales decline as more contemporary-looking rivals with V-8 engines—Oldsmobile and Buick included—chipped away at its position. On the other hand, Superior-Pontiac production in Kosciusko, Mississippi, increased from 34 units in 1953 to 195 the following year. With an attractive crinkle-finished roof and Art Deco wreath, the service car was almost certainly the rarest bod style.

Richard J. Conjalka collection

With 109 new features, it was claimed that the 1955 Pontiacs touted more changes than any single model since the marque's debut in 1926. A modern overhead-valve V-8 displacing 287 cubic inches superseded both the side-valve six and straight-eight engines, and its more compact profile allowed a hood that was 3.75 inches lower than the 1954 models. This limousine-style 1955 National hearse was aggressively priced at $5,750 to counter similar coaches from Barnette, Comet, Economy, Memphian, and Superior.

The Memphis Coach Company, formerly known as Economy Coach, applied the "Memphian" name to its Pontiac professional cars for the first time in 1955. Patients and operators alike benefited from Pontiac's change to tubeless tires, 12-volt electrics, and longer rear leaf springs spaced 3.25 inches further apart. With U.S. market Pontiac sedan deliveries discontinued since 1953, a Chieftain station wagon served as the basis for this style 862 ambulance with wraparound corner windows and a rather elaborate-looking rear bumper step.

Walt McCall collection

White sidewall tires, chrome wheel discs, tunnel lights and two-tone paint optional extra equipment.

From the beginning, Pontiac's new V-8 was designed to accommodate displacement increases in the future, and the future arrived more quickly than anticipated, when 1956 models were bored out to 317 cubic inches for a minimum of 227 horsepower. Superior Coach's Southern Division offered seven different Pontiac Regency models that year, ranging in price from $5,805 for a service car to $6,525 for a landau ambulance/funeral coach combination.

Richard J. Conjalka collection

Walt McCall collection

In 1957, side trim remained a good way to tell one coachbuilder's Pontiac professional cars from another's. The National Body Manufacturing Company of Knightstown, Indiana, put all of Pontiac's four-pointed stars on its rear fenders (promotional renderings show both three-star Chieftains and four-star Star Chiefs), while Superior and Memphian divided their stars between the rear side door and quarter panel in 1/2, 1/3, 2/2, and even 3/1 ratios, depending on the individual vehicle or catalog illustration.

257

The big news in 1958 comes from **SUPERIOR** coach

on Pontiac chassis

The Criterion Funeral Coach

Bernie Weis collection

Accented by Bonneville front fender louvers and Star Chief ornaments for the quarter panel coves, 1958 Superior Pontiacs adopted Criterion styling with Beau Monde limousine or traditional landau window treatments. The new look coincided with a 3-inch-longer, 147.5-inch wheelbase and a change in marketing strategy, where the Pontiacs were no longer treated as a separate "Southern Division."

Richard J. Conjalka collection

Ideal for funeral homes and rescue squads without the funds or space for an extended-chassis coach, Memphian's "OWB" ambulance conversion was made from a heavy-duty 1958 Pontiac four-door sedan instead of a station wagon. 1958 Pontiacs got a 370-cubic inch V-8 on top of 1957's displacement increase to 347 cid.

Terry Lange photo

Superior's dramatic Criterions got a platform to match in 1959, when Pontiac adopted "Wide Track" wheels (increased from 58.74 to 63.72 inches up front and from 59.43 to 64 inches in the rear) and "Strato-Star" styling with a split grille and twin fin fenders. Now stretching 245.25 inches on a 148-inch wheelbase, the "Performance Tested" Superior-Pontiacs were 9.25 inches longer, 6 inches wider, and 6 inches lower than the 1958s. Fitted with a Federal "Q" siren and oversized "West Coast" mirrors, this Criterion Surburban high-top was operated by St. Francis Ambulance of Winnipeg, Manitoba.

W.R. Church photo, Richard Litton collection

Attempting to expand its clientele to airport and hotel livery operators, Superior launched the nine-passenger Pontiac Cargo Cruiser as a 1959 model. Renamed the Caravelle for its last year on sale in 1960, its stylish Criterion body boasted a smoother ride and 50 percent more cargo space than the typical factory station wagon, but it was still not a great success. Side and tailgate trim unique to this model could be filled with Di-Noc panels simulating mahogany, limed oak or walnut.

Establishing his first plant about 10 miles southeast of Memphis along U.S. 78 in Olive Branch, Mississippi, former Comet Coach Company partner Jack W. Pinner started building Pontiac professional cars under his own name in 1960. Pointing to its unaltered 124-inch Star Chief wheelbase, 220.7-inch overall length, and partitioned-off 98-inch-long casket compartment, he billed his model 60-419 "Big Junior" as "a coach that is as easy to drive and park as your personal car yet roomy enough to handle the largest shippers."

Richard J. Conjalka collection

259

Beyond its rear door opening, the Pinner "Big Junior" combination was plainly trimmed, but patently functional, with sliding "airline" drapes, a flush-folding attendant's seat (extended-wheelbase models got two), and handy storage compartments. Headroom totaled 41 inches with 50 inches of inside height from the step well, while Pontiac's Wide-Track design allowed a 50-inch-wide floor and 61 inches of clearance between the windowsills.

Richard J. Conjalka collection

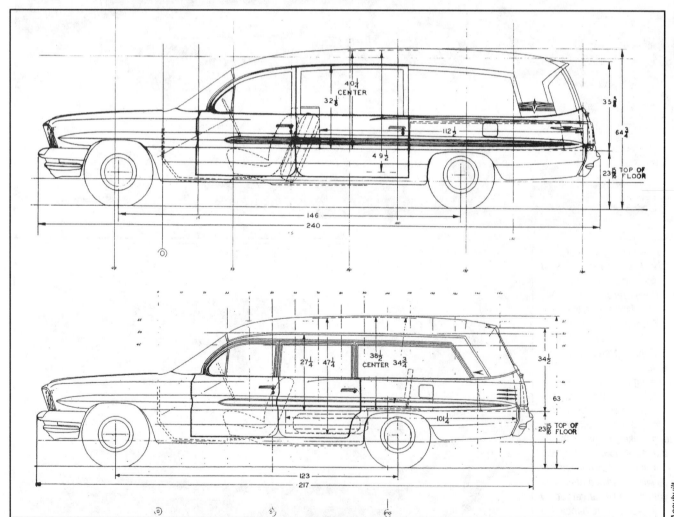

Accubuilt

1961 Pontiacs featured trimmer exteriors with modest vertical tailfins and a new windshield that dispensed with the entry-hampering "dogleg" corners. It was also the first year for Superior's standard-wheelbase Consort series, which sported a convertible-style chamfered roof that differed significantly from the one used on extended-wheelbase Criterions.

Accubuilt

While it retained the stock 123-inch wheelbase, the 1961 Superior Pontiac Consort was by no means a converted station wagon. Its construction started with a heavy-duty Bonneville chassis/cowl unit touting bigger brakes and uprated front and rear springs. This was welded to a steel framework topped by die-formed roof bows. Superior was the only firm that received this special Pontiac platform.

Richard J. Conjalka collection

Pontiac's switch to a perimeter-type frame in 1961 enhanced the stiffness of extended-wheelbase professional cars like this eight-door airport limousine constructed by National Coaches of Knightstown, Indiana. Like many of the firm's promotional photos, this image was taken in the backyard of company founder Vernon Perry's house.

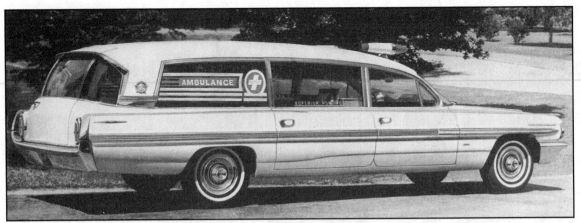

As Pontiac's new crescent-shaped taillights looked odd without their connecting recess, 1962 Superior Criterions and Consorts used vertically re-oriented Oldsmobile lenses. The body, featuring die-formed pillars, structural wheelhouses and dovetail joints in the side and rear door jambs to ensure alignment and eliminate rattling, was precision-built as a complete unit in a jig before being mounted on an exclusive chassis/cowl platform.

With 27 examples built, compared to 144 combinations and 68 ambulances, a 1962 Superior Pontiac hearse on the extended 146-inch wheelbase is a relatively rare sight. The roof covering on this Criterion Landaulet is not vinyl, but a crinkled texture paint that Superior dubbed a "Morocco" finish.

Superior added a Bonneville limousine to its 146-inch-wheelbase lineup in February 1962. While Superior Pontiac funeral coach owners were enticed by the idea of a perfectly matched procession, the $7,713 starting price also posed a tempting proposition to hotels, resorts, and tour companies that were in the market for a $9,722 Cadillac Fleetwood Seventy-Five sedan.

Richard J. Conjalka collection

Richard J. Conjalka collection

Muscular "Venturi" styling with Coke bottle fenders, straightened-out A-pillars, and forward-thrusting headlight hoods propelled Pontiac to a record 8.4-percent share of the U.S. new car market in 1963 (besting the 7.67 percent record set in 1941). But Superior lost the momentum above beltline level with a strange new roof for its $7,713 nine-passenger limousine.

Accubuilt

In 1963, the Kosciusko, Mississippi, plant that manufactured Superior's Pontiacs underwent an expansion that increased total production space to nearly 300,000 square feet. The Bonneville in this photo appears to be a military ambulance with the government-mandated all-metal roof cap.

Richard J. Conjalka collection

By the time Pinner photographed one of its standard-wheelbase 1963 Pontiac Star Chief hightops at the Memphis Municipal Airport, the company had relocated its plant to Victoria, Mississippi, with a sales office in Memphis. Cost-wise, this coach was a sensible intermediate step between the Catalina Amblewagons built by Automotive Conversion Corporation and the Bonneville-based Superior Consort. The base vehicle is likely a sedan, and the side windows also appear slightly taller than stock.

National Coaches of Knightstown, Indiana, built this impressive-looking 1963 Pontiac Catalina long-wheelbase ambulance, which was operated in Maryland by the Marlboro Volunteer Fire Department Rescue Squad. Pontiac brakes were now self-adjusting, and handling also benefited from a track increase to 64 inches.

Steve Lichtman Collection

Richard J. Conjalka collection

The body may have been in the last season of a four-year cycle, but the Kingwood Rescue Squad's 1964 Superior Pontiac 46-inch headroom Rescuer ambulance was still an undeniably attractive rig with its rocket-tipped roof lights, 146-inch wheelbase and freshly supersized Coke-bottle contours.

Richard J. Conjalka collection

Standard-wheelbase Consorts accounted for 209 of the 448 Pontiac professional cars built by Superior in Kosciusko, Mississippi, during the 1964 model year. The rarest variant remained the Model 308 Service Car with its stylized chrome wreath (used since 1949) and $6,360 sticker. Most prospective customers felt its functions could be handled by a $3,203 six-passenger or $3,311 nine-passenger Pontiac Safari station wagon with some first-call modifications by the funeral director's local body shop.

Richard J. Conjalka collection

Sharing structural componentry with the company's all-new Cadillacs, 1965 Superior Pontiacs got a commercial glass windshield flanked by reduced-angle "A" pillars for the first time. Slimmer, straighter carriage bows were added to the Landaulet, which was priced at $8,805 as a Model L204 straight hearse, or $9,044 as an L205 combination with reversible casket rollers.

Accubuilt

Superior's Pontiac Embassy limousine received an elegant new formal roofline for 1965, which nicely complemented the pronounced Coke-bottle contours also seen on this 1966 example. To achieve comfortable seating for nine passengers, this model had a 3.9-inch-longer center stretch than the funeral coaches and ambulances, creating a 150.7-inch wheelbase. It was last offered in the 1967 model year.

Accubuilt

Per government regulations, the Pontiac ambulances built by Superior for the military had special roof caps made of steel. These were distinguished by forward-leaning front faces. Equipment levels were otherwise minimal to save money, with an under-hood siren, one central beacon, and a single swiveling spotlight mounted over the driver's compartment. A two-speed roof vent and overhead stretcher hooks complete the specification on this 1966 model.

Stressing the scale of production at its Southern Division plant in Kosciusko, Mississippi, Superior posed one of its 48-inch-headroom 1967 Pontiac high-tops with a fleet of Kaiser-Jeep M-109 military ambulances manufactured under the same roof. Superior's 1969 acquisition by the Sheller-Globe auto parts conglomerate moved the Pontiacs to the Lima, Ohio, plant by decade's end.

Accubuilt

Accubuilt

The Kosciusko plant also served as headquarters for Superior's Export Division, which prepared this pair of standard-wheelbase 1967 Pontiac Consort ambulances for delivery to the Philippines.

With their twin grilles divided by a prominent chrome center prow, 1968 Pontiacs had horizontal headlights for the first time since 1962. Lacking a rooftop center beacon, this high-headroom Superior Model 207 is rather basically equipped, besides its two-tone paint, and probably sold for close to its $10,039 starting price.

Richard J. Conjalka collection

Confirming they did not take a back seat to Superior's Cadillacs in the realm of customer choice, 1968 Superior Pontiac landau hearses were available with both traditional Sovereign styling (top) and as a Royale with wraparound corner windows (bottom). The three-window limousine style cars that were also offered proved ideal for service as funeral coach/ambulance combinations.

Steve Loftin collection

The 1969 model year marked the fifth birthday for the basic Superior-Pontiac body shell. Notable styling changes included a dent-resistant Endura nose and flush-fitting landau bows adopted in anticipation of Federal regulations that would have banned exterior trim projecting more than one half-inch beyond the body's surface. This example, identified as a Royale by the curved rear corner windows, was owned by Steven E. Silver of Kingston, Ontario.

Tim A. Fantin photo

Having purchased a 36-percent stake in Superior Coach for $13,261,520 in August 1968, the Toledo, Ohio-based auto parts conglomerate Sheller-Globe Corporation used a stock swap to complete its acquisition on June 2, 1969. That this would prove a detriment to long-term prospects was not yet apparent when the company's 1970 Pontiacs debuted. This 40-inch-ceiling combination was used by the Marvel Memorial Chapel in Arco, Idaho. It is currently owned by Wayne Guy of Clarksboro, New Jersey.

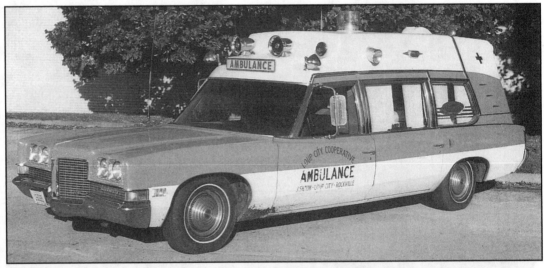

All-new Superior Pontiacs, sharing squared-off body shells and a Lima, Ohio, plant with the company's Cadillac coaches, bowed as 1971 models, but a three-month strike against General Motors slashed the series' output to 194 vehicles after 350 were built in 1970. In addition to dispensing with the front vent and wraparound rear corner windows, Superior increased wheelbases to 127 inches on the Consorts and 152 inches on the Sovereigns. This 54-inch-headroom Model 226 ambulance was used by the Loup City Cooperative in rural Sherman County, Nebraska.

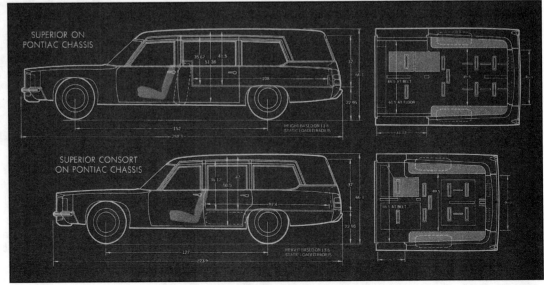

Accubuilt

Costing $8,834 as a funeral coach, $9,092 as a combination, or $9,159 as an ambulance, this limousine-style 1972 Superior Pontiac Consort on the standard 127-inch wheelbase used an under-floor spare tire to allow a 97.4-inch-long rear floor that gave up only 10.6 inches to the partition-equipped 152-inch-wheelbase Sovereigns.

Accubuilt

A representative of the Loewen Funeral Chapel takes delivery of a Pontiac Sovereign Landau in front of the executive garages at Superior's East Kibby Street factory in Lima, Ohio, on July 19, 1972. The longer cars were much more popular by 1972, when 259 Sovereigns were completed, compared to just 61 Consorts.

With a phone call or letter to Stageway Coaches of Fort Smith, Arkansas, 1972 Superior Pontiac funeral coach owners could procure themselves a matching limousine with four or six doors. Ironically, company president Milt Earnhart's son, Tom, would end up purchasing Superior Coach from Sheller-Globe in 1981.

When it came to really large eight-door, 12-passenger Pontiacs targeted at resorts, school sports teams, and airport taxi services, Stageway Coaches asserted that 45 years of limousine building experience gave it "the edge over the rest of the field." These 1972 models were true beasts of burden with their "West Coast" mirrors, full-length luggage racks, and (in the case of the station wagon shown) high-capacity rooftop air conditioners.

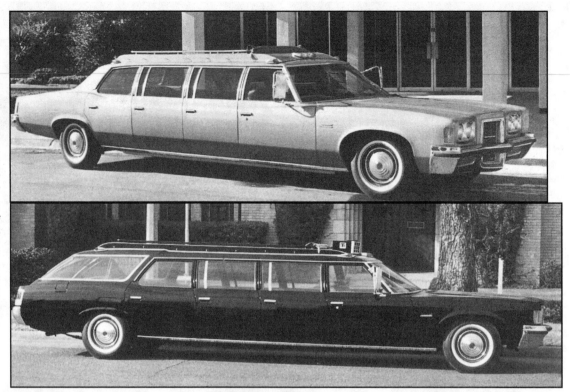

Deciding it was no longer profitable to build, Superior dropped its standard-wheelbase Pontiac Consort after the 1973 model year. This rare example was exhibited by Premier Coach Sales of Clear Lake, Iowa, at the Professional Car Society's 1996 International Meet in St. Paul.

These 1973 and 1974 Superior Pontiacs were photographed with a pair of 1974 Cotner-Bevington Oldsmobiles shortly after Winnipeg, Manitoba, passed a law ending private ambulance service in its environs. The city inherited all the units from seven or eight independent operators, scrapped many of them immediately, and put the rest into service wearing lime and white.

Terry Lange photo

Superior 54 on Pontiac chassis features
54" headroom and choice of floor plans.

With van and pickup cab-based modular units taking over the ambulance market, the last Superior Pontiacs appeared in the 1975 model year and just 60 units were built in ambulance, combination, and funeral coach forms. This 54-inch-headroom Model 226 ambulance (the 51-inch version was designated Model 221) embodied everything Superior had learned from building Pontiac professional cars on a continuous basis since 1953—even though the 1975 catalog shots had airbrushed-in corner lamps instead of fresh photos.

When the Eureka Coach Company Ltd. of Concord, Ontario, dedicated its new manufacturing facility on March 22, 1985, the highlight of the opening ceremony was the introduction of a commercial glass Pontiac Chieftain funeral coach and matching limousine on an extended rear-wheel-drive Parisienne chassis.

Thomas A. McPherson collection

NAHC, Detroit Public Library

GMC

Once America was "Over There," the General Motors Truck Company earmarked 90 percent of its output for the World War I, delivering 8,512 vehicles to the U.S. Army through 1919. Essentially an upgraded version of the Model 15 that served "Black Jack" Pershing's Mexican campaign against Pancho Villa, this GMC Model 16 3/4-ton ambulance first appeared in 1918. Its chassis featured a 132-inch wheelbase, 56-inch front and rear tread, and a 30-horsepower L-head four-cylinder motor with a Yale-locked 25-mph automatic speed governor. In the interest of simplicity, the headlights, cowl lamps and single taillight were oil-fueled by a running board-mounted Prest-O-Lite tank.

271

This plainly finished 1951 GMC model 101-22 half-ton 4x2 ambulance was photographed at Fort Jackson, South Carolina, on June 21, 1952. Suburbans with this basic body styling initially appeared in the summer of 1947 and stayed current through 1954, adding squared-off parking lights in 1953 and a one-piece curved windshield for their final year on sale.

Bernie Weis photo

Launched in March, 1955, the GMC "Blue Chip" models offered truck-tuned Pontiac V-8 engines as an option and sleek new bodies with panoramic windshields, flow-through fenders and double-bar grilles with pod-like bumper guards. Helped by these dramatic changes, GMC's registrations climbed 127.4 percent over 1954. During 1955 or 1956, the Christopher Company of New York City delivered this "RES-Q" combination squad car, ambulance and rescue vehicle to the West Bend, Wisconsin, Fire Department.

Rich Litton collection

Fitchburg, Massachusetts, took advantage of Federal Civil Defense funding to obtain this four-wheel-drive GMC rescue truck bodied by the Gerstenslager Company of Wooster, Ohio. GMC debuted the innovative heavy-duty V-6 engine powering this vehicle in a variety of displacements for the 1960 model year, while straightened windshield pillars eliminating the dogleg arrived in 1964, and squared-off grille lettering was phased-in during 1965.

Steve Lichtman collection

Steve Lichtman collection

The GMC pickup cab on this Fasco-bodied heavy-duty ambulance was used from 1967 to 1972, with the black grille sections further narrowing the date of manufacture to 1971 or 1972. The fully modular "Type I" body could be fitted to a new chassis when the old one wore out. This unit was operated by the East Rockaway, New York, Fire Department.

1973 GMC pickups and chassis/cab units were completely redesigned with more glass area, an energy-absorbing steering column with a locking ignition switch, and a three-section grille flanked by single-lens headlamps for the first time since 1957. Star-Line Enterprises of Sanford, Florida, offered this "Star Mod" Type I ambulance. The body was constructed from heavy-gauge unitized steel framing with an electrically welded floor and heavy-gauge aluminum exterior panels that were riveted to the frame after an electrolysis barrier was installed.

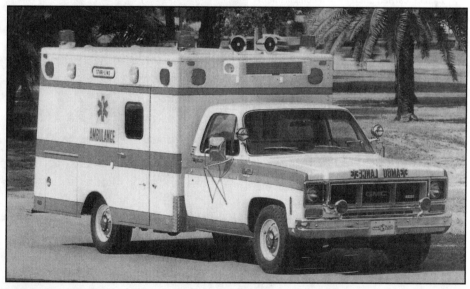

An aerodynamic, aluminum-framed fiberglass body, tandem rear wheels with all-independent air suspension, and a front-wheel-drive Oldsmobile Toronado power train, affording a low floor and car-like handling, made the 1973-78 GMC MotorHome (known as the GMC Transmode Commercial Vehicle in non-recreational applications) an ideal foundation for advanced emergency units. This Safety Lime-colored example served on Long Island, New York, with the Melville Fire Department

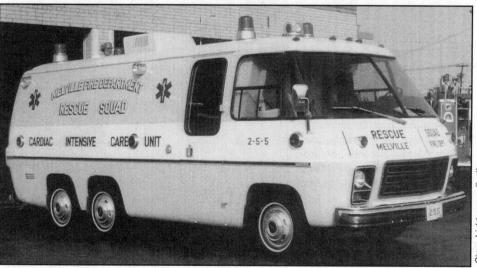

Steve Lichtman collection

273

Bay Ridge, Brooklyn, funeral director Gerard R. McLaughlin, revived the World War I era idea of a funeral omnibus when he replaced a hearse and two limousines with this 14-passenger GMC "Luxury Coach." It was modified to his specifications by the Rico Company of Warren, Ohio. The casket, carried laterally in a compartment behind the rear wheels, could be loaded or unloaded from either side of the vehicle, while the family and friends of the deceased were given tinted privacy glass, 76 inches of headroom, an entertainment center, swiveling captain's chairs with plush blue fabric and an air suspension levelizer that lowered the door opening to curb level. The rear compartment could be used for luggage when the casket rack was covered with an upholstered tray. The Luxury Coach had also transported the bridal party at McLaughlin's daughter's wedding and "the entourages of such entertainers as Frank Sinatra and Phyllis Diller.

Crestline Coach Ltd. of Saskatoon, Saskatchewan, has built considerably more ambulances than funeral vehicles since it was founded in 1976, but it did a fine job preparing this 1981-82 GMC C-1500 two-wheel-drive Suburban for first-call duty. It had fender skirts, a 3/4-padded vinyl roof with landau bows and coach lamps, elaborate front door medallions, and a fully finished casket compartment.

Chapter 10

"Best of The Rest"

The history of funeral cars and ambulances in North America may have ended as a saga dominated by Chrysler, Ford, and especially General Motors-based platforms, but there were many years in the 20th century where the so-called "independent" makes made a similarly important mark on the industry. In a roughly two-decade period spanning the World War I era, the Roaring 1920s and the first years of the Great Depression in the 1930s, leading stand-alones like Hudson, Nash, Reo, White and Pierce-Arrow enjoyed an especially strong reputation for innovative engineering, distinctive exterior styling, or uncompromising craftsmanship—all of which proved to be potent inducements for funeral directors and livery operators who wanted to stand apart from their competitors or make sure that their equipment would never let a customer down.

There were, in turn, a number of independent carmakers that recognized how hearses and ambulances were an excellent image builder at the community level and accordingly joined forces with leading bodybuilders. Some of the most memorable and admired team-ups were the Eureka-bodied 1928-30 Kissels and Henney-bodied 1931-33 Reos offered by the traveling salesmen of the National Casket Company, and the exclusive, 1938-54 partnership between Packard and Henney that was chronicled in Chapter Eight.

As far as market coverage and volume were concerned, it is certain that the most-successful venture in this idiom was the 1925-37 alliance between the Superior Body Company and the Studebaker Corporation—a firm which would, in addition to chalking up such design-

Bernie Weis collection

Steam- and electric-powered ambulances had seen limited service since the turn of the century, but the Cunningham Model 774 became America's first commercially built gasoline-powered auto ambulance when it was unveiled on April 15, 1909. Resting on a 126-inch-wheelbase chassis built in-house at the 71-year-old Rochester, New York, firm, the body featured a stained mahogany interior with four electric dome lights, two attendant seats, a linoleum-covered floor, a semi-closed driver's compartment with a windshield, roll-down side curtains, and foot-operated warning gong. Power came from a Continental-supplied four-cylinder engine making 32 horsepower, though a 40-horsepower overhead-valve unit built by Cunningham took its place within a year.

related successes as the "coming or going" 1947 coupes and the 1963 Avanti, became a "top five" auto industry player by the early 1920s.

Founded in Lima, Ohio, to construct wood-framed aluminum-paneled bus bodies for the Garfords manufactured in narby Elyria, Superior was only 2 years old when it launched a line of professional cars designed for the Studebaker Big Six and Cadillac V-8 chassis in early 1925. But its workmanship standards and thoroughly contemporary "limousine" styling impressed Studebaker management to the point that they promptly forged a pact where the firm would manufacture standardized funeral coach and ambulance bodies to South Bend's specifications and mount them on a purpose-designed, Studebaker-built 156-inch long wheelbase Big Six chassis. After purchasing the completed cars from Superior, Studebaker would handle marketing and distribution through its 3,000-strong nationwide dealer network, with the added incentive of an installment financing program specifically targeted at funeral directors.

In its 1926 professional car sales brochure, Studebaker would report that more than 1,200 funeral directors, "Recognizing an opportunity to bring their equipment up to date at an exceptionally moderate cost," had selected the Big Six chassis for hearse and ambulance bodies during the first year of the collaboration. The $3,550 price initially asked for both ambulance and hearse variants quickly dropped in ensuing seasons as Superior realized new efficiencies by expanding its East Kibby Street manufacturing facility and added less-expensive models based on Studebaker's entry-level Dictator. Well aware that many funeral directors embraced a matching fleet ideal, Superior also modified Studebaker's factory-built seven-passenger sedan into a "Combination Ambulance and Pallbearers Car" priced at $2,875 in 1926 (the conversion required just two minutes to remove the right front seat, unclamp the right side center pillar and load a Bomgardner folding chair cot). In 1927, Superior took advantage of its bus experience to introduce a 12-passenger "Mourners Sedan" with two driver's side doors, four passenger's side doors and four rows of seats.

The 1930s would see Superior mount more bodies on General Motors chassis and begin to advertise and distribute its products independently. The alliance with South Bend had played an indisputably important role in placing the company on a path where it would emerge as the world's largest volume coachbuilder. Studebaker, narrowly avoiding liquidation after entering receivership

in March, 1933, frequently believed that the high-profile, relatively-stable funeral business would help its dealers keep their doors open during the darkest days of the Depression. Not only did the company consider mortuary customers to be low-risk credit-wise, its statistical research also calculated that every Studebaker funeral vehicle placed in service spurred the sale of two Studebaker passenger cars. These inducements remained potent even after Superior dropped its Studebakers in favor of Pontiacs after the 1937 model year, compelling South Bend to call on the Cleveland-based Bender Body Company for more ambulances and funeral coaches in the 1938-40 period.

No "Best of the Rest" list would be complete without a retrospective of the early days when firms like Sayers & Scovill, Crane & Breed, Riddle, Rock Falls, Henney, and Meteor constructed their own chassis as well as their own bodies. While the Continental engines, Delco electrics, Stromberg carburetors, Timken axles, Eaton gears, Westinghouse shock absorbers, and other outsourced components proved entirely capable of delivering reliable service, James Cunningham, Son & Company trumped them all by building virtually everything that went into its professional cars in-house.

By the time this venerable, Rochester, New York, concern unveiled America's first commercially manufactured gasoline ambulance on April 15, 1909 (a Mosque deck bodied auto hearse, initially mounted on a White steam car chassis, appeared the following August and took part in New York City's first all-car funeral procession in the autumn), it had already been building premium quality horse-drawn carriages for more than 70 years. Company founder James Cunningham, an 18-year-old Scotch-Irish immigrant who demonstrated promise as a carpenter and wood worker, got his start in the industry after leaving his family's farm near Cobourg, Ontario, Canada in 1833. Settling in the rapidly growing town of Rochester, New York, he secured an apprenticeship with the newly established Hanford and Whitbeck carriage works in 1834.

In 1838, when he was 23 and newly married, Cunningham joined forces with fellow employees James Kerr and Blanchard Dean to purchase the business and, after his partners resigned in 1842, assumed sole responsibility for the company's day-to-day management and then-substantial $6,000 debt. The unassailable reputation that Cunningham's coaches, buggies and one-horse sleighs (also known as "cutters") acquired for quality and durability allowed him to quickly reverse the enterprise's fortunes. Prospective customers were especially impressed to learn that he preferred to make his own springs, axles, carriage lamps and folding steps instead of purchasing them from outside suppliers.

In the early years it was not unusual for Cunningham to hitch a string of buggies together, venture into the New York countryside on a demonstration trip, and return home on horseback after selling the entire sample. His elevation to a national-level player was only temporarily hindered by an 1848 factory fire (the construction of an all-new facility on Canal Street was accomplished with impressive speed) and the 1857 financial panic that decimated his Western sales market and pushed him into a bankruptcy that resulted in a 3-year reorganization. Large orders of carriages for the Union Army certainly played a large role in improving Cunningham's balance sheets during the Civil War years, though it benefited just as much from the hiring of a financially savvy young man named Rufus Dryer, who would marry James' daughter Margaretta and become a company partner in 1875.

While the exact year that Cunningham built its first horse-drawn hearse is open to conjecture, it is known that the company completed an exceptionally elaborate example for a Pittsburgh undertaker (at an almost unheard-of cost of $2,300) sometime prior to 1865 and earned a special medal with another one of its beautifully carved creations at the Philadelphia Centennial Exposition of 1876. By this time, the firm, formally incorporated as James Cunningham, Son and Co. in 1882, could claim to be the largest industry in Rochester with more than 400 employees, a total capitalization of $800,000, and sales branches in such major U.S. cities as Chicago, Louisville, Nashville, New Orleans, Kansas City, Topeka, Denver and San Francisco. Its high-end buggies, sleighs, and Victorias built for private customers were complemented by a complete line of ambulances, invalid wagons, casket wagons and pallbearers' carriages for the undertaking trade. These imposing-looking conveyances, exemplified by the four-column "funeral car" that Cunningham debuted at the 1884 New Orleans Cotton Exposition and the even more-ornate six- and eight-columned hearses that followed later, played an important role in steering undertakers' tastes away from the comparatively dainty gooseneck frames, Ostrich plumes, and oval windows that had dominated American hearse design since the 1830s. By any measure, Joseph Cunningham, born in 1843, had plenty to be proud of and much to look forward to when he assumed the company presidency after his father James expired in 1886.

Despite the sterling reputation acquired in the carriage trade, the founder's grandsons Francis E. and Augustine J. Cunningham were well aware that the 20th century would be a "horseless age," so the pioneering Duryea Brothers were approached as early as 1896 to explore the prospect of the two families teaming up to manufacture motor vehicles in Rochester. Though these plans never came to fruition, Cunningham completed an experimental electric vehicle of its own by the turn of the century and constructed three more prototype electric runabouts prior to its 1907 introduction of gasoline cars that, at a lofty asking price of $3,500, initially combined the company's superbly constructed custom bodies with Continental or Buffalo four and six-cylinder engines. Within 3 years, however, Cunningham was manufacturing its own 40-horsepower, four-cylinder overhead-valve engines, transmissions, axles and even radiators. The 1909-12 time frame also saw a number of its coupe, landaulet and taxi cab bodies utilized by other auto makers including Empire Electric, Ideal Electric, Cadillac, Chalmers, Gaeth, Peerless, Velie, and Locomobile.

The intricately carved funeral coach and lavishly equipped ambulance models that debuted in 1909 were, in common with Cunningham's passenger cars, designed to be the very best that money could buy, and their positioning as prestige offerings was further enhanced by the 1915 debut of a 442-cubic inch V-8 engine producing 90 hp at a relaxed 2400 rpm. Only a few months, ironically, had elapsed since the company had stopped cataloguing horse-drawn carriages, but the similarly stately and conservative character of Cunningham's motor cars ensured a steadfastly loyal base of well-heeled customers. With the Rochester factory employing about 450 craftsmen who produced only 375 to 650 vehicles annually on average at transaction prices ranging from $5,000 for the chassis alone to $9,000-$12,000 for completed cars, there was virtually no customer request that Cunningham would not satisfy, including a 1923 commission from a New York mortician who wanted his massive "White Angel" horse-drawn hearse remounted on the latest V-Series motor chassis, after which it rendered many more years of distinguished service. It was also common practice for the company to store and refurbish a local customer's open touring body after fitting its chassis with a closed body for the winter months, or dispatch a factory mechanic to a distant city on a service call, or appoint a funeral director or hospital official that used Cunningham equipment as a dealer.

Walt McCall, recalling the company's history in a 1981 issue of *The Professional Car*, was certainly justified in asserting that, "Aside from the U.S.-bodied Springfields, the classic Cunningham was probably as close to an American Rolls-Royce as any production automobile this country has ever seen." This lofty reputation, as was the case with so many other prestige automakers like Pierce-Arrow, Marmon, Stutz and Duesenberg, would be of little value once the Great Depression made the display of wealth unfashionable. Cunningham responded to the hard times as best it could by concentrating on funeral coach and ambulance production after 1931 (some of the leftover passenger cars did not find buyers until 1933), introducing a "W" series model powered by a Continental straight-eight engine and, starting in 1934, mounting its professional coachwork on Oldsmobile, Cadillac and Packard chassis.

With its final funeral cars completed in the autumn of 1936, the company's diversification efforts also spurred a run of town car bodies adding $2,000 to the $600 price of a 1936 or 1937 V-8 Ford, a Cunningham-Hall Aircraft subsidiary that produced civilian sports and military planes from 1928 through 1938, the manufacture of aircraft safety belts and diving helmets, and the creation of an innovative armored vehicle with lightweight, rubber-block tracks that achieved a cross-country speed of 50 mph in a 1935 test. The company's

defense-related employment rolls dramatically increased from six men in January, 1940, to 360 in 1942 and 800 in 1943 as it initiated production of machine gun mounts and servo-operated gear boxes for controlling wing surfaces and gunner's turrets. Its post-World War II endeavors included gasoline-powered farm and garden implements, Pullman-type toilets and plumbing fixtures for house trailers, and electro-mechanical crossbar switches that found wide application in the automatic machine tool control, communications, power transmission and aerospace industries.

Even after the 1960s saw Cunningham open a brand-new, 20-acre plant situated some 15 miles south of Rochester in Honeoye Falls, New York, and become a component of the multinational Gleason Works that also has its world headquarters in Rochester, the company could still creditably clam to be one of the oldest continuously operated industrial enterprises in the United States. Even after 60 years pursuing unrelated ventures, its status as one of country's greatest carmakers can never be disputed.

Bernie Weis collection

While a gasoline-powered model arrived soon afterwards, Cunningham's first auto hearse combined a Style 793 Mosque deck body with a torquey, quiet-running White steam car chassis. After appearing in White's Manhattan showroom in the autumn of 1909, this vehicle was loaned to leading funeral director Frank E. Campbell for New York City's first all-car funeral. The carefully stage-managed procession to Rosehill Cemetery in Linden, New Jersey, which also featured a matching fleet of White steam limousines, was photographed by Franz E. Jensen for a feature published in the December, 1909, issue of The Sunnyside.

Nathan Lazernick photo, NAHC, Detroit Public Library

Auto hearses were a subject of public curiosity at early exhibitions. In January 1910, this Model 1112 Combination Casket Delivery Wagon and Ambulance built by Crane & Breed of Cincinnati was displayed at the Philadelphia Auto Show prior to entering service with Fithian Simmons of Camden, New Jersey.

Richard J. Conjalka collection

Audacious publicity stunts are rare in the ultra-conservative funeral car business. One of the best-remembered ones remains a cross-country trip commenced by a Great Eagle motor hearse in August 1913. Though this Columbus, Ohio-built coach weighed 6,560 lbs. when it left the House of Lanyon undertaking firm in San Francisco bound for New York City, its 72-horsepower Rutenber six-cylinder engine and sturdy Hoover springs conveyed embalmed remains across the virtually roadless continent without mechanical difficulty. The feat did not, however, prevent the United States Carriage Company from falling into the receiver's hands in February 1915.

Bernie Weis collection

Having built carriages since 1838 and horse-drawn funeral coaches since the Civil War, James Cunningham, Son & Company regarded the transition to motor hearses as no excuse to lower its traditional standards of construction or aesthetics. Anyone who saw this Style 914 enclosed-drive hearse built on a 1913 M-Series chassis for Wann & Son of Chattanooga, Tennessee, would agree that these objectives were achieved admirably. Intricately carved curtains, draped column pedestals, ornate carriage lamps, and an elaborately filigreed "Berline Front" all worked beautifully together to create a vehicle of unrivalled stature in the community.

279

Whether it was intended or not, a distinctly automotive look that shared no visual vocabulary with horse-drawn vehicles was a notable achievement on this limousine-style Cunningham Model 915 funeral coach built for C. Edwin Walley on the 1913 Model M chassis. The leaded-glass panels along the top of the body recalled the ones seen on the era's private railroad cars.

Bernie Weis collection

While the combination of a rounded cowl with a flat front radiator dates this Cunningham as one of the last four-cylinder cars—either a 1914 Model R or a 1915 Model S—this distinctive and attractive 991 funeral coach with oval-shaped, diamond-pattern beveled glass windows was available during the company's V-8 era.

Bernie Weis collection

Bernie Weis collection

In September 1915, not long after it discontinued horse-drawn coaches, Cunningham replaced its four-cylinder motor with a 442-cubic inch V-8 making 90 hp at a relaxed 2400 rpm. Opting for oval quarter windows, an open driver's compartment, and massive Westinghouse shock absorbers at each corner of the chassis, the Rochester Homeopathic Hospital was one of the first recipients of an ambulance built on this new V-1 platform.

NAHC, Detroit Public Library

Founded by Jonas Swab in 1868 and still in business today as a builder of firefighting/rescue vehicles, refrigerated delivery bodies and animal transport trucks, the Swab Wagon Company of Elizabethville, Pennsylvania, became a Studebaker dealer in 1916. The company celebrated the endeavor by creating this glass-sided, eight-column, carved hearse with lotus-style pedestals on an ED-6 chassis.

American Funeral Director

Afforded a distinctive front-end appearance with "coal scuttle" hoods and fender-mounted headlights, several Pierce-Arrow funeral omnibuses were operated by the Fifth Avenue Coach Company of New York City. The casket was carried sideways in its own compartment behind the driver's seat, with space for flowers on the level above. Though this concept had promise as a successor to the somber funeral trolleys used between urban centers and suburban cemeteries for a number of years, its popularity pretty much peaked in the World War I period when individual car ownership was not yet universal.

Bernie Weis collection

Prepared for any casualties the Kaiser might inflict, a group of nurses pose with their driver and commanding officer beside a Cunningham V-Series U.S. Navy Medical Department ambulance (officially designated Design 47-A) in New York City's Washington Square Park. A rounded radiator shell, most-often body colored, was the biggest visual difference between the first half dozen years' worth of V-8 Cunninghams and the earlier four-cylinder models.

This port-side photo of a V-8 Cunningham Design 47-A ambulance constructed for the U.S. Navy Medical Department during World War I shows the foot-operated bell mounted on the running board and the massive spotlight on the driver's door pillar. Cunninghams had used left-hand steering since the 1913 Model M. Three-drop down windows were fitted to each side of this body for effective ventilation, while the rooftop tire-carrier was flanked with Red Cross pennant staffs.

NAHC, Detroit Public Library

Having forged a reputation for superlative coachwork since its founding in 1877, the Rock Falls Manufacturing Company of Sterling, Illinois, made use of a heavy-duty Velie six-cylinder chassis built in nearby Moline, Illinois, for this dignified Design 135 carved hearse constructed around 1918.

Museum of Funeral Customs, Springfield, Illinois

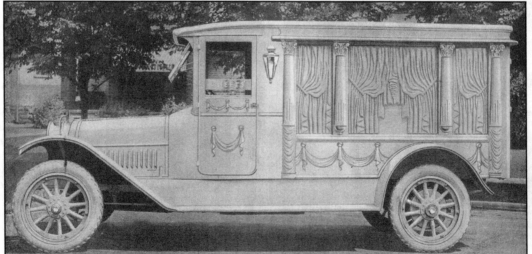

Museum of Funeral Customs

To limit the cost of this 1919 Model 80 carved-panel hearse to $2,200 plus a 5-percent War Tax, the Meteor Motor Car Company of Piqua, Ohio, relied on direct-mail marketing. It also relied on proven mechanical components, such as a 50-horsepower Continental "Red Seal" six-cylinder engine with Stromberg carburetion, Delco electrics, and a Borg & Beck clutch attached to a Covert three-speed transmission.

Bernie Weis collection

Wire wheels and a twin-oval backlight gave this 1918-20 V-3 Series Cunningham Style 992 invalid coach a limousine-like ambiance that the customers of a high-class private ambulance service like Scully-Walton of New York City would have certainly appreciated. As a vehicle like this was intended for non-emergency transfers, the running board-mounted Van Duesen bell and the illuminated ambulance sign above the windshield would not have been used on every call.

Bernie Weis collection

Cunningham's uncompromising craftsmanship is reflected in the carefully finished, contrasting color moldings covering the lower quarter panels of this Style 987 ambulance built for the Shelley-Loring Company in the late teens. On some cars the shield design integrated into the side window leading was painted to proclaim the operator's name.

Resplendent with its glass-walled casket compartment and vine motif pillar carvings, this 1919 Reo Speed Wagon bodied by the Finch Carriage Company of Ridgeway, Ontario, earned the Funeral Directors' Choice Award at the Professional Car Society's 2000 International Meet in Kingston, Ontario. Owner Larry Williams recalled this car was more "like a pickup truck" when he bought it sight-unseen in Grimsby, Ontario, but an old nameplate from the Chris & Burt Climenhage Funeral Home in Stevensville, Ontario, allowed him to track down a granddaughter who had photos of the car when it was in service. All in all, it took two years to locate parts and one year to assemble the vehicle at Great Lakes Auto Restoration in Tillsonburg, Ontario.

283

Don Lunn

When W.N. Lunn of the Merkel-Lunn mortuary in Wichita Falls, Texas, switched to motorized equipment in1920, he went all the way with top-of-the-line vehicles built by Sayers & Scovill of Cincinnati, Ohio, and James Cunningham, Son & Company of Rochester, New York. Posed for posterity after being unloaded from railroad cars, the S&S Model 345 ambulance (center) and Model 245 Masterpiece 12-column carved hearse (right) stayed in Wichita Falls, while the Cunningham Style 992 combination coach with wire wheels (left) was sent 40 miles south to the firm's other home in Olney.

Sporting the disc wheels and drum-style headlights that were coming into vogue at the start of the 1920s, this Cunningham style 137-A Mosque deck hearse combined solid carved sides with ceiling-level beveled glass windows to let a little light into the casket compartment. Note how the small upkick in the beltline behind the driver's door is complemented by a similar curve on the underside of the windshield visor.

Bernie Weis collection

Donald F. Wood

The so-called "V-4" series V-8 Cunninghams launched in 1921 introduced a flat-front radiator shell, but the old round-shouldered design was still being installed on some cars two years later. This style 138-A ambulance from 1923 also fitted ceiling-level forced-air ventilators in place of drop-down patient compartment windows previously used, and the mechanical siren on the running board certainly had more volume and range than an old-fashioned bell or gong.

Silver-Knightstown is believed to be the builder of this all-white 1922 Studebaker Big Six child's hearse owned by David Neitzel of Logansport, Indiana. A large metropolitan livery service, as opposed to an individual funeral director, would have been the most-likely original owner of this extremely specialized vehicle. The robust L-head six made 60 hp from 353.8 cubic inches, while the exterior had a one-piece windshield and, carried over from 1921, a graceful reverse curve on the back edge of the rear fenders.

Walt McCall collection

This 1924 S&S Kensington invalid coach had carefully pinstriped double rear doors with a bowed beltline and fold-down step. Westinghouse air shock absorbers and solid aluminum disc wheels with demountable rims were standard equipment. The exterior could be finished in any color desired, though recommended treatments included a pearl gray hood and body panels with black, maroon or dark blue fenders, light and dark blue with gold striping or, if a darker scheme was preferred, maroon with black moldings, fenders and chassis.

NAHC, Detroit Public Library

A horse-drawn Riddle had attended to the funeral of President William McKinley in 1901, and the Ravenna, Ohio, builder (in business from 1831-1926) received a similar honor when one of its elaborately carved Number 1082 Pilaster motor hearses was used to carry President Warren G. Harding through the streets of Marion, Ohio in August, 1923. Escorted by a military honor guard, this stately vehicle was borrowed from an Indiana mortuary as the H. Schaffner Company in charge of the arrangements was having a new hearse built at the time.

Keith Marvin collection

The Superior Motor Coach Body Company of Lima, Ohio, was only 2 years old when it added hearse and ambulance bodies to its lineup in 1925. Studebaker forged a deal where Superior would manufacture standardized, limousine-style professional car bodies to Studebaker's specification, mount them on a Studebaker-built, 156-inch-long-wheelbase Big Six chassis, and sell them directly to Studebaker for distribution. Fitted with a Meritas-covered "Landau back" at extra cost, one of the early ambulances went to J. Walter Wills & Company of Cleveland, Ohio—a prominent mortuary still in business today after five generations as The House of Wills.

George Hamlin collection

George Hamlin collection

Standardized design and mass production held the price of Superior's 1925-26 Studebaker professional cars to $3,550 for both the funeral coach and ambulance models, and a doubling of factory capacity during 1926 set the stage for added efficiency and even lower prices in the future. Body frames were fashioned from kiln-dried Northern white ash and hard maple that was glued together and reinforced with bronze corner brackets and dowel-pinned mortise and tenon joints, which was then finished with 20-gauge steel exterior panels, aluminum sill plates, felt-lined steel window channels and lacquer paintwork. Beyond a sliding glass partition with a roller shade, the rear compartment featured frosted dome lights, a 37-inch-wide right-hinged rear door with a 31-inch loading height, and 36-inch-wide front-hinged side doors.

This imposing 1927 Pierce-Arrow, likely a top-of-the-line Series 36 judging from the vacuum-boosted four-wheel brakes and the hood louvers divided into six groups of three, was used as an ambulance by the North Arlington, New Jersey Fire Department. The shape of the windshield, vent windows and side window reveals suggest that this was a factory-built vestibule sedan or limousine fitted with an extended rear roof and quarter panels by a local body shop.

Frank Fenning, Jr. photo, Rich Litton collection

American Funeral Director

In March, 1927, the Superior Studebaker line was expanded into the budget market with an Arlington funeral coach and Bellevue ambulance (shown) combining a 146-inch wheelbase chassis with the 50-horsepower, 241.6-cubic inch L-head six-cylinder engine from the Series EU Dictator.

George Hamlin collection

Superior's top-of-the-line Studebaker DeLuxe on the 158-inch wheelbase Big Six chassis received several appearance changes for 1927, including chrome-plated, bullet-shaped headlights, and a simpler one-piece windshield underneath a flowing, French-style sun visor. This photo with the car's window shades rolled up gives a good look at the sliding glass partition behind the driver's seat and the arched walnut-finish flower tray.

Bernie Weis collection

An Aztec pyramid might have inspired the unusual, step-style deck on this late 1920s Cunningham Series V casket wagon built for the Thomas F. Burke funeral home of Perth Amboy, New Jersey. An extra set of side doors made it easier to load a church truck or chairs, while a railing around the back of the body allowed flowers to be transported externally.

J.T. Hinton & Son of Memphis spent an incredible $13,000 constructing this armored ambulance on a Cunningham V-Series chassis. The interior had hot and cold running water, a complete lavatory, and a "perfect ventilation system" with electric fans. "Our purpose in designing and building this remarkable ambulance is to give our patrons absolute protection against the carelessness and recklessness of other motorists," Frayser Hinton told *American Funeral Director.*

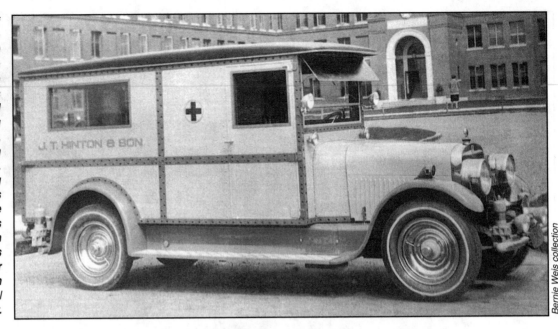

Bernie Weis collection

Walt McCall collection

1927 Meteors, such as this maroon-and-black funeral coach shown by K.K. Hamsher of Fox Lake, Wisconsin, at the Professional Car Society's 1985 International Meet in Toronto, touted a $600 across-the-board price reduction that brought stickers into the $2,385-$2,650 range. While proven outside suppliers provided the mechanicals, the steel-sheathed, Duco-finished coachwork was constructed entirely within Meteor's Piqua, Ohio, plant from laminated second-growth straight-grain ash.

The Model 858-A Service Car may have been Meteor's least-expensive 1928 offering at $2,250, but it still featured the new 80-horsepower Continental Red Seal straight engine for effortless full load performance. The interior also came standard with Wilton carpeting, a removable flower tray, protective window grilles and an exclusive slide-out extension sill roller built into the threshold of the split rear doors.

American Funeral Director

American Funeral Director

Facing increasingly stiff competition from General Motors and Chrysler during the 1920s, the Kissel Motor Car Company of Hartford, Wisconsin, was one of several well-regarded independents that turned to the high-profile funeral business for additional sales. While Kissel dealers were distributing Eureka-bodied professional cars as early as 1926 the initiative was taken to a more-ambitious level by a 1928-30 alliance where the National Casket Company of Boston marketed these vehicles directly through its huge corps of traveling salesmen. Two-hundred funeral cars, ambulances, service cars and combinations were sold annually during the first two years.

George Hamlin collection

Still constructed on a 146-inch-wheelbase commercial chassis, the Superior-Studebaker Arlington funeral coach got another $200 trimmed from its price in January 1928, taking its starting tab to $2,385 while the Bellevue ambulance set the buyer back just $2,560. These entry-level coaches now directly rivaled Meteor as the industry's least expensive full-sized professional cars.

George Hamlin collection

As Superior-bodied Studebakers used only six-cylinder engines in 1928, the Turner Mortuary in Cedar Rapids, Iowa, turned to the Eureka Company of Rock Falls, Illinois, for this Model 194 ambulance on the new straight-eight Studebaker Series FA President chassis. This basic body was distinct from Superior's design in such details as the leaded glass quarter window pattern and the differing height of the windshield base and side windowsills.

George Hamlin collection

The Turner Mortuary in Cedar Rapids, Iowa, also used the 1928 Studebaker President chassis for this Ereka Model 40 Sideway Burial Coach. In 1926, Eureka was the first to offer curbside loading. The seat on the side being opened folded forward so the casket table, supported by a series of ball bearings, could swing out along a Y-shaped guide track.

In mid-1929, the DeLuxe Big Sixes at the top of Superior's Studebaker lineup were superseded by a Samaritan ambulance and Westminster funeral coach powered by an 80-horsepower, 250.4-cubic inch, nine-bearing straight engine from the FD Series Commander. The interior of this Lincoln, Nebraska-based Samaritan was well-equipped with an electric fan, a hot water heater, a pair of fold-away attendant's seats with swiveling bases, and a partition-mounted first-aid cabinet with two Thermos bottles.

George Hamlin collection

Bernie Weis collection

Shunning the period's streamlining trends with its perpendicular windshield, drum headlights and demountable-rim spoked wheels, this Cunningham style 306A combination flower and service car on a late V-Series chassis was apparently completed for the Sampson mortuary in 1931. In spite of this traditional detailing, the low, coupe-like, leather-covered roof and graceful landau bows endowed the finished body with a surprisingly sleek appearance.

Finished in an attractive cream-and-coffee two-tone paint scheme accented by intricately leaded quarter windows, this 1930 Meteor ambulance owned by the Joseph Pray Funeral Home of Charlotte, Michigan, is entirely original. With its straight-eight Continental *"Red Seal"* engine, this car served actively in Grand Ledge, Michigan, until the 1960s.

George Hamlin collection

Priced at $3,160 sans such options as dual spotlights, red lens cowl lamps, and a suspended stretcher, this 1931 Superior Samaritan ambulance delivered to the city of Mishawka, Indiana, shared its sleeker styling, longer 154-inch wheelbase, Free Wheeling gear set, and increased horsepower rating with the Arlington funeral coach.

Moby's Eureka Autos

Dropping its six-cylinder cars to focus on a line of Lycoming-built, straight-eight models priced from $945 to $1,395, Auburn defied The Depression by selling a record 29,536 cars and posting a $3.5 million profit in 1931. In 1932, Smith and High sent an eight-cylinder Auburn to Superior's Lima, Ohio, facility for the fitment of this dashing ambulance body. Head-turning touches included knockoff wire wheels, four rear-hinged side doors, and two-tone paintwork where the belt moldings, radiator shell and fenders were finished in a lighter shade than the rest of the body.

George Hamlin collection

After Studebaker purchased Pierce-Arrow for $5.7 million in 1928, it was perhaps inevitable that Superior would launch a line of "Pierce-Superior" funeral cars and ambulances in May, 1932. This 1933 Model 836 delivered to the Roy D. Klinker Mortuary of Huntington Park, California, benefited from Stewart-Warner power brakes, lower-profile 17-inch wheels, and a more-powerful 135-horsepower engine with the industry's first hydraulic tappets. Fender-mounted headlights had been a Pierce-Arrow trademark since 1913, but the 1933 models were the first since 1914 where the housings followed the same arc as the fenders.

Having lost money in 1932 for the first time in its 80-year history, Studebaker entered receivership in March 1933 and endured the suicide of President Albert R. Erskine in July. The relatively stable funeral business was more important than ever. This 1933 Superior Samaritan ambulance was delivered to the Diffly Funeral Home in Prattville, Alabama. The gracefully curved siren bracket was a clever response to the prow-like lower grille, and Superior offered a town car roof as a $300 option just in case two-tone paint didn't turn enough heads.

Moby's Eureka Autos

Switching to Buick's trusty straight-eight chassis, but disguising the fact with their own split grille design, Meteor joined the ranks of professional car builders that no longer assembled their own frames in 1933. This ambulance model, sporting the deeper fender skirts and steel spoke artillery wheels that were new on all 1933 Buicks, was still serving with the Pittsford, New York, Fire Department when it was photographed on October 6, 1951.

Bernie Weis photo

Dubbed "Kenosha Duesenbergs" by noted automotive historian Dave Brownell, one of the Depression era's great performance bargains was the twin-ignition, nine-bearing, overhead-valve straight-eight engine debuted by Nash in the 1930 Series 490. For 1934, Count Alexis de Sakhnoffsky further emphasized the Ambassador's streamlined look with bullet-shaped headlights, two horizontal rows of hood louvers, eyelash-like fender valances, and a beavertail rear end. All were put to good use when A.J. Miller of Bellefontaine, Ohio, created this long, low, limousine-style funeral coach for Emmett Cole of Rome, Georgia.

Cunningham's final in-house chassis, designated the W-1 and powered by a Continental Red Seal straight eight engine, was introduced in November 1931, and produced until the end of 1933. As the company no longer made passenger cars, the sole purpose of this 149-inch-wheelbase frame was to serve as an ambulance and funeral coach platform, and even with 15 body styles cataloged it is still thought that only a dozen-or-so were built at prices in the $6,500 range. This style 341-A carved hearse, beautifully finished in two-tone gray to highlight its Ionic-style columns and matte-finish draperies, was originally sold to Ingimire & Thompson of Rochester, New York, in 1934.

Bernie Weis collection

In October 1933, the National Funeral Directors Association held its annual convention in Cunningham's home town of Rochester, New York, so the company pulled out all the stops by displaying this awe-inspiring style 336-A eight-column "Carved Cathedral" town car hearse. It was likely constructed on the last Series W chassis built. After the convention, the car was sold to Buffalo funeral director A.L. Orlowski.

George Hamlin collection

The "flying goose" radiator mascot was about the only carryover styling element seen on the 1934 Superior Studebakers when they first appeared at the NFDA Convention in the fall of 1933. The headlamps were bullet shaped and body colored, while springs and other mechanicals were concealed by fuller fenders. The forward-leaning rear door made space for a covered church truck well that could still be accessed when a casket was on board.

George Hamlin collection

Horizontal hood louvers distinguished the 1934 Superior Westminster from the less-expensive Arlington, but its Studebaker-built 152-inch-wheelbase Commercial Chassis and 110-horsepower, 250.4-cubic inch, nine-bearing straight eight were now considered to be part of a smaller, lighter President series. This shot shows off the interior's tasseled velvet draperies and arch-shaped walnut flower trays.

Richard J. Conjalka collection

Searching for a relatively stable market, Auburn announced the addition of a limousine-style funeral car to its line in 1935. Reasonably priced at $1,895 including a 115-horsepower Lycoming straight-eight engine, the Model 856 featured a 163-inch-wheelbase X-type frame that was 3 feet longer than the standard Auburn sedan, and a 98-inch-long casket floor accessed through a horizontally split rear door with two sections hinged at the top and bottom.

Walt McCall collection

Though Henney had no reason to regard its Reo, Olds, and Packard-based professional cars with anything but pride, there was still nostalgia for the coaches the Freeport, Illinois, firm had built on its own chassis prior to 1934. In response, the company rolled out this intriguing 1936 hybrid that combined Auburn front-end sheet metal with Cadillac bumpers, Oldsmobile rear fenders and a Lincoln-like grille with a leaping greyhound hood ornament.

Walt McCall collection

Traveling from town to town calling on funeral directors, the Derby-wearing salesman in this photo had plenty of improvements to point to in this limousine-style Silver-Knightstown funeral car constructed from a 1936 Hudson Custom Eight. The exterior design was pumped up with domed fenders, prow-shaped grille accents, and an angled windshield, while the chassis added hydraulic brakes and an all-new "Radial Safety Control" front suspension.

In late 1936, the Bowersock & Chiles Funeral and Ambulance Service of Lima, Ohio, had a front-wheel-drive Cord 810 sedan converted into a side-loading ambulance by Owen Brothers of Lima, Ohio. The idea that Gordon Buehrig's coffin-nosed masterpiece would be put to work in this way is ironic, but mechanical problems forced it to return many times to the Cord factory in Auburn, Indiana, for repairs. It was eventually scrapped and parted out in 1946.

Richard J. Conjalka collection

For 1936, Superior joined in the industry-wide carved-coach revival with this intriguing "4-Purpose" Studebaker, offered as a $250 option on the eight-cylinder Westminster (shown) or six-cylinder Arlington. Split into two pieces per side weighing about 30 lbs. each or 120 lbs. in total, the rubber-cushioned decorative panels were made of cast aluminum and secured to the body with thumbscrews. As had been the case with Dictator-based Superiors since 1931, the straight-eight President chassis used for this Westminster was now delivered to Superior's plant in a standard-wheelbase form that was subsequently extended and reinforced for funeral service.

Moby's Eureka Autos

George Hamlin collection

Enhancing its status as Superior's costliest Studebaker at $2,630, this 1936 Samaritan ambulance touted a more stately grille design and a two-piece V-shaped windshield. Front-hinged front doors were also added for enhanced safety, and Superior could still equip the body with a town car style driver's compartment for an extra $511.25. Given that straight Samaritan ambulances used squared-off #2 doors incorporating the coach lamps, the curved openings on this car suggest it was a combination outfitted for Superior's new "4-Purpose" removable carved hearse panels.

This is a $2,032 Arlington funeral car offering a 239-inch overall length and a 90-hp 217-.8-cubic inch L-head six-cylinder engine with four main bearings. The 1937 Studebakers lineup also had a $1,919 Elhurst service car, $2,452 Westminster funeral car, $2,242 Elmwood service car, and $2,592 Samaritan ambulance using a straight-eight President platform stretched to 247 inches overall.

Walt McCall collection

Used for first calls and flower transport in Tulare, California, this 1937 Terraplane Series 70 Custom Panel Delivery was fitted with distinctly angled quarter windows by the Crown Coach Body Company of Los Angeles. Its chrome-alloy-block, 212-cubic inch, six-cylinder engine would have been a sparkling performer offering 96 or 107 horsepower, depending on the cylinder head fitted.

Walt McCall collection

After Superior discontinued its Studebakers in 1937, South Bend turned to Bender Body of Cleveland for its funeral cars and ambulances. While the association lasted only from 1938 to 1940, it was fruitful, judging from the attractive, Lincoln Zephyr-like flavor of this all-white 1940 President ambulance. Bender would become better known for the open-topped sightseeing busses it constructed on White chassis for the National Park Service.

Steve Lichtman collection

The 1949-53 Kaiser Traveler and 1951 Frazer Vagabond "utility sedans" were America's first hatchbacks, and the sales department at Willow Run suggested that their low cost and flexibility made them ideal for rural doctors, accident patrols, and funeral directors seeking a family sedan that could handle first calls.

American Funeral Director

297

Added to Studebaker's low-slung, Loewy-styled lineup in 1954, the Conestoga station wagon was offered with a factory-fitted $60 Ambulet package aimed at budget-conscious rescue squads, law enforcement agencies, industrial plants, Civil Defense Corps, and rural doctors who made house calls. The Shasta White paintwork on this 1954 model would have cost another $10, while the "Red Cross Decalomanias" in the rear quarter windows were $2.50 per pair plus a 75-cent installation charge.

George Hamlin collection

Studebaker postponed its demise by nearly a decade when it launched the compact Lark as a Rambler rival in 1959, nearly tripling model-year sales to 126,000 cars. Its "central" body shell dated to 1953, but smaller overhangs and shortened wheelbases of 108.5 inches for the sedans and 113 inches for the two-door station wagon respectively trimmed their overall lengths to 175 inches and 184.5 inches. Ambulet equipment remained available on wagons through 1964, with the "Lark VIII" tailgate badging on this car announcing that a 180-horsepower, 259.2-cubic inch, overhead-valve V-8 was fitted in place of the Lark VI's L-head six.

A raised roof cap and diamond-treaded front and rear bumpers enhanced the capabilities of this practical International Travelall operated by the Branchville, Maryland, Rescue Squad. The horizontally oriented quad headlights and anodized aluminum concave grille behind the massive Federal "Q" siren date this as a 1961 or 1962 "C" Series model. Note that the fuel filler is located in the cowl.

Steve Lichtman collection

Given a raised roof and a lengthened 140-inch wheelbase by the Springfield Equipment Company of Springfield, Ohio, this 1968 International Travelall was among the last to use a body shell that traced its origins to the 1957 model year.

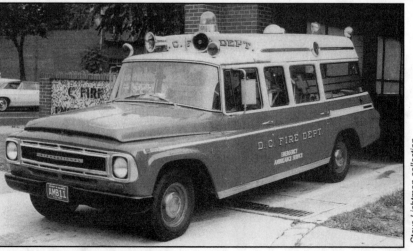

Steve Lichtman collection

Steve Lichtman collection

The Springfield Equipment Company prepared this 1969-70 International Travelall for Miami's challenging new paramedic program by extending the wheelbase to 149 inches and covering the patient compartment with a high-headroom roof cap. A stock wheelbase Interne 119 and an intermediate-stretch Interne 139 were also offered by this Springfield, Ohio, builder.

Steve Lichtman collection

A modern suburban community like Levittown, New York, practically demanded state-of-the-art ambulances like this Clark Cortez Motor Home conversion, which offered significantly more working and storage stage space than a traditional car-based unit. Vehicles like these were instrumental in the late 1960s movement to deliver training and equipment previously found only in a hospital's cardiac care unit directly to a heart attack victim.

Steve Lichtman collection

Also known as a manufacturer of bookmobiles, the Gerstenslager Company of Wooster, Ohio, was responsible for building this high-visibility emergency rescue unit used in Rotterdam, New York, by the Carman Fire Department. Flashlights and fire extinguishers on the front bumper made them easy to reach for after rescuers arrived at an accident. The electric winch and hood-mounted spotlight also came in handy in roadside extrication situations.

Richard J. Conjalka collection

Fashioning a virtual stretch limousine for emergencies, the Springfield Equipment Company extended the wheelbase of this 1972-73 International Travelall by 20 inches to create its "Interne 139" ambulance. A high-capacity rooftop air conditioner, downward-pointing ditch lights, and trapezoidal side markers made from stock Travelall taillamps turned sideways were other distinctive features of this individual unit.

Comprehensively equipped to deliver shock trauma assistance, coronary care, and multi-patient transport capability on the west end of Allentown, Pennsylvania, this gigantic 1974 Grumman was in service with the Cetronia Ambulance Corps through 1991. A bumper-mounted winch, running water, and an interior that was tall enough for attendants to stand up made this rolling emergency room far more capable and comfortable than earlier ambulances.

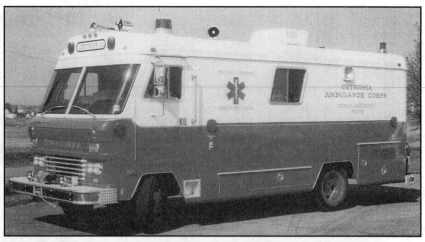

Steve Lichtman collection

American Funeral Director

Connelly-McKinley Ltd. of Edmonton, Alberta, placed its first funeral omnibus into service in 1918, when it fitted a casket-carrying 14-passenger body to a solid-tired, chain-drive Reo army truck chassis. In 1981, company president W.J. Connelly took delivery of this 40-foot Prevost Le Mirage of Sainte Claire, Quebec, fitted with a pull-out casket table and 42-inch-high side windows. This Quebec-built bus was particularly useful for distant internments and the funerals of retirement home residents.

A San Francisco artist adorned this 1961 Superior Cadillac hearse with Norse-style shields, swords, helmets and stern ornaments, completing the eclectic composition with an open driver's seat, Gothic quarter windows, trumpet-like taillight appendages, a roof-mounted cross, and skulls for the instrument panel and the corners of the front bumpers.

Craig Watley photo/The Professional Car

With a hand-held remote control re-distributing hydraulic pressure through 62 feet of piping in the chassis, Ronald Dermotta can get his 1961 Flxible-Buick Premier low-rider landau hearse to do a little dance. Fender skirts, side exhausts and knockoff-style wheel spinners complete the custom look.

Nick Bliss, Indiana Chapter PCS

Billing itself as the "Home of the Chicken Car," Love Auto Sales of Indianapolis placed a giant rooster on the roof of this 1974 Superior Cadillac Chateau Baronet combination coach. It's part of a six-vehicle fleet of old funeral cars and limousines, otherwise topped with a duck, a pig, hen, turkey, or a triple-tier wedding cake, that's rented out for parties, parades, and proms.

Courtesy Western Reserve Historical Society

Rod Heitman designed and built this hot rod hearse that was displayed at the Crawford Auto-Aviation Museum in Cleveland, Ohio. The 1770 vintage wooden hearse body, originally outfitted as a horse-drawn sleigh, was found in a Gettysburg, Pennsylvania, field in 1985, fully restored and mounted on a specially constructed chassis with a 1977 Chevrolet Camaro sub-frame. A 454-cubic inch V-8 and Turbo-Hydramatic 400 transmission were installed behind the hand-fabricated cow catcher with its centrally mounted fire truck headlight, while the casket compartment was finished in plush red velvet with a brass-trimmed rosewood Formica floor.

Gregg D. Merksamer photo

Dr. David Bressler, who runs the largest children's dental practice in Philadelphia, drives this 1965 Miller-Meteor Cadillac "Cavity Buster" when he performs magic shows at area schools. The giant tooth on the roof is actually a waiting room stool for kids.

Sandy Grossman photo

Promising clients go-anywhere advertising that can literally drive through the visual clutter of New York City's streets, Sandy Grossman of emergencyads.com converted this 1959 S&S Cadillac ambulance into a rolling billboard with backlit roof signage, an LED message center, and a BOSE sound system for playing pre-recorded jingles for commercials. It was fully restored and featured authentic lights, two-way radios, oxygen tanks, a fire extinguisher, and a stretcher.

301

BIBLIOGRAPHY

"Armored Ambulance Introduced in Memphis." *American Funeral Director*, August, 1927, p. 51.

"The Auto-Hearse In Operation." *The Director*, April, 1909, p. 10.

Barkley, Katherine Traver. *The Ambulance: The Story of Emergency Transportation of Sick and Wounded Through the Centuries*. Load N Go Press, Kiamesha Lake, New York, 1990.

"Barnette Cars Shown At State Conventions." *American Funeral Director*, July, 1949, p. 84.

Becker, Mark. "Certification Programs Indicate a Commitment to the Coachbuilder." *Limousine & Chauffeured Transportation*, November, 1997, pp. 38-46.

Belson, Ken. "America's Favorite Hearse To Join the Dearly Departed (Cadillac Fleetwood)." *The New York Times*, October 27, 1996, Section 11, p.1.

Benson, Don M., M.D.; Dirsch, Jerry, M.D.; Esposito, Gerald, M.P.H.; Safar, Peter, M.D.; and Whitney, Raymond, M.D. "Mobile Intensive Care by 'Unemployable' Blacks Trained as Emergency Medical Technicians (EMTs) in 1967-69." *The Journal of Trauma*, Williams & Wilkins Co., Volume 12, No.5, May 1972, pp. 408-420.

"Bringing Defibrillation to the Public." Retrieved December 5, 2003, from http://www.chainofsurvival.com/cos/Cardiologist_detail.asp.

"British Funeral Cars." *American Funeral Director*, August, 1976, pp. 31-34; September, 1976, pp. 59-62.

Burness, Tad. *Ford Spotter's Guide, 1920-1980*. Motorbooks International, Osceola, Wisconsin, 1981.

Burness, Tad. *Chevy Spotter's Guide, 1920-1980*. Motorbooks International, Osceola, Wisconsin, 1981.

Burness, Tad. *Pickup and Van Spotter's Guide, 1945-82*. Motorbooks International, Osceola, Wisconsin, 1982.

Butler, Don. *The History of Hudson*. Crestline Publishing, Sarasota, Florida, 1982.

Caroline, Nancy L., M.D. "Emergency! 'Freedom House' saved lives—yours and theirs, but now it is mostly shunted aside and forgotten." *Pittsburgh* magazine, April 1977, pp. 43-86.

Carr, Virginia Spencer. *(John) Dos Passos, A Life*. Doubleday, New York City, 1984, pp. 117-139. Excepts regarding service in Norton-Harjes Ambulance Corps, World War I, retrieved November 26, 2003 at http://www.ku.edu/carrie/specoll/AFS/library/DosPassos.html.

Casteele, Dennis. *The cars of Oldsmobile*. Crestline Publishing, Sarasota, Florida, 1981.

Clark, Henry Austin Jr. and Kimes, Beverly Rae. *Standard Catalog of American Cars 1805-194*. Second Edition, Krause Publications, Iola, Wisconsin, 1989.

Conjalka, Richard J. "Knightstown... Famous for Fine Coaches since 1900 – Revisited." *The Minute Man Monitor*, Indiana Chapter PCS, Volume 1, #7 (2001).

Conjalka, Richard J. "Merrillville Man Remembers Childhood Trip to K-town." *Knightstown Banner*, November 7, 2001, p. 13.

Conjalka, Richard J. "A Most Rare Combination (1957-9 S&S Park Place)." *The Minute Man Monitor*, Indiana Chapter PCS, Volume 1, Issue #9, autumn, 2002.

Conjalka, Richard J. "A Unique Indiana Professional Car (1936 Cord by Owen Brothers)." *The Minute Man Monitor*, Indiana Chapter PCS, Issue #10, January, 2003.

"A Conversation With Robert Peterson." *Limousine & Chauffeur*, January/February 1986, pp. 79-85.

Crabtree, Jim. "Combination Cars, Part II." *The California Collector*, Southern California Chapter PCS, issue #23, May-June, 1999, pp. 2-8.

Dammann, George H. and Wagner, James K. *The Cars of Lincoln-Mercury*. Crestline Publishing, Sarasota, Florida, 1987.

Dammann, George H. *Seventy Years of Buick*. Crestline Publishing, Sarasota, Florida, 1973.

Dammann, George H. *Seventy Years of Chevrolet*. Crestline Publishing, Glen Ellyn, Illinois, 1972.

Dammann, George H. *Seventy Years of Chrysler*. Crestline Publishing, Sarasota, Florida, 1974.

"Development of the Funeral Car." *American Funeral Director*, March, 1935, pp. 30-34.

DeWinter, Bernie IV. "Packard Replicoaches." *The Professional Car* #55, First Quarter 1990, pp. 3-7.

DeWinter, Bernie IV. "The Surprisingly Simple Flxidoor." *The Professional Car* #108, Second Quarter 2003, pp. 3-7.

Diehl, Digby. "The Emergency Medical Services Program." Retrieved December 5, 2003, from the Robert Wood Johnson Foundation Anthology, http://www.rwjf.org/publications/publicationsPdfs/anthology2000/chapter_10.html.

Dunham, Terry B. and Gustin, Lawrence R. *The Buick: A Complete History*. Revised 5th Edition, Automobile Quarterly Publications, Kutztown, Pennsylvania, 2000.

Dunne, Jim and Norbye, Jan P. *Pontiac: The Postwar Years*. Motorbooks International, Osceola, Wisconsin, 1979.

Dunne, Jim and Norbye, Jan P. *Oldsmobile: The Postwar Years*. Motorbooks International, Osceola, Wisconsin, 1981.

Ebert, Robert R. *Flxible: A History of the Bus and the Company*. Antique Power, Inc., Yellow Springs, Ohio, 2001.

Ebert, Robert R. "Motorcycles, Model Ts, Buicks, Buses, and 'Boss Kett': Flxible's Early Years (1913-42)." SAH's *Automotive History Review*, Summer 2000, pp. 4-19.

"Economy Coach to Make Meteor-Pontiac Models." *American Funeral Director*, December, 1953, p. 74.

Ehmer, John. "Owner's Pride: 1940 Superior Pontiac Combination." *The Professional Car* #72, Second Quarter 1994, pp. 11-12.

"A Fine Funeral Car (1914 Cunningham)." *Automobile Dealer and Repairer*, January, 1914, p. 53.

"FFDA Reports: Average Profit Slipped To 7.63% In 2002." *American Funeral Director*, June, 2003, pp. 56-60.

Flammang, James M. and Kowalke, Ron. *Standard Catalog of American Cars 1976-1999*. Third Edition, Krause Publications, Iola, Wisconsin, 1999.

Foster, Kit. "The Black Line: American Purpose-Built Hearses." *Classic Car Mart* (UK), March, 1998, pp. 88-91.

"From Carriages to Crossbars: Rochester's Oldest Manufacturing Concern Moves with the Times Through a Variety of Product Lines." James Cunningham, Son & Company press release, Rochester, New York, 1960.

Gale, Paul. "Hearse company was 'style leader' in funeral industry." Sauk Valley (Illinois) *Sunday News*, July 16, 2000.

Geller, L.D. "The American Field Service Archives of World War I, 1914-1917." Greenwood Press, Westport, CT, 1989. Retrieved November 26th, 2003 at http://info.greenwood.com/books/0313267/0313267944.html.

Getts, Joe. *The Flower Car; Origin & Design*. NAFCOA Publishing Company, Miamisburg, Ohio, 1994.

"The GMC in U.S. Army Service." GMC Trucks brochure, General Motors Corp., 1918.

Godshall, Jeffrey I. "The Ghia Crown Imperials." Appendix 1 of *Chrysler & Imperial 1946-1975: The Classic Postwar Years* (Langworth, Richard M., author). Reissued edition, Motorbooks International, Osceola, Wisconsin, 1993.

Gunnell, John. *GMC: The First 100 Years*. Krause Publications, Iola, Wisconsin, 2002.

Gunnell, John. "GMC followed President Wilson into war." *Old Cars Weekly*, November 14, 2002, p. 37.

Gunnell, John. "Pontiac Hearses And Ambulances." *Old Cars Weekly*, January 21, 1982, pp.14-17.

Gunnell, John. *75 Years of Pontiac-Oakland*. Crestline Publishing, Sarasota, Florida, 1982.

Gunnell, John. *75 Years of Pontiac: The Official History*. Krause Publications, Iola, Wisconsin, 2000.

Gunnell, John A., Editor. *Standard Catalog of American Cars 1946-1975*. Krause Publications, Iola, Wisconsin, 1982.

Hamlin, George L. "1942nd M*A*S*H (Monstrous Antique Showstopping Henney)." *The Packard Cormorant*, Winter 1978-9, pp. 22-25.

Hamlin, George L. "The Professional Packard: Commercial Bodies on Packard Chassis." In *Packard: A History of the Motor Car and the Company* (Kimes, Beverly Rae, Editor), Princeton Publishing, General Edition, Second Printing, Princeton, New Jersey, 1978, Appendix III, pp. 696-713.

Hamlin, George L. "Whatever Happened to the Super Station Wagon?" *The Packard Cormorant*, Number 43, Summer 1986, pp. 16-21.

"Happenings (The last Cadillac ambulance to be manufactured ...)." *Registry* (Newsletter of the National Registry of EMTs), Vol. 11, No. 1, April, 1980.

Hendry, Maurice D. Cadillac: *Standard of the World. The Complete History*. Fifth Edition update, Automobile Quarterly Publications, Kutztown, Pennsylvania, 1996.

Hinrichs, Noël. *The Pursuit of Excellence*. James Cunningham, Son & Co.,1964, retrieved January 23, 2004 at http://www.obs-us.com/people/karen/cunningham.

Huntington, Richard and Metcalf, Peter. *Celebrations of Death: the anthropology of the mortuary ritual*. Cambridge University Press, 1979.

Hutchings, H.V. "Princes, Presidents, Potentates and Popes: Cal Beauregard Remembers."

Special Interest Autos #150, November/December 1995, pp. 46-58.

"Introducing the 1956 Funeral Coaches and Ambulances." *American Funeral Director*, November, 1955, pp. 67-71.

Isard, Daniel M. "Automobiles, Who Needs 'em." *American Funeral Director*, November, 2002, pp. 54-56.

Johnson, Hannah. "Wildangers: Builders of 'Suburban' Bodies." *Monmouth Register*, November 4, 1984.

Keel, John R. "The History of Sayers & Scovill, Part 4: 1946-1956." *The Minute Man Monitor*, Indiana Chapter PCS, Volume 1, #7 (2001).

Kimes, Beverly Rae, Editor. *The Classic Car: The Ultimate Book About the World's Grandest Automobiles.* Classic Car Club of America, Des Plaines, Illinois, 1990, distributed though Motorbooks International.

Kimes, Beverly Rae, Editor. *Packard: A History of the Motor Car and the Company.* Princeton Publishing, General Edition, Second Printing, Princeton, New Jersey, 1978.

Kowalke, Ron. "Auburn Ambulance Incident." *Old Cars Weekly*, April 17 2003, p.22.

Langworth, Richard M. *Chrysler & Imperial 1946-1975: The Classic Postwar Years.* Reissued edition, Motorbooks International, Osceola, Wisconsin, 1993.

Kraft, Ralph F. "The All-Purpose Pickway." *The Professional Car* #11, Spring, 1979, pp. 2-7.

Larson, Jonie. "Eureka Building In Rock Falls Will Soon Be Only A Memory." *Daily Gazette* (Sterling-Rock Falls, Illinois), August 22, 1987.

Larson, Matt and Van Gelderen, Ron. *"LaSalle: Cadillac's Companion Car."* Turner Publishing Company, Paducah, Kentucky, 2000.

Lee, David. "A Short History of the Amblewagon." *The Professional Car* #104, Second Quarter 2002, pp. 7-12.

"Lehmann-Peterson Lincolns." *Special Interest Autos* #187, January/February 2002, p. 37.

Lichtman, Stephen. Letter to the Author regarding U.S. DOT Specification KKK-1822, Mt. Airy, MD, March 26th, 2003.

"LIMO Members Commit to Safety." Limousine Industry Manufacturers Organization press release, Falls Church, VA, July 26th, 1990.

"A Little History (timeline of EMS)." Retrieved December 5th, 2003 from http://www.angelfire.com/co/fantasyfigures/710history.html.

Logan, Robert. "How to Increase Profits for Funeral Homes and Limousine Operators." *Limousine Digest*, October, 2002, pp. 36-38.

"Major Model Changes Mark New Professional Cars." *American Funeral Director*, November, 1976, pp. 22-45.

"Manufacturers Present 1959 Funeral Cars and Ambulances." *American Funeral Director*, October, 1958, pp. 62-64.

"Many Improvements Noted in 1953 Barnette Line." *American Funeral Director*, January, 1953, p. 92.

"Many Innovations in 1957 Line of Automotive Equipment." *American Funeral Director*, November, 1956, pp. 78-84.

Martin, Patrick J. "Professional Cars from Kalamazoo (Checker)." *The Professional Car* #103, First Quarter 2002, pp. 9-21.

Marvin, Keith. "Cunningham (i) (US) 1907-36." From *The Beaulieu Encyclopedia of the Automobile* (Georgano, Nick, Editor)," Volume 1 (A-L), pp. 357-8. The Stationery Office, London, 2000.

Marvin, Keith. "Meteor: Kills 'Em With Music and Hauls 'Em Away." *Antique Automobile*, March 1966, pp. 26-36.

Marvin, Keith. "S&S: Fit for the Final Ride." *Upper Hudson Valley Automobilist*, April 1993.

McCall, Walter M.P. "The Acme Motor Company." *The Professional Car* #100, Second Quarter 2002, pp. 5-7.

McCall, Walter M.P. "Ambulance On Ice." *The Professional Car* #87, First Quarter 1998, p. 13.

McCall, Walter M.P. *The American Ambulance, 1900-2002, An Illustrated History.* Iconografix, Hudson, Wisconsin, 2002.

McCall, Walter M.P. "The Arrowline—And Other Non-Packard Henneys." *The Professional Car* #95, First Quarter 2000, pp. 5-17.

McCall, Walter M.P. "The Cunningham Story." *The Professional Car* #20, Summer 1981, pp. 4-11.

McCall, Walter M.P. "The Demise of the Flower Car." *The Professional Car* #7, Spring 1978, pp. 2-7.

McCall, Walter M.P. "The Downsized 1977-1979 Professional Cars." *The Professional Car* #51, First Quarter 1989, pp. 1-15.

McCall, Walter M.P. *80 Years of Cadillac-LaSalle.* Crestline Publishing, Sarasota, Florida, 1982.

McCall, Walter M.P. "Flower Cars: A glance at a forgotten funeral vehicle." *Limousine and Chauffeur*, January/February, 1990, pp. 66-68.

McCall, Walter M.P. "The Forgotten Factories." *The Professional Car* #101, Third Quarter 2001, pp. 7-19.

McCall, Walter M.P. "Funereal Fords from the Shop of Siebert." *The Professional Car* #28, Summer 1983, pp. 3-12.

McCall, Walter M.P. "A History of the Commercial Chassis." *The Professional Car* #62, 4th Quarter 1991, pp. 5-15.

McCall, Walter M.P. "Mopar Professional Cars." *The Professional Car* #52, Second Quarter 1989, pp. 3-13.

McCall, Walter M.P. "News of the Industry." *The Professional Car* #37, Fall 1985, pp. 19-20.

McCall, Walter M.P. "News of the Industry." *The Professional Car* #46, Winter 1987-8, pp. 13-14.

McCall, Walter M.P. "News of the Industry." *The Professional Car* #71, First Quarter 1994, pp. 17-21.

McCall, Walter M.P. "Our Heritage— Part One: The Evolution of the Contemporary Funeral Car." *Canadian Funeral Service*, September, 1972, pp. 7-11.

McCall, Walter M.P. "Our Heritage—Part Two: The Funeral Coach Industry in Canada." *Canadian Funeral Service*, November, 1972, pp. 7-12.

McCall, Walter M.P. "Our Heritage—Part Four: The Rise and Decline of the Carved Panel Hearse." *Canadian Funeral Service*, November, 1973, pp. 7-10.

McCall, Walter M.P. "Our Heritage—Part Five: From Casket Wagon To Service Coach." *Canadian Funeral Service*, July/August, 1974, pp. 6-9.

McCall, Walter M.P. "Our Heritage—Part Seven: The Economy Model Funeral Coach." *Canadian Funeral Service*, December, 1975, pp. 6-13.

McCall, Walter M.P. "Our Heritage—Part Eight: Fifty Years Of Side-Servicing." *Canadian*

Funeral Director, November, 1976, pp. 7-12.

McCall, Walter M.P. "Our Heritage—Part Nine: The Landau At Forty." *Canadian Funeral Director*, November, 1977, pp. 6-10.

McCall, Walter M.P. "Petal-Packin' Packards: A History of the Henney-Packard Flower Cars." *The Packard Cormorant*, Number 68, Autumn 1992, pp. 22-29.

McCall, Walter M.P. "A Portfolio of Professionals." *The Packard Cormorant*, Number 21, Summer 1983, pp. 4-7.

McCall, Walter M.P. "The Professional Cadillac." T*he Self-Starter*, Cadillac-LaSalle Club, August, 2001, pp. 6-12.

McCall, Walter M.P. "The Rise (and Fall) of the Eureka Coach Company." *The Professional Car* #52, Second Quarter 1989, pp. 3-13.

McCall, Walter M.P. "The Service Car - Then and Now." *The Professional Car* # 65, Third Quarter 1992, pp. 5-11.

McCall, Walter M.P. "The (Short) History of the Gothic-Panel Carved Hearse." *The Professional Car* #71, First Quarter 1994, pp. 3-12.

McCall, Walter M.P. "The Side-Servicing Coach Marks its Fiftieth Year." *American Funeral Director*, November, 1976, pp. 28-31.

McCall, Walter M.P. "Side-Servicing at Sixty." *The Professional Car* #41, Fall 1986, pp. 6-16.

McCall, Walter M.P. "Superior's Hardtop Hearses." *The Professional Car* #46, Winter 1987, pp. 6-10.

McCall, Walter M.P. "Those S&S Hood Bars." *The Professional Car* #74, Fourth Quarter 1994, pp. 5-14.

McCall, Walter M.P. "The Ultimate Ambulance (1937 Meteor Cadillac V-16)." *The Professional Car* #63, First Quarter 1992, pp. 1-12.

McCall, Walter M.P. "Weller Brothers of Memphis." *The Professional Car* #47, Spring 1988, pp. 6-13.

McCracken, J. Paul. "Owner's Pride: 1962 McClintock Chrysler Sedan Ambulance." *The Professional Car* #88, Second Quarter 1998, pp. 17-18.

McPherson, Thomas A. *American Funeral Cars & Ambulances Since 1900.* Crestline Publishing, Glen Ellyn, Illinois, 1973.

McPherson, Thomas A. *The Dodge Story.* Crestline Publishing, Glen Ellyn, Illinois, 1975.

McPherson, Thomas A. *The Eureka Company: A Complete History.* Specialty Vehicle Press, Don Mills, Ontario, 1994.

McPherson, Thomas A. "America's First Automobile Funeral." *The Professional Car* #91, First Quarter 1999, pp. 13-30.

McPherson, Thomas A. *Flxible Professional Vehicles: The Complete History.* Specialty Vehicle Press, Don Mills, Ontario, 1993.

McPherson, Thomas A. "The Kunkel Carriage Works, 1875-1928." *The Professional Car* #83, First Quarter 1997, pp. 17-25.

McPherson, Thomas A. "National of Knightstown." *The Professional Car* #93, Third Quarter 1999, pp. 5-22.

McPherson, Thomas A. "Professional Cars From Knightstown." *The Professional Car* #92, Second Quarter 1999, pp. 5-25.

McPherson, Thomas A. *Superior: The Complete History.* Specialty Vehicle Press, Don Mills, Ontario, 1995.

Merksamer, Gregg D. "The Last Ride: The history and future of the American funeral coach." Directed Research Project, Pratt Institute Graduate Industrial Design Program, Brooklyn, New York,

December 17, 1991.

Merksamer, Gregg D. "The Launch of a New Era: Cadillac Prepares For Front Wheel Drive." *American Funeral Director*, October, 1996, pp. 48-158.

Merksamer, Gregg D. "The 1994 Professional Vehicles." *American Funeral Director*, October, 1993, pp. 48-146.

Merksamer, Gregg D. "The 1995 Professional Vehicles." *American Funeral Director*, October, 1994, pp. 40-138.

Merksamer, Gregg D. "1996 Professional Car Preview: Entertaining to Drive, Easy to Maintain." *American Funeral Director*, November, 1995, pp. 22-77, and December, 1995, pp. 44-48.

Merksamer, Gregg D. "1997 Professional Car Preview: Front-Wheel-Drive Hearses Without Excuses." *American Funeral Director*, November, 1996, pp. 18-59.

Merksamer, Gregg D. "1998 Professional Car Preview: An Intriguing Revolution." *American Funeral Director*, November, 1997, pp. 22-74.

Merksamer, Gregg D. "1999 Professional Car Preview." *American Funeral Director*, November, 1998, pp. 22-58.

Merksamer, Gregg D. "2000 Professional Vehicle Preview." *American Funeral Director*, November, 1999, pp. 22-58.

Merksamer, Gregg D. "2001 Professional Vehicle Preview: Coachbuilders Focus on Refinement, Personal Service to Pursue Customers." *American Funeral Director*, November, 2000, pp. 22-56.

Merksamer, Gregg D. "2002 Professional Vehicle Preview: Coachbuilders Poised to Reinvent Their Wheels in Pursuit of Discriminating Customer." *American Funeral Director*, November, 2001, pp. 24-57.

Merksamer, Gregg D. "2003 Professional Vehicle Preview: Quality, Innovation in the Face of Uncertainty." *American Funeral Director*, November, 2002, pp. 22-52.

Merksamer, Gregg D. "2004 Professional Vehicle Preview: Touting New Models And Refined Features, Coachbuilders Expect to Turn The Corner." *American Funeral Director*, November, 2003, pp. 20-51.

Merksamer, Gregg D. "The Wheels of Angels: Funeral Cars for the New Millennium." Masters Thesis Project, Pratt Institute Graduate Industrial Design Program, Brooklyn, New York, February, 1993.

Merksamer, Gregg D. "Wilner Welcomes the PCS." *The Criterion*, PCS Northeast Chapter, Third Quarter 1997, pp. 3-5.

"Miller-Meteor Coach is No More." *Canadian Funeral Director*, September, 1979.

"More on the Paramedic Program and 'Emergency!'" Retrieved December 5, 2003 from Randy Mantooth's Official Web site, http://www.randymantooth.com/paramedic.html.

Morrow, Bob. "Amblin' About Ambulances (as told by Willard C. Hess)." *The Self-Starter*, Cadillac-LaSalle Club, November/December 1999, pp. 12-15.

"New Ambulance For Hospital." *Chester Times*, Chester, Pennsylvania, Wednesday, July 20, 1938, pp. 1-5.

"New Funeral Car and Ambulance Models." *American Funeral Director*, February, 1954, pp. 57-62.

"New Professional Cars Emphasize Elegance." *American Funeral Director*, October, 1984, pp. 51-64.

"1993 Professional Car Preview." *American Funeral Director*, October, 1992, pp. 47-62.

"1999 EMS Fact Sheet: 25 Years of Meeting the Challenge." Retrieved November 26th, 2003 at http://www.mcg.edu/ems/emsResources/pdffiles/EMS_week_fact_sheet.pdf.

Nowak, Joe. "Eureka Closes—80 Lose Jobs." Norwalk, Ohio *Reflector*, Friday, July 16, 1999.

Obert, Genevieve. "Amblewagon: Arriving at the E.R. in style in a 1958 Edsel Passenger-Car Ambulance." *Special Interest Autos* #184, July/August 2001, pp. 32-37.

O'Dell, John. "New Line Is No Big Stretch: Anaheim's Krystal Koach has expanded from making limos into the hearse business." *Los Angeles Times*, January 12th, 1995, pp. D1, D6, D7.

Osman, Jeffrey. "Armbruster/Stageway Rolling Through the 1980s." *Limousine & Chauffeur*, January/February 1984 (reprint).

Page, James O. "The Paramedics: An illustrated history of paramedics in the first decade in the U.S.A." Retrieved December 5, 2003 from Journal of Emergency Medical Services Web site, http://www.jems.com/paramedics.

Parker, Vern. "Life goes on for an old funeral flower pickup." *Motor Matters*, www.phillyburbs.com/automall, article # 63, 2002.

Pinner Coach Company, Olive Branch, Mississippi. Miscellaneous correspondence between Jack Pinner, Win Parker and Franz Ridgway, February 11-December 12, 1960.

"Preview of the 1955 Line of Funeral Coaches and Ambulances." *American Funeral Director*, December, 1954, pp. 45-49.

"Pre-View of the 1958 Line of Funeral Automotive Equipment." *American Funeral Director*, November, 1957, pp. 68-72.

Ralston, Marc. *Pierce-Arrow*. A.S. Barnes and Company Inc., San Diego, California, 1980.

"Rebirth of the 3-way funeral coach." *The Professional Car* #62, Fourth Quarter 1991, pp. 16-18.

"Recapturing the past: Oscar Seagle's '36 Siebert-Ford combination car." *Old Cars Weekly*, July 9, 1998, p. 37.

"Recent Deaths: John W. Henney." *American Funeral Director*, December, 1946, p. 90.

"The Red Cross Symbol on Ambulances." *On Call*, PCS Mid-Atlantic Chapter newsletter, August 1993, p. 5.

Roduck, Kent. "Re-Birth Of A Classic (re: John Little 1941 Cadillac Gothic-carved hearse)." *Canadian Funeral Director*, June 1988, pp. 38-39.

Ruediger, Steve. "Literary Ambulance Drivers—World War I." Retrieved November 26th, 2003 at http://www.angelfire.com/indie/anna_jones1/drivers.html

Skinner, Phil. "Nixon birthplace receives Lincoln from Ford." *Old Cars Weekly*, November 21, 1996, pp. 3-13.

"CLAFMA Online: Squad 51." Retrieved December 5th, 2003 from County of Los Angeles Fire Museum Association Web site, http://www.clafma.org/squad51.html.

Srikameswaran, Anita. "Pioneer medics to gather again." *Pittsburgh Post-Gazette*, November 7, 1997, pp. B-1, B-2.

Stannard, David E., editor. *Death in America*. University of Pennsylvania Press, Philadelphia, Pennsylvania, 1975.

Stewart, Craig. "Owner's Pride: 1976 Miller-Meteor Cadillac Lifeliner Ambulance." *The Professional Car* #76, Second Quarter 1995, pp. 13-17.

Stewart, Craig. "Owner's Pride: 1978 Miller-Meteor Cadillac Lifeliner Ambulance." *The Professional Car* #84, Second Quarter 1997, pp. 17-18.

Strauss, Ed. *The BUS World Encyclopedia of Buses*. Strauss Publications, Woodland Hills, California, 1988.

Studebaker Funeral Cars and Ambulances. The Studebaker Corporation of America, South Bend, Indiana, 1926.

"Studebaker Offers New Funeral Cars." *Automobile Topics*, April 19, 1930, p. 877.

Swab Wagon Company Web site. History retrieved August 4, 2003 from http://www.swabwagon.com.

"To Sell Winton Auto Hearse." *Cycle and Automobile Trade Journal*, September, 1911, p. 194.

Trebilcock, Michael. "City of Miami Department of Fire-Rescue: Our History." Retrieved December 5, 2003 from http://www.ci.miami.fl.us/fire/history.asp.

"Two Unusual Flower Cars." *The Professional Car* #64, Second Quarter 1992, pp. 9-11.

Van Beck, Todd W. "The 1,100-Year History Of the Ambulance." *American Funeral Director*, May, 1992, pp. 44-63

Van Beck, Todd W. "From the Hearse's Mouth." *American Funeral Director*, November, 1997, pp.32-36.

Weiss, Michael J. "Dead But Not Necessarily Buried." *American Demographics*, April, 2001.

Wheeled Coach Industries Web site. Ambulance specifications retrieved December 13, 2003 from http://www.wheeledcoach.com.

Whitmore, Betsy. History of Riddle Manufacturing Company, Ravenna, Ohio, online at http://www.geocities.com/riddlecah.

Winnewisser, Peter. "Model T ambulances in World War I." *Old Cars Weekly*, August 17, 2000, p. 6.

Wolbrink, Lowell R. Undated letter to Steve Wolbrink regarding family's involvement in establishing Allendale, Michigan's funeral and ambulance services, Zeeland, Michigan.

Woudenberg, Paul R. *Lincoln & Continental: The Postwar Years*. Motorbooks International, Osceola, Wisconsin, 1980.

Yengst, W.G. "Recollections and findings in connection with the dispersal of the records of Jas. Cunningham, Son & Co." Summary of research conducted at Detroit Public Library, compiled Rochester, New York, May 1, 1973.

Zavitz, R. Perry. *Canadian Cars, 1946-84*. Bookman Publishing, Baltimore, Maryland, 1985.

Zimmerman, Bob. "Henney Introduces its Postwar Models." *The Professional Car* #87, First Quarter 1998, pp. 5-11.

Zuchniewicz, Glen. "Glen's Contemporary Corner: The 1980-1985 DeVilles and Fleetwoods." *The Self-Starter*, Cadillac-LaSalle Club, February, 2003, pp. 8-25.

Zuchniewicz, Glen. "Glen's Contemporary Corner: The 1986-1992 Brougham." *The Self-Starter*, Cadillac-LaSalle Club, May, 2003, pp. 8-21.